PLANNING AND CONDUCTING NEEDS ASSESSMENTS

PLANNING AND CONDUCTING NEEDS ASSESSMENTS

A Practical Guide

Belle Ruth Witkin
James W. Altschuld

SAGE Publications
International Educational and Professional Publisher
Thousand Oaks   London   New Delhi

For information address:

SAGE Publications, Inc.
2455 Teller Road
Thousand Oaks, California 91320
E-mail: order@sagepub.com

SAGE Publications Ltd.
6 Bonhill Street
London EC2A 4PU
United Kingdom

SAGE Publications India Pvt. Ltd.
M-32 Market
Greater Kailash I
New Delhi 110 048 India

Printed in the United States of America

Library of Congress Cataloging-in-Publication Data

Witkin, Belle Ruth.
    Planning and conducting needs assessments : A practical guide /
Belle Ruth Witkin, James W. Altschuld.
        p. cm.
    Includes bibliographical references and index.
    ISBN 0-8039-5809-9 (alk. paper). — ISBN 0-8039-5810-2 (pbk. :
alk. paper)
        1. Planning. 2. Needs assessment. I. Altschuld, James W.
II. Title.
HD30.28.W595   1995
658.4′012—dc20   95-16786

This book is printed on acid-free paper.

97 98 99 10 9 8 7 6 5 4 3

Production Editor: Tricia K. Bennett   Typesetter: Christina M. Hill

Contents

Foreword

Sometimes a book appears on your desk that successfully defines a field. You look at the book and say "Thank you." *Planning and Conducting Needs Assessments: A Practical Guide* is just such a book.

For too long, researchers and practitioners have seen the term "needs assessment" used as a descriptor for virtually any kind of study. In the mid-1980s, I heard one presenter compare conducting needs assessment to "pinning jello to the wall." Any kind of study, from a simple opinion poll, to a feasibility study, to a market survey for a product, could be called a needs assessment. Trying to explain to students why one study was a "program evaluation" while another was a "needs assessment" has been difficult. On the other hand, focusing a definition for needs assessment too narrowly can be deadly, since this type of study is frequently applied in a variety of fields under vastly different conditions.

It is to the credit of these authors that they have steered a careful course between the amorphousness of some earlier formulations and the over-prescriptiveness of others. The book is clearly grounded in program planning and is not an afterthought or add-on to some other field. I am excited to see this book appear in print. It clearly fills a niche that has been empty for some time: a practical approach to learning about and conducting needs assessments.

I foresee that educators, health specialists, and workers in other human service areas will be the book's primary audience. Although both authors' careers have been in education, I believe that the examples chosen and the methods covered will appeal to a broader audience and will have applicability in a variety of contexts. It may also serve as a text in a course on needs assessment, evaluation, or instructional design. Practitioners in many other areas will find it to be most helpful. I believe the book helps put needs assessment back on the map.

The chapters are logically arranged, with excellent coverage of both the basics of planning needs assessment and various methods, such as focus groups, strategic planning, and futuring techniques. The topics are covered in sufficient detail to make the book usable in practice.

I like the flow of the book. I particularly like the extensive description of the model in Chapters 2 through 4 and the elaboration in later chapters. It is one of the more enjoyable books about research methods that I have read in the past few years. But most important, I think it does what it sets out to do in providing practical advice for someone conducting a needs assessment.

I appreciate the authors' clear use of examples. There are many, and they make the points evident. Overall, they contribute in a major way to the practicality of this work.

This book is strong on practical applications and does a nice job of demystifying needs assessment. Nothing sounds overwhelming. Although any particular person may lack the expertise required to use some of the tools, the book contains sufficient explanation for people to see what the limits of their own knowledge are and when they will need to draw on the expertise of an outside expert.

This is a marvelous book that should make a significant contribution to the field. I plan to make extensive use of it both in my work as a practitioner and in my teaching. To Drs. Witkin and Altschuld: Thank you for writing this book.

NICK EASTMOND
Utah State University

Preface

In 1984, Belle Ruth Witkin wrote:

> The central decision for [all organizations] is, What is the best way to portion out the available resources, including time, money, and organizational efforts, to meet all the demands—the needs—that compete for them?
>
> Such decisions may be based on intuition, political pressures, past practices, or personal preferences, and they may be made by boards or managers. But the most effective way to decide such issues is to make needs assessment the first stage in planning. (Witkin, 1984, p. ix)

This statement still holds true 11 years later. It constitutes the core of our beliefs and forms the underlying theme for this book. We see *Planning and Conducting Needs Assessments: A Practical Guide* as providing a framework for systematically investigating critical or unmet needs or problems, agreeing on needs-based priorities, understanding probable causes of those needs, and using the information to develop quality programs—that is, programs that have high probability of leading to resolution or improvement of the needs situation.

Point of View

The term *guide* is central to our approach. Although we furnish specific steps for many procedures, we did not intend to provide a "how-to" cookbook for needs assessment (NA). Rather, we describe a structure for understanding and managing the process and options for gathering and analyzing data on needs. The three-phase model that forms the basis for the structure grew out of both theory and practical experience in many kinds of settings. The processes that we describe are also based on both theory and practice, and the vignettes that illustrate the processes are all drawn from life, except for a couple of hypothetical situations that are so noted.

This book focuses on assessing needs of organizations and other groups, rather than those of individuals. The groups may range from loosely knit associations, such as residents of a retirement community, to highly structured corporations or government institutions.

Another basic concept is that NA is not a "top-down" activity, in which a few people decide the needs to be addressed. Rather, it engages the active involvement of a wide cross-section of recipients of service, providers of service, and representatives of the organization or system under whose aegis services (or goods) are provided. The involvement ranges from providing information or opinions to having an integral part in making decisions on needs and priorities.

There are two other concepts that we cannot overemphasize—*priorities* and *democratic involvement*. NA does not end with the gathering of information; it should lead to decisions about priorities of needs as well as priorities of action to meet the needs. Furthermore, the active involvement of many groups of stakeholders not only ensures that the information will have a broad base from many perspectives but also increases the likelihood that the results of the NA will be used in appropriate programs or other action. Finally, we strongly endorse using two or more methods of gathering data on which to base the assessment.

The topics and treatment are as comprehensive as we could make them and still maintain a unified focus. We tried to provide as much information as possible for carrying out the NA, but we could not treat each topic exhaustively. Most of the tools suggested for gathering data, such as surveys, interviews, social indicators, small group processes, and the Delphi, are not unique to NA, and many books have been written about each. We focused on those aspects that are particularly relevant to the NA task.

Audiences for the Book

If you are a needs assessor for an organization, a program planner, an evaluator, or a consultant in planning or evaluation, you will find the NA model, methodological discussions, and vignettes applicable to your work. If you teach NA at a university, the book is usable as a text, and the references supply further resources. If you are a board member or an administrator with responsibility for implementing needs-based decisions in the political and social contexts of your organization or community, you will find particularly helpful the treatment of uses of the NA, through specific methods for assigning priorities and translating NA results into action plans.

Although our own experience in NA has been mainly in the context of educational planning or evaluation, we have directed or consulted on NAs in other areas as well. The book draws on the expertise of people in such diverse fields as library services, business and industry, organizational training and development, health and mental health services, public education, higher education planning and research, and city and community planning, among others. The book is also applicable to the fields of public administration and public policy.

Organization and Content

The book is divided into two parts. Part I (Chapters 1 through 4) focuses on planning and managing the NA. Chapter 1 describes a three-phase plan, defines "need" and "needs assessment," places NA in a systems context, and provides a method for choosing options in the plan. Chapter 2 describes Phase 1, the Preassessment, during which the needs assessor and needs assessment committee (NAC) do preliminary data gathering on what is already known, design the main assessment and an evaluation plan, and consider the political and contextual factors of their NA.

Chapter 3 explains the tasks for Phase 2, Assessment, and provides guidelines for collecting, analyzing, and interpreting data. It also raises concerns about sociolinguistic and cultural factors that are often overlooked, and considers aspects of conducting NAs in different contexts. Chapter 4, Postassessment, focuses on providing a bridge from the main NA to use of the results. The first section of Chapter 4, "Major Tasks for Phase 3," describes methods of setting priorities on needs, selecting solution strategies, preparing an action plan, evaluating the NA, and preparing reports. The second section of Chapter 4, "Techniques for Phase 3," describes four techniques applicable to Phase 3.

Part II of the book consists of six chapters, five of them on methods for conducting an NA. Chapter 5 explains the use of records, social indicators, and other existing databases. Chapter 6 is devoted to surveys, interviews, and the critical incident technique. Chapter 7 describes three of the most widely used group processes: community forums, the nominal group technique, and the focus group technique. Chapter 8 continues with five specialized survey and group techniques: DACUM, the mailed Delphi survey, the group (modified) Delphi, electronic groups, and concept mapping. Chapter 9 presents five future-oriented NA procedures: strategic planning, scenarios, cross-impact analysis, future wheels, and trend analysis.

Chapter 10 deals with special tools for analysis, rather than with data gathering. It discusses three types of causal analysis: fishboning, cause and consequence analysis, and fault tree analysis. It shows how causal analysis may be used to discover needs, to analyze contributing factors to identified needs, and to provide a basis for avoiding failure and enhancing the success of a plan to meet critical needs. It also shows how fault tree analysis may be used in planning and managing the NA itself.

The book concludes with a Postscript, which is both a personal reflection of the authors and a prediction of the role of NA in the coming decades.

How to Use the Book

We recommend that all users read Part I, particularly to become familiar with the general flow of events in the three phases; to understand the three-level schema for focusing the assessment (service recipients or clients, service providers, and the system level); to recognize the distinction between *needs* and *solutions*; and to note the different contexts in which NAs occur. We also suggest a careful reading of Chapter 10, on causal analysis. If you are a practitioner, you may want to skim Chapters 5 through 9 in Part II to choose the assessment methods that fit your situation. They can be read independently, not necessarily in order. We have cross-referenced sections in Parts I and II as appropriate. If you are a student, we recommend that you read all of Part II in order and work out two or three scenarios for planning and conducting an NA in different contexts and with different data-gathering processes.

Unique Features of the Book

All needs assessment books have many features in common, but we believe that there are several unique features in this guide. Among them are comprehensiveness, with applications to many different contexts and disciplines; the treatment of sociolinguistic and cultural factors; the analysis of group processes in terms of communication factors, including listening; the advocacy and explanation of uses of causal analysis; the role of different contexts for the NA; the emphasis on laying a basis for the NA from previous assessments or existing records; and the importance of providing a clear bridge to action planning. We have also described several specialized techniques, including DACUM and concept mapping, that are not generally known in NA but that hold promise for the future.

Acknowledgments

Although much of this book draws directly on the experiences of the two authors, it could not have been written without the contributions to the field of many others. Since the 1960s, Roger Kaufman has led the way in providing many of the fundamental concepts of NA and has generously shared ideas as his own work has developed. Jack McKillip has also contributed substantially to our thinking on NA. Kent Stephens has been our principal source for updates on fault tree analysis and risk assessment. We also thank Madelaine Georgette for her insights on community involvement and applications of force field analysis.

We also wish to thank professor Nick Eastmond of the Department of Educational Technology at Utah State University and John Theiss, in the Texas Department of Mental Health and Mental Retardation, for their thoughtful reviews of the original text. Their perspectives helped us sharpen our focus, and we attempted to address their concerns as much as possible.

Neither of us could have collaborated on the book without plenty of practical support. At The Ohio State University, we owe thanks to Arthur White and Michael Klapper, codirectors of the National Center for Science Teaching and Learning, for the Center's support and enthusiastic endorsement of this endeavor; to Barbara Heinlein, who spent many hours creating tables and providing other support services; and to the many graduate students who contributed information through their own work on NA, in particular Phyllis Thomas, Jung Sook Yoon, Michael Jones, and Kathy Limes.

We are also grateful for the assistance of a cadre of creative people in the Puget Sound area: Kim Casado (Dandelion Graphics) for her intelligent rendering of the figures that illustrate our concepts; Valerie Pace, for invaluable assistance with organizing research files; Barbara Pozner, Marilyn Campbell, and Cathy Brownell, research librarians at the Renton Public Library, who spent many hours tracking down technical references; Keith Mifflin, for his expert assistance on the intricacies of a new computer program; and the dozen or so people on the Microsoft "help" line who over several months patiently answered scores of questions whenever one of the writers got lost cruising in cyberspace.

We also wish to thank Christine Smedley, our editor at Sage, Frances Borghi, assistant editor, and Claudia Hoffman, managing editor, for their encouragement and support for this project.

Finally, we owe more than we can say to our families for their encouragement and willingness to put up with our moods and lack of communication as the work progressed to completion. To our respective families with deep gratitude and affection: Joe Witkin and Sheryl Killman; and Ruth, Steven, and David Altschuld.

BELLE RUTH WITKIN
JAMES W. ALTSCHULD

PART I

Planning and Managing
the Needs Assessment

∞

ONE

A Three-Phase
Model of Needs Assessment

A library system in a large city investigates the information needs of the community, both its patrons and potential library users.

A federal task force collects data to examine the health care and health-related needs of the American population.

A school district seeks community consensus on educational goals in order to set directions for future planning.

A city of 125,000 engages its citizens in a visioning process that results in a "future focus" designed to lead to a community action plan. The future focus is used as a guide to determine needs and programs in education, health and social services, transportation, and land use.

A statewide university system conducts a needs assessment to determine how best to meet community goals and allocate resources in the coming decade.

These examples are only a few of the many types of needs assessments (NAs) that are conducted for a variety of purposes. This chapter provides a general background on what NAs are and why they are conducted and presents a three-phase plan or framework as a general guide.

Some Background
on Needs Assessment

What Is a Needs Assessment? In our perspective, NA may be defined broadly as

> a systematic set of procedures undertaken for the purpose of setting priorities and making decisions about program or organizational improvement and allocation of resources. The priorities are based on identified needs.

A *need* is generally considered to be a discrepancy or gap between "what is," or the present state of affairs in regard to the group and situation of interest, and "what should be," or a desired state of affairs. Kaufman (1988, 1992) emphasizes that need is the discrepancy between current and desired results or consequences. The concept of need is discussed in more detail in a later section. A needs assessment, then, seeks to determine such discrepancies, examine their nature and causes, and set priorities for future action.

Who Conducts NAs? Many types of organizations or agencies do: governmental agencies, school systems, social service agencies, business corporations, cities, hospitals, universities. NAs also grow out of citizen action groups that want to participate more directly in making decisions about their community: control of growth, improving the infrastructure (roads, utilities), or obtaining better recreational facilities.

Why Conduct NAs? The question arises, "Don't we already know what we need?" The answer is, yes and no. There is plenty of information from the press, the broadcast media, and reports of special commissions on social and economic indicators of need. Examples abound regarding low achievement in schools, drug abuse, incidence of major health problems, violence, homelessness, and family breakdowns, among others. These areas are not wanting for proposals to meet the needs, such as the war on drugs or illiteracy or homelessness. So the question remains, "Why conduct an NA?"

One clear reason is that populations that seem quite similar demographically often perceive their needs as being very different from each other. As an illustration, a large metropolitan region of more than

2 million set up a countywide council for long-range planning on growth. Recently, eight of the involved suburban and unincorporated communities requested permission to elect their own local councils, in addition to or instead of the county council. They believed that their needs were unique to their own geography and demography.

An NA is conducted to derive information and perceptions of values as a guide to making policy and program decisions that will benefit specific groups of people. Although NAs are often undertaken for other purposes (research studies of the NA process itself, identifying needs of special groups such as handicapped children and people with Alzheimer's disease, or justifying decisions already made—a practice we do not recommend), the focus of this book is on assessments done in a specific organization or community that are intended to lead to action, change, and improvement. NAs are shaped by and take their characteristics from their specific contexts. The NAs cited at the beginning of this chapter were all conducted for policy or program purposes in behalf of specific groups.

The word *group* is important. The doctor or teacher assesses needs daily in dealing directly with patients or students. But an NA is not intended to provide diagnostic information about individuals. Its purpose is to make decisions regarding priorities for program or system improvement. This can be accomplished sometimes by aggregating data that have been gathered for individuals, but it can also occur by asking questions of and about people served by the system that are never asked by the health professional or teacher. NA, in the broadest sense, is concerned with policy and programs, not individual diagnosis. If the NA is done well, however, it should lead to measures that will directly benefit the individuals with the needs.

We make no sweeping claims for NA. Rather, our proposal is modest: that NA offers a useful and rational approach to identifying and describing specific areas of need, discovering factors contributing to perpetuation of needs, and devising criteria for plans to meet or ameliorate the need.

How Is an NA Done? We propose a plan consisting of three phases—preassessment, assessment, and postassessment. These are briefly explained in this chapter and are further delineated in Chapters 2, 3, and 4. In Chapters 5 through 10 (Part II), we describe many procedures for data gathering, analysis, and interpretation and discuss their applicability to the three phases.

Who Benefits From an NA? We believe that the primary beneficiaries are the people whom the organization or agency serves: patients, customers, students, citizens served by government agencies, and other groups in both the public and private sector. From this perspective, we suggest that there are both *valid* and *nonvalid* NAs.

Some purposes of a valid NA would be (a) laying the groundwork for designing a new or improved program of service or education, (b) restructuring an organization in light of better understanding of its goals, (c) setting criteria for hiring training personnel, or (d) determining possible solutions to a complex problem.

A nonvalid NA purpose would be to benefit only the organization itself. An NA may have the hidden agenda of improving public relations or promoting a course of action that has already been decided on. In past years, pertinent literature included the idea that a good reason for an NA was to have the community approve of or validate a program or action. In our view, that is not a legitimate reason for an NA.

How Does NA Relate to the Allocation of Resources? Resource allocation is an important part of organizational or community planning. In the best of all possible worlds, a school or university system, social service agency, or corporation would have all the money they desire to accomplish their goals. Furthermore, all people involved would be working at their highest level of ability and striving to fulfill their potential.

In the real world, there is never enough money to meet all needs, nor do programs and people function perfectly. A major function of policymakers and management is to decide where to put the organization's resources—what programs or services to add, what to maintain, what to cut back or delete. Some things work well, but a lot of others do not. To a large extent, NA grows out of a dissatisfaction with the present state of affairs, whatever that is, and the desire to make improvements. It may also serve the function of analyzing which elements of present programs are working well but need additional support for maintenance or what new services or programs should be added.

For social service agencies, one purpose of NA is to develop a basis for outreach to people who might benefit from the services but who are not now being served. Agencies require data on both unexpressed (or latent) need for services and expressed demand to allocate their resources to programs and groups with the greatest needs.

What Is the Unique Focus of NA? NA focuses on the *ends* to be attained, rather than the *means*, although the data can form the basis for guidelines and criteria for selecting the means or solutions. It also provides a broad base among stakeholders for decision making. One of the reasons for the rise and popularization of NA in the late 1960s and 1970s was that school systems and public agencies saw it as a way of involving the school community in setting goals and priorities, whereas previously, decisions were all too often made unilaterally by governing boards or councils or by individual administrators. NA cannot always prevent decisions made for personal or political reasons, but it does provide a mechanism whereby broader-based decisions are more likely to occur.

Point of View of the Book

This guide presents a three-phase model that combines a logical structure with flexibility and choices to fit the circumstances. It assumes that NA occurs best within an ongoing or cyclical process of strategic planning, program implementation, and evaluation, both formative and summative. We believe that NA offers a useful and rational approach to identifying and describing specific areas of need, discovering factors contributing to its perpetuation, and devising criteria for plans to meet or ameliorate the need.

The book also uses concepts from many disciplines, including organizational communication theory and communication strategies applied to group sensing and deliberation. It furnishes examples of actual NAs from human resources agencies, education, industry, health, city planning, recreation, and social services. Our model also builds in an evaluation of the NA process and methods for enhancing the likelihood of success and the use of the recommendations.

When organizations initiate an NA, they typically take a top-down approach. They define their goals and reasons for the NA, decide what information they should have, and plan and manage the NA. When community groups initiate NA, they take a bottom-up approach. In the latter case, the community may already feel that it knows its needs, and the assessment is often based not so much on getting information about previously unrecognized needs as on seeking widespread community input to refine an understanding of the needs, suggest alternate solutions to known needs, or support certain courses of action.

This book focuses mainly on NAs managed by organizations. Although we recognize the importance of grassroots efforts in NA, the book is intended mainly as a guide for people (usually within an organization) who have the responsibility for designing NAs as an integral part of short- and long-range planning or in concert with program evaluation. Nevertheless, we recognize and emphasize the importance of widespread stakeholder participation in the entire process. We have included many examples that show such participation.

STRENGTHS OF THIS BOOK

A study of several hundred NAs conducted in the United States during the 1980s and early 1990s showed that many had serious shortcomings (Witkin, 1994). Chief among these were the following:

- Confusing means with ends or needs with wishes
- Using only one method for gathering information
- Equating the opinion survey with an NA
- Confusing levels of need (see the following section)
- Failing to use the data to set priorities

This book addresses all of these problems. It seeks to strike a balance between the "right" way(s) to conduct an NA and what is doable and feasible in the context of agencies and institutions and their constraints. We believe that following the three-phase plan results in information that is valid and that will lead to constructive action.

HOW TO USE THIS BOOK

For both newcomers and experienced needs assessors, we recommend reading all of Part I (Chapters 1 through 4) carefully to become familiar with the general model and the three phases of NA. Refer to Chapters 5 through 10 in Part II as the different processes are suggested in Part I.

Needs—Core Concepts

DEFINITIONS OF NEED

The most difficult concept to grasp is the whole idea of "need," in the sense that it has become widely accepted for NA (following Kaufman's work; see Kaufman, 1988). Part of the reason may be due to ambiguity in the language. In NA, the noun and the verb have quite different meanings.

Need as a noun refers to the gap or discrepancy between a present state (what is) and a desired end state, future state, or condition (what should be). The need is neither the present nor the future state; it is the gap between them. Therefore, a need is not a thing in itself but, rather, an inference drawn from examining a present state and comparing it with a vision of a future (better) state or condition. In a sense, a need is like a problem or concern.

Need as a verb points to what is required or desired to fill the discrepancy—solutions, means to an end. There is an important difference between needs and solutions. If you find yourself saying, "I (we, they) need child care, hot lunches, a phonics program, money to hire recreation directors in our parks program, stiffer penalties for drunk driving," you can be sure you are discussing solutions, not needs. The child care or hot lunches or stiffer penalties are means to achieve some desired end—in effect, they are solutions to the underlying problem or concern.[1]

The major drawback to many NAs is that the two meanings of need are often confounded. It will become clearer how to avoid the confusion when we explain the three levels of need.

Unmet Needs. NAs are predicated on the assumption that groups of people have needs that are not being met or not being addressed adequately. When they are aware of such needs, the awareness is often expressed as demands. When they are not aware, the needs are said to be unexpressed or latent. NAs seek to uncover unmet needs, both recognized and latent.[2]

DEFINITION OF NA

At the beginning of this chapter, we proposed a definition of NA in terms of its general purposes. It can also be viewed as a series of procedures for identifying and describing both present and desired states in a specific context, deriving statements of need, and placing the needs in order of priority for later action.

Some writers make a distinction between need identification, needs analysis, and needs assessment. In our approach, identification and analysis of needs are parts of the total process of NA.

Earlier, we stated that an NA was a systematic procedure for setting priorities and making decisions about programs and allocation of resources. Let us look at the components of the definition.

An NA is a *systematic* approach that progresses through a defined series of phases. It gathers data by means of *established procedures and methods* designed for specific purposes. The kinds and scope of methods are selected to fit the purposes and context of the NA. NA *sets priorities and determines criteria for solutions* so that planners and managers can make defensible decisions. NA leads to *action* that will *improve* programs, services, organizational structure and operations, or a combination of these elements. NA *sets criteria* for determining how best to allocate available money, people, facilities, and other resources.

TARGET GROUPS AND LEVELS OF NEED

We have said that NA should be focused on the people in the system, but that statement can be confusing. One way of clarifying the idea is to think in terms of three *levels of need*, each of which also represents a target group for the NA. Figure 1.1 shows two schemas for relationships of the three need levels to a system of interest and to external influences.

Here are examples of components at the three levels:

Level 1 (primary)—*service receivers*: students, clients, patients, information users, commuters, potential customers

Level 2 (secondary)—*service providers and policymakers*: teachers, parents, social workers, caretakers, health care professionals, plant workers, postal employees, librarians, administrators, supervisors, managers

Level 3 (tertiary)—*resources or solutions*: buildings, facilities, equipment, supplies, technology, programs, class size, surgical procedures, information retrieval systems, transportation, salaries and benefits, program delivery systems, time allocations, working conditions

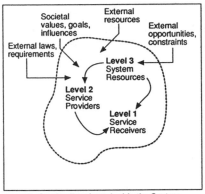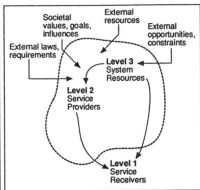

A. Service Receivers Inside the System   **B. Service Receivers Outside the System**

Figure 1.1. Two Schemas Showing Relationships of Three Levels of Target Groups to the System and to External Influences

The people in Level 1 are those for whom the system ultimately exists; they are at the heart of the NA process. Those in Level 2 either have some direct relationship to those in Level 1, providing information, services, training, or nurture, or they perform planning, technical assistance, or oversight functions that affect others in Level 2 as well as, indirectly, those in Level 1. People in Level 2, however, may also have unmet needs related to the functions they perform in relation either to their colleagues (such as managers) or to groups in Level 1.

Therefore, although the prime target for NA—the ones who will ultimately benefit—should be Level 1, NAs can also be performed at Level 2—principally for training needs—or at Level 3, when the needs of the organization *as an organization* or the resources it provides are the focus of the assessment. These distinctions will become clearer in subsequent chapters, through descriptions of NAs at different levels and for different purposes.

Figure 1.1 also shows the three levels in two different system contexts and with different relationships to persons in Level 1. Schema A depicts an organization such as a university or the clients (members) of a health maintenance organization in which the service receivers, the primary focus of the NA, are within the system on a regular basis. Services and resources are focused on the students or clients. The people in Level 1 constitute a known, or "closed," group. In Schema B, the service receivers are outside the system. Examples are potential clients of social service agencies within a catchment area or potential customers of a business. The exact numbers and characteristics of such persons are to a large extent unknown, and they therefore constitute a "fuzzy" group. (Market research in business is an example of an attempt to discover the characteristics and wishes of fuzzy groups.)

In both schemas, the system (agency, organization) is subject to various external influences: societal goals and values, economic and social forces, funding sources, family, religious organizations, the physical environment, political factors, legislative mandates, and other opportunities and constraints. The needs assessor takes such influences into account when planning and monitoring the NA.

We reiterate that, ideally, a valid NA is focused first of all on Level 1. It seeks to determine the needs of the people for whom the organization or system exists. The brief descriptions at the beginning of this chapter are of Level 1 NAs. Other examples of Level 1 NAs are those conducted to (a) assess the career planning needs of psychology majors at a large university, (b) identify personal and schooling needs of learning disabled children, and (c) analyze the physical and mental health needs of persons over age 55 who are enrolled in a health maintenance organization.

Many NAs, however, are conducted at Level 2. Examples are to determine preservice training needs of counselors, determine inservice needs of elementary teachers where a new math program is being instituted, and determine training needs of electrical workers in a manufacturing plant that is adopting new processes. Organizations in which the service receivers are outside the system often conduct Level 2 NAs in areas such as the physical and mental health needs or training needs of their staff—the service providers. Level 2 NAs may also be conducted to serve the information needs of an emerging field of technology, to perform a task analysis in a changing field, or for policy reasons in a specific context.

Level 3 needs often masquerade as Level 1. That is, educators may assert that a school system "needs" more school buses, a different reading program, a longer school day, or computers in every classroom. But those are really solutions to Level 1 needs. Many Level 3 NAs in public agencies focus on the "need" for different types of transportation or maintenance of buildings. There are legitimate reasons for conducting such assessments. Our point of view, however, is that NAs at the second and third levels should grow out of adequate Level 1 assessments, or at least be consciously based on an understanding of Level 1 needs from prior investigation.

The ideal NA, then, begins at Level 1 and is related to societal and organizational goals.[3] Beginning at Level 1 is particularly important if the agency or organization has not previously conducted an NA. If previous NAs have been conducted, however, cyclical updating or other requirements may make it advisable to start at Level 2 or 3. For example, a large health maintenance organization undertakes yearly assessments of its buildings' and facilities' needs for repairs, maintenance, new facilities, and the like, but these Level 3 NAs are implicitly related to needs at Levels 1 and 2 (see Chapter 3 for details).

The previous history of NAs or evaluations of programs and services in the system is relevant to present NAs and their focus. If prior data collection has occurred, the needs assessment should take advantage of it. The important factor is that the needs assessor and needs assessment committee (NAC; see Chapter 2) should be fully aware of what is being assessed, why, and at what level. Assessments of training or facilities needs are by no means complete NAs, and care must be taken that solutions or programs are not confused with the ultimate needs (Level 1) that they are intended to meet.

THE IDEA OF A SYSTEM

A *system* is a regularly interacting or interdependent group of people forming a unified whole and organized for a common purpose. In this text, we use system to refer to the organization or group involved with the NA.

An important characteristic of a system is that all parts are interdependent. Anything that affects one part of the system has consequences for the whole. We advocate an approach to NA that identifies processes and functions that cross organizational lines, with the goal of increasing chances for success and reducing chances for failure. Our approach also recognizes that systems such as schools and social agencies exist within the broader context of the community and that they must take that context into account in NA.

Typical systems that conduct NAs are educational (K-12 schools, universities, private training institutions), health related (hospitals, health agencies), social services (departments of health and welfare, counseling agencies, relief organizations), trade and commerce (manufacturers, retail businesses), and public service and government (municipalities, park and recreation districts, state governments and agencies).

The boundaries and scope of the system whose needs are being assessed are determined by definition. An NA could be conducted of a state library system, a regional or county library system, the libraries in one city, or a specific program in a library, such as school outreach or on-line services for the public via computers.

Finally, problems of systems are also often messy, ambiguous, ongoing, and rarely completely solved. They stem from multiple and interacting causes. Needs assessors must be cognizant of this complexity as they carry out their work.

A Three-Phase Plan for Assessing Needs

Figure 1.2 displays a general plan for assessing needs in three phases. They occur in sequence, and each phase concludes with a written product. The boundaries between them are not fixed, however; they merely suggest a time progression of a given set of tasks.

Phase 1, *preassessment* (described in Chapter 2), is exploratory. Its function is to determine what is already known about needs in the system; to identify issues and major areas of concern; and to decide on system boundaries, focus and purpose of the NA, potential sources of data, how the information will be used, and what kinds of decisions will be made on the basis of the findings. In Phase 1, the needs assessor also develops the design and management plan for Phase 2 and sets criteria for evaluating the whole needs assessment.

In Phase 2, the *main assessment* (data gathering) occurs. The needs assessor and NAC gather and analyze information and opinions on the needs, set preliminary priorities, and analyze causes related to all three system levels (see Chapter 3).

Phase 3, *postassessment*, is the bridge to use of the data and plans for action. The principal tasks are to set priorities and criteria for solutions, weigh alternative solutions, and formulate action plans for program changes or other interventions. Information on the NA design, results, and recommendations for action are communicated to decision makers and other stakeholders, and relevant information is prepared for archives and other uses (see Chapter 4). The evaluation of the NA itself also occurs in Phase 3.

PHASE 1 Preassessment (exploration)	PHASE 2 Assessment (data gathering)	PHASE 3 Postassessment (utilization)
Set up management plan for NA	Determine context, scope, and boundaries of the NA	Set priorities on needs at all applicable levels
Define general purpose of the NA	Gather data on needs	Consider alternative solutions
Identify major need areas and/or issues	Set preliminary priorities on needs—Level 1	Develop action plan to implement solutions
Identify existing information regarding need areas	Perform causal analyses at Levels 1, 2, and 3	Evaluate the NA
Determine: • Data to collect • Sources • Methods • Potential uses of data	Analyze and synthesize all data	Communicate results
Outcomes:	**Outcomes:**	**Outcomes:**
Preliminary plan for Phases 2 and 3, and plan for evaluation of the NA	Criteria for action based on high-priority needs	Action plan(s), written and oral briefings, and reports

Figure 1.2. Three-Phase Plan for Needs Assessment

Contexts of Needs Assessments

To a certain extent, NA takes its character and methods from the context in which it is done. In an organizational context, NA ideally occurs as an integral part of a cycle that consists of planning, program installation and implementation, and evaluation. Viewed in its simplest form, there is a circular relationship in which evaluation of the adequacy and effects of programs that were installed to meet certain needs leads logically to a new phase of NA and planning. In practice, this circular relationship is more complex and interrelated than it at first seems. NA may occur in any phase of the cycle (see Figure 3.3 in Chapter 3).

We have identified five context-embedded perspectives of organizations that influence NAs and the collection of needs-related data. They are planning, evaluative, cyclical, ongoing for a management information system (MIS), and collaborative. The five perspectives are described in detail in Chapter 3.

Planning and Conducting the NA

An NA, like other purposeful and systematic activities, is planned, monitored, and evaluated (see Chapter 2). *Planning* includes deciding on the objectives, focus, and scope of the assessment; obtaining commitment to the effort and the use of its results; appointing a NAC; and designing and implementing NA procedures. Planning can also include a causal analysis of the NA itself, to predict potential problems and to redesign the plan if necessary.

Monitoring consists of periodic checks to see that the NA is proceeding in a timely fashion along the lines desired, particularly in Phase 2 (assessment); making necessary adjustments in time lines or data-gathering procedures; and ensuring that all requisite communication and action linkages inside and outside the system are kept operative. Monitoring alerts the needs assessor to the need for corrective action before a problem escalates.

We have found that monitoring can be enhanced by posting on a wall a large flowchart (or success map—see Chapter 10) of the planned activities, with indications of target dates and persons responsible for various activities. Both professional and support staff involved in the NA can use the chart to see how their work fits into the whole picture and to give feedback to the needs assessor on contingencies that may arise.

Evaluation is designed with criteria such that when the NA is complete, the NAC and the policymakers have a clear picture of the extent to which the NA met its stated goals—and if some of the goals were not met, the reasons why. Certain methods of causal analysis described in Chapter 10 can be used to predict potential problems in completing the NA as planned and to suggest areas to redesign.

KEY FACTORS IN CONDUCTING NAs

Before discussing the three phases in detail, we call attention to some factors that are basic to a successful NA:

- Keep in mind the value and necessity of broad-based participation by stakeholders.
- Choose appropriate means of gathering information about critical issues and other data.
- Recognize core values in the group whose needs are being assessed.
- NA is a participatory process; it is not something that is "done to" people.
- NA cannot ignore political factors. Some people may view the process as causing a loss of control. The priorities derived may be counter to entrenched ideas in the system.
- Data-gathering methods by themselves are not an NA. The NA is a total decision-making process, in which the data are but one component.

Every NA situation is different. There is no one "right" way that applies to every NA, although there are a few general principles to guide the needs assessor. Chapter 2 suggests some ways to start from where you are, then branch out, depending on the previous history of the system and other relevant factors.

A CAUTION BEFORE BEGINNING

The notion that there is or should be a systematic and rational way to obtain information and set priorities is an ideal that may be difficult to achieve in practice. People who have closely observed how skillful decision makers behave and the conditions under which they work suggest that "actual decision makers face:

1. ambiguous and poorly defined problems;
2. incomplete information about alternatives;
3. incomplete information about the baseline, the background of the problem;
4. incomplete information about the consequences of supposed alternatives;
5. incomplete information about the range and content of values, preferences, and interests; and
6. limited time, limited skills, and limited resources." (Forester, 1989, p. 50)

Forester (1989) points out that there is a continuum of decision making running from the idealized situation of the rationalist to highly politically structured and distorted situations. One task for the needs assessor is to determine where along this continuum the organization lies. To a large extent, the structure of the situation will determine what is practical as well as rational to do in it. The framework we propose provides tools for improving the definition of problems and information about their causes and possible consequences. It also suggests alternative paths and procedures to adapt to the situation, without sacrificing clarity of purpose.

SUMMARY

The major purpose of NA is to gather information for setting priorities on needs of people in relation to a system of interest. Data from the NA are used to set criteria for allocating resources and for developing new or improved programs or services to meet the needs.

This guide presents a three-phase plan for conducting an NA. We advocate viewing NA and target groups from three levels, to clarify distinctions between needs of primary recipients of services or programs (Level 1) and the people and resources that exist because of them (Levels 2 and 3). The activities of the NA are carried out with the help of a management design for planning, monitoring, and evaluating the project.

Chapters 2, 3, and 4 of Part I explain the three phases: preassessment, assessment, and postassessment. In Part II, Chapters 5 through 9 describe methods appropriate to gathering data for assessing needs, and Chapter 10 describes three methods for causal analysis.

Notes

1. Many NAs at Level 3 do focus on solutions or demands for programs, products, or services. Unless they are consciously based on data regarding Level 1 needs of the target population, we regard them as essentially market research. The question is, What is really the nature of the need that the program or service is expected to fulfill or solve?

2. An in-depth discussion of needs definitions can be found in Witkin (1991).

3. For elaboration of this point of view, see Kaufman's Organizational Elements Model (Kaufman, Rojas, & Mayer, 1993). Kaufman also discusses levels of need, but in a different conceptual framework.

⊗

TWO

Phase 1—Preassessment

Purpose of the Preassessment Phase

The purpose of the preassessment phase is to investigate what is already known about the needs of the target group; to determine the focus and scope of the assessment; and to gain commitment for all stages of the assessment, including the use of the findings for program planning and implementation. The preassessment also provides the basis for determining the most appropriate kinds of data-gathering methods for the assessment. The following vignette shows the context, original design, and focus of an NA planned by a school district, and how a preassessment changed the elements of the NA the district had previously decided on.

The Waverly Valley Joint School District is in a rapidly growing region about 30 miles from a large city. The city of Waverly (until recently, a small town in the midst of farms and orchards) was undergoing a rapid spurt in growth, which the city council resisted by trying to pass legislation to prevent newcomers from moving in; it didn't work. The families of the students were a mix of farmers (some transient), middle-class retirees, and affluent couples with young children. A large percentage of the latter worked at the nearby research laboratory (an arm of the state university) or put up with a long commute to the large metropolis in exchange for quiet living and a good school system. The most prominent minority in the district (about 18%) was Hispanic.

The Waverly District had four elementary, two intermediate, and two high schools. Seeing the writing on the wall and anticipating an enrollment increase of at least 2% per year, the district board decided to conduct an NA survey.

The criteria for the NA set by the administrative council of the district were (a) minimal time expenditure by site administrators, (b) minimal cost (no more than $700 to conduct the survey), and (c) usefulness of information to individual schools as well as to the district as a whole.

The superintendent asked the county schools office that served the area for help in designing an NA survey. The county superintendent appointed two consultants from the office of planning and research to assist the district. They submitted a proposal, in accordance with the district's request, to construct a questionnaire to be sent to teachers, parents, and the community. The consultants suggested that the district appoint a steering committee representing teachers and administrators across all school levels and including a district administrator and a board member. They also submitted a procedural statement and a suggested time line for the NA activities.

The school board adopted the proposal with an appropriate budget and appointed a steering committee of 19, which included parents and two citizens at large in addition to staff and administrators.

After a preliminary meeting with the administrative council, however, the consultants persuaded the steering committee to engage in some preassessment activities before committing to a survey. As a result, the steering committee, which had now become the needs assessment committee (NAC), decided to take a different approach and to use a survey as only one part of NA data gathering. The consultants submitted a revised NA proposal, which the board accepted.

What occurred to change the minds of the NAC? After the first meeting with the administrative council to explore the reasons for the NA and what the district hoped to gain from it, the consultants realized that much of the basic data was already available in district files or elsewhere. They also believed that the survey contemplated by the administration was too broad and unfocused to form an adequate basis for action on needs.

Therefore, they submitted a revised proposal to conduct a pre-assessment consisting of two half-day sessions with the NAC, held about a month apart, with data gathering in the interim. The following section explains the format of those sessions.

A Two-Session Preassessment Process

The two-session process used at Waverly is applicable to many NA contexts. This section gives examples of the kinds of information gathered and decisions made in the two preassessment meetings. The total elapsed time, including gathering data in the interim, was about 2 months. No special costs were incurred by the district (interim data gathering was done by supervisory staff, and there were no costs for the two county office consultants), and time commitments of the NAC were relatively small.

PLANNING FOR SESSION 1

In their original interviews with the administrative council, the consultants found that the district had a written statement of philosophy and 18 goals. The philosophy statement pledged to "provide the necessary educational opportunities to help each student realize his or her potential. To do this, the district will be responsive to each student's academic, intellectual, emotional, physical, and social needs."

Six goals were at Level 1, directly related to student outcomes or values. Two were Level 2 goals, for staff and support services. The rest were at Level 3: four related to curriculum programs, two to school-community relations and communication, and one each to equipment, facilities, the learning environment, and management planning. Prior to Session 1, the NAC members were asked to (a) review the goals and (b) list those that appeared to be most closely related to unmet student needs.

SESSION 1 PROCEDURES

Table 2.1 shows the schedule for Session 1.

TABLE 2.1 Schedule for Preassessment Session 1

Time	Group Configuration[a]	Activity
8:30–8:45	A & B	Introduction and overview
8:45–9:30	A/B	Generate list of concerns: Identify top six goals with five concerns for each
9:30–10:00	A & B	Share goals and concerns: Select top four goals with five concerns each
10:00–10:15		Break
10:15–11:00	A/B AAA/BBB	Decide on major concerns Write data resources list
11:00–11:30	A & B	Share and discuss list
11:30–12:00	A & B	Designate people and tasks for interim data quest; final discussion and questions

a. A & B designates one large group; A/B designates two groups working independently; AAA/BBB designates possibility of groups dividing into dyads or triads and working independently.

The consultants explained the reason for the preassessment session and how the group would work. The NAC was divided randomly into groups A and B, which worked separately as well as together. After they reached consensus on the six goals of most importance in terms of unmet needs, they brainstormed a list of concerns for each of those goals. The group then narrowed the list to the top four goals and, after much discussion, decided on the major concerns for each goal (for small group techniques, see Chapters 7 and 8).

The NAC then discussed indicators that could verify that the concerns existed, the people affected, what was already known about the concerns, what kinds of further information would be helpful, and where to get the data. The information for "what is known" was collated on a wall chart, and the NAC listed additional facts to be gathered in the intersession period. The material was displayed in a Data Resources List depicted in Table 2.2.

Each member volunteered to gather and bring to Session 2 specific information on indicators such as incidence of fights and vandalism, attendance records, and the like. Such data would give clues as to the

TABLE 2.2 Data Resources List Format for Preassessment

Goal:

Concern:

What Is Known		Data to Gather	
Facts	Sources	Facts	Sources
		Opinions	Sources

NOTE: Additional columns may be added to indicate who will be responsible for gathering the data and target dates.

extent of the problem—whether it was widespread or limited to a few highly visible incidents. They also decided what kinds of opinions about the concern area should be collected—as to importance of the concern, frequency of occurrence, and the like—and from whom to gather them.

Chapter 5 gives examples of several kinds of information available for preassessment. The group analyzes concerns, indicators of the problem, and who is affected by the problem. At Waverly, one of the concerns related to the goal that students would respect authority and the rights of others. Some indications that a problem existed were observations of student fights, vandalism, and a sense of disorder in many classrooms. The NAC decided to document incidents (numbers, types, times of occurrence, etc.) and to gather indicators of success in the goal area as well.

INTERIM PERIOD BETWEEN SESSIONS

In the 2-week period between Sessions 1 and 2, both the NAC and the consultants were busy. The consultants organized the information from Session 1 and circulated a summary to the NAC and key administrators. They also designed charts for Session 2. The NAC members examined district records related to the issues. Some of the NAC conducted informal mini-surveys among teachers and students to get a sense of how closely their opinions about some of the issues matched the actual data. Results were used later in designing a questionnaire.

SESSION 2 PROCEDURES

When the data were collated at Session 2, the NAC discovered that enough was already known about some of the concerns that further formal NA on those issues was unnecessary. The remaining issues formed the basis for Phase 2 data gathering through two questionnaires. One was designed for parents, students, and staff based on school goals related to high-priority concerns, and one was for a community sample regarding recreational needs of both students and residents in the district and the region.

The plan for Phase 2, which narrowed the scope and focused the NA on high-priority areas of concern, included the two questionnaires and a focus group interview with the NAC and other stakeholders. The consultants assisted a writing team in designing the questionnaires; the staff conducted the survey and analyzed the data.

Functions of the Preassessment Phase

In summary, the major functions of Phase 1 are the following:

- To set up planning and management groups, define obligations of all parties, and develop group ownership of the NA process and outcomes
- To conduct a preliminary investigation of what is known about the need
- To identify the purposes and scope of the NA, to set the focus, and to clarify potential uses of the NA findings
- To devise and obtain approval for a preliminary plan for Phases 2 and 3, including target dates, timelines, and budget, with contingency clauses permitting modification as more information is gathered
- To deal with relevant matters in the political context of the organization, institution, or agency desiring the NA
- To build in procedures to ensure use of the findings in Phase 3 in terms of commitment by management to implement an action plan

A caution about preassessment is in order here. We strongly recommend a preassessment to prevent reinventing the wheel. But NAs that build on previous work may easily become tied to the status quo. That is, the needs assessors may decide that the needs have not changed in character or scope, or that some needs have already been solved by programs that were installed earlier. The work of the preassessment phase is to find hard data that indicate the presence and nature of a set of needs and then to suggest the kinds of data and investigative methods that go beyond present knowledge and either verify the continuation of past needs or identify the emergence of new ones. Chapter 9 discusses methods of anticipating future needs.

Managing the Preassessment Phase

Phase 1 activities, as well as the plan for Phase 2, depend to a large extent on what has already occurred in the system, such as prior NAs, the context of the NA activity, and the purposes for which the results will be used. Figure 2.1 suggests a way of focusing and narrowing the scope of the assessment.

The order in which the preassessment activities occur also partially depends on who initiates the request for the NA and whether the needs assessor is internal to the organization or is an external consultant retained for that purpose. In addition, the authority and role of the needs assessor relate to the size of the organization. In small or medium-sized agencies, the NA is often conducted in-house, and the person in charge may be a planner, evaluator, or a mid-level administrator assigned to the task.

Large organizations frequently hire an external consultant or firm to design and conduct the NA. The organization may employ a consultant to design the NA and develop data-gathering processes but use its own staff to gather the data.

THE NEEDS ASSESSMENT COMMITTEE
(NAC—PLANNING GROUP)

The NAC works with the needs assessor to set policy, assist with designing procedures and instruments, and provide general direction and support for the NA. It is broadly representative of the stakeholders in the assessment and drawn from the target population or service

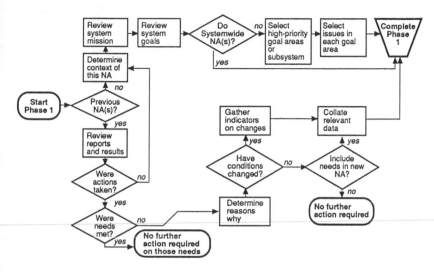

Figure 2.1. Decision Flow for Focusing the Needs Assessment, Phase 1

receivers, the service providers, and interested community members. It may also include people who have specialized knowledge about the general concerns of the NA.

A NAC for a school system could consist of students and parents as well as teachers, administrators, clerical and support staff, and community persons from the area served by the schools. The committee for a social agency planning an NA of a certain category of clients might include representatives of the target group in addition to agency staff persons.

The state parks and recreation field furnishes an example of a NAC primarily consisting of individuals external to the system conducting the NA. Consider the case of the need and possible plans for a new state park. Here the NAC might come from representatives of organized camping and recreational vehicle groups, hikers, steelhead fishers, kayakers, equestrians, the Audubon Society, the Nature Conservancy, retailers of recreational and sporting goods, and neighbors of the site.

Although the NAC should represent as broad a constituency as possible, too large a group may become unwieldy and not able to reach consensus easily. A compromise is to divide the work between two groups: the NAC, which might contain 20 or 25 people who act in an advisory and policy-making capacity, and a core committee composed of 8 to 12 persons drawn from the NAC who do most of the actual work of Phase 1. In practice, we have found that the NAC might need only three or four meetings: the first to set the broad direction of the NA, one or two for progress reports, and one to review and approve the plan for Phase 2. Later, in Phase 3, the NAC is a prime source of support for action plans to meet high-priority needs.

MEMORANDUM OF AGREEMENT

Regardless of whether the needs assessor is a staff member or an external consultant, the direction and limits of the NA are best spelled out in a written memorandum that has been negotiated between the needs assessor and the NAC or other oversight committee. The agreement defines the obligations of the needs assessor, the NAC, and the sponsoring organization or agency. The act of putting expectations and obligations in writing clarifies ambiguities and documents the consensus of expectations. Essentially, the memorandum attests to the commitment of top management to support the NA and to follow through with the use of its findings.

A preliminary memorandum specifies the purpose of the assessment, measurable objectives, and criteria for evaluating the fulfillment of NA activities. It clarifies the roles and duties of the needs assessor, the roles and obligations of the NAC, and the lines of responsibility and authority within the system for administrative support and approval at critical stages. It includes dates for completion of phases and objectives, resources needed, and a budget.

With a Phase 1 agreement, the needs assessor can control the types and levels of data input in Phase 2 without being tied to an unworkable plan. This is done by stipulating that certain decisions or tasks in Phase 2 be contingent on the outcomes of Phase 1. At the end of Phase 1, a modified agreement will embody the final plan for Phases 2 and 3. Thus, the memorandum provides for appropriate changes in focus or scope or for alternative data collection strategies in Phase 2.

If the principal needs assessor is an external consultant, these components are included in a formal contract. In this case, it is particularly important to be specific about target dates, deliverables, budget, and criteria for evaluation.

GROUP OWNERSHIP

A major outcome of Phase 1, preassessment, is a sense of commitment to the NA at both high and low levels in the organization and an assurance that decision makers will follow up the findings with appropriate and timely action. If the NA is conducted in the context of long-range strategic planning, such commitment is built into the process. Unfortunately, many NAs have no such context but are conducted for other reasons—to satisfy a funding source, to make the organization look good with its public, or to sway public opinion in favor of a program or policy already decided on by top management. As noted in Chapter 1, these types do not qualify as valid NAs.

The active use of a representative NAC is one important method for gaining commitment to the process and the results. Timely reports to top management and other important stakeholders, with opportunity for interaction on crucial issues, also are critical. The more that people feel that they are involved from the beginning, the greater the sense of ownership of the results.

Preliminary Data Gathering— What Is Known

The case of Waverly, cited earlier in this chapter, shows one way of gathering preliminary NA data. In summary, the tasks to be accomplished are these:

1. Identify issues related to the NA area(s). How this is done depends to a certain extent on the context.

   - If the NA is part of strategic planning (see Chapter 9) and overall organizational renewal, begin with a review of the system goals; if necessary, update or modify them. Use focus group interviews (Chapter 7) with key informants to pinpoint goals that are not being met or areas in which the system has lost direction.
   - If a high-risk area has already been identified (due to environmental factors, system changes, or poor performance), use it as a starting point. Issues identified as belonging to one goal area or part of the system often have ramifications in other parts, so don't assume that identification of a given goal area at this point irrevocably sets the parameters of Phase 2 assessment.

- The NA may be part of an ongoing or cyclical planning-monitoring-evaluation process, and previous NAs may have been conducted. Phase 1, then, investigates what high-priority needs were identified earlier, what actions were taken, and how well the needs were met or ameliorated as a result. If no actions were taken or if they were ineffective, the NAC ascertains what causal factors (Chapter 10) and barriers might have operated.

- The organization might have conducted an NA several years prior to the present one, but not as part of an ongoing plan. What were the purposes and focus then? Why? Sometimes organizational memory is short, due to turnover in key management or staff positions. In Phase 1, the NAC reviews reports of previous NAs and finds out what actions, if any, were taken as a result and whether the present situation reflects any improvement of those needs.

No matter which of the foregoing circumstances are relevant, an NA does not occur in a vacuum. Investigating the history of previous efforts will pay off in the long run.

2. Determine indicators of need in each issues area.
3. Identify what is already known about the need from archival data and current wisdom.
4. Identify what kinds of information would more clearly define the need.
5. Identify the best potential sources of the information and methods of obtaining it.
6. Set general preliminary priorities for each area at the three levels of need (as appropriate) as a focus for gathering data.

Note that preassessment activities not only define potential sources of data but also indicate probable best methods for data collection. For example, analysis of information on existing sources might show the need for amplification or verification with specific informants, leading to targeted surveys or focus groups.

Designing Phase 2—Assessment

Once the preliminary analysis has been made, the NAC is in a position to design the activities for Phase 2, Assessment. The following steps are included in the design.

1. Describe the purposes and scope of the NA.

   - Why is the NA being undertaken? Who will use the results? What decisions will probably be made on the basis of the information? Will the NA cover a whole system (organization, agency, institution, school district) or one or more subsystems, such as a program, unit, or department? What is the rationale for the scope?
   - *If the scope is too broad,* the usual results are unwieldy data, over-expenditure of time and other resources (at the risk of curtailing subsequent action to alleviate the needs), the difficulty of establishing priorities and a focus for action to meet the needs, and so forth. The NA may attempt to deal with too many concerns in too superficial a manner and fail to analyze any area in sufficient depth to provide meaningful criteria for action. The NA may take so long to complete that exhaustion sets in.
   - *If the scope is too narrow,* the study may fail to uncover significant needs. If limited to the most obvious areas of need, it may result in wasted effort and failure to go beyond the conventional wisdom of what is already known or perceived to be true.

2. Define the focus for Level 1 and, if necessary, for Levels 2 and 3. What are the Level 1 target groups (service receivers) whose needs are being assessed? How are those needs related to the major issues and concerns raised in Phase 1? If the NA is to focus on Level 2 or Level 3 needs, what is the rationale? What Level 1 needs are implied?

3. Determine types of data to be gathered, best sources, and methods (see Chapters 5 through 10 for data-gathering and analytic processes).

4. Lay out target dates and timelines for completion of the Phase 2 tasks.

5. Describe resources needed and a budget.

6. Identify potential users of the results and methods that will be used to communicate with them—reports, oral briefings, and the like (see Chapter 4 for suggestions).

7. Describe briefly how the NA will be evaluated in terms of its stated objectives. For guidelines on this step, see the section, "Designing an Evaluation Plan for the NA."

8. Include a contingency clause for modification of the Phase 2 plan based on findings from Phase 1, and explain the reasons.

9. Obtain approval for the plan.

Boundary Considerations for Phase 2

RATIONALE FOR DOING A SUBSYSTEM NA

In the Waverly example, the scope of the NA covered general concerns of interest applicable to all the schools. But sometimes a preassessment reveals system constraints that make it difficult to conduct a comprehensive NA of an entire organization. In such cases, it may be advisable to begin with one or two units and later to expand to the whole system. An example of the desirability of beginning with a subsystem is illustrated by the Templeton experience.

The Templeton school district wanted to develop a cyclical NA for its high schools focusing on gathering a database for improvement of departmental programs. The district retained a consultant to design an NA plan in cooperation with an advisory committee of teachers, department heads, and parents.

Prior to this time, the advisory committee had conducted a brief survey of parents as to their perceptions of the greatest academic needs of students in the high schools. Their opinion of the highest priority need was in the area of reading, which was surprising because the students scored very high on state and national reading tests; almost all of the students intended to go to college. It was evident that their parents, who had academic or professional careers, were responding to what they read in the papers about the deplorable state of education in general rather than to actual needs of the majority of students in the district. In informal interviews with some English teachers and the English department chair, the consultant verified the fact that the majority of students (except for a very few with learning disabilities) had little need for basic reading skills, although many of them could benefit from assistance with difficult material in science and social studies. (See Chapter 6, for discussion of defects in superficial surveys of perceptions of need.)

The committee also found that few people were aware of the district goals, which would be used to base the "vision" aspect of the NA. Accordingly, the consultant and the committee designed two preassessment activities:

1. The committee examined the list of district goals and filled out forms indicating in which department(s) and course(s) each goal was ad-

dressed or implemented. They discovered that some goals were not implemented anywhere in the curriculum and that some courses reflected implied goals that did not occur anywhere in the district list. As a result, the advisory committee recommended a long-range curriculum review and that the present NA be limited.

2. The high schools in the district were highly departmentalized, with each department having almost complete autonomy; only a few departments elected to participate in the NA. Therefore, the first round of NAs was conducted with those departments only. A NAC was formed of the chairs of the most interested departments in one high school: English, foreign languages, mathematics, physical education, science, and history. The activities of the preassessment occurred over a 3-month period. The issues and data from separate departments were later collated, and schoolwide issues were defined as the basis for a comprehensive NA. Plans were made for other departments to participate in subsequent years.

STEPS IN A DEPARTMENTALIZED (SUBSYSTEM) NA

Figure 2.2 shows the general flow of events for a departmentalized NA derived from goal-based issues.

Following is an explanation of the steps shown in Figure 2.2.

1.0 The status of system goals relevant to the department was analyzed. This was accomplished in meetings with department heads. They were asked the question, "If you walked into a classroom in your department, how could you tell whether the class was meeting certain goals? What would be observable indicators?"

1.1 The department heads identified indicators of success in reaching the goal, either from student performance in the classroom or from other evidence such as work portfolios, projects, or test scores.

1.2 The department heads also identified indicators of failure to reach the goal.

2.0 On the basis of success and failure indicators, the department heads listed sets of issues for each goal area in the department.

3.0 They then selected the highest-priority issues by department. Criteria included importance of the issue in reaching the goal, risk to the students if the goal was not met, and frequency of occurrence of the issue.

4.0 They set standards on each issue—standards for adequacy and for excellence. In other words, two levels of need were postulated: a basic

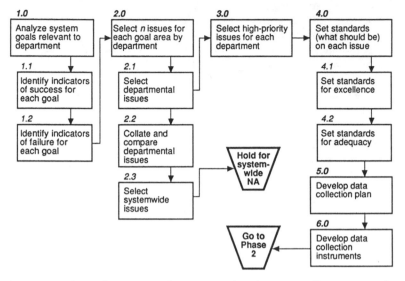

Figure 2.2. Flow of Events in Phase 1, Based on Issues in a Departmental System

need level, defined by the degree to which performance fell below adequate, and a need level related to excellence. The latter was proposed because, in general, students performed at above-average levels, yet many failed to reach levels of excellence that were within their individual abilities.

5.0 The department heads specified a data collection plan.

6.0 They developed data collection instruments and processes.

At a later date, issues and priorities for NA of the different departments were compared and collated, and a systemwide NA was planned using similar steps. At the individual departmental level, most of the issues and needs were student-centered (Level 1), although some Level 2 needs emerged. At the system level, issues related to both Level 2 and Level 3 were appropriate.

For example, one of the issues that appeared in the foreign language department related to the ability of students to converse fluently in the language. Many of the students studying French had the opportunity to travel to France, yet the instructional program focused almost entirely on reading and writing the language, with little opportunity for listening and speaking. The preliminary analysis indicated that one source of the problem was that teachers were more comfortable teaching the language for academic rather than communication purposes. Consequently, students seldom or never attained oral proficiency.[1]

The Templeton experience is an illustration of one way to focus the NA for Phase 2 as well as a rationale for narrowing the scope. Another instance when a limited NA is appropriate is if the organization has already done one or more comprehensive NAs based on its mission and major goals.

The cyclical aspect of the NA is found in the fact that departments are added to the NA on a rotating basis. After the first NA was completed, the district administrator who had requested the NA drew up a plan for a cyclical NA model for the district. The plan proposed adding three or four new departments each year until all departments had participated, using the same model as the first year; the earlier departments updated their data yearly. After the cycle was complete, all departments updated their data about every 3 years. The results of the schoolwide surveys were also used to refine the focus for subsequent years, and information from the surveys was recorded in a computerized database.

Political and Contextual
Factors to Consider for Phase 2

NAs require a democratic process, but, ultimately, the search for an objective, nonpolitical approach may be doomed (Witkin & Eastmond, 1988). NA requires a weighing of political factors, either overt or covert. The greater the number of people to be served, the more complex the organization, and the more critical the needs and issues appear to be, the more likely that political factors will play a part. That is, decision makers may take certain positions for reasons of ideology, protection of "turf," or commitment to certain courses of action, or to be an advocate for a particular cause.

Single-issue groups can also be a major political factor in NA. Such groups tend to see issues only through the prism of their particular concerns, whether it be child abuse, housing for the homeless, or a phonics program as the ultimate answer to illiteracy.

One place to begin is with the reasons for the NA. How will the results be used? What groups will be affected? Are there hidden agendas, such as a desire for improved public relations or a way to rationalize projected cuts in programs or staff? Has the administration already decided on the scope and focus? Does it want to use procedures that might be inappropriate? Is the NA process simply a guise for justifying the installation of a program or service that has already been decided on?

The needs assessor who is an administrator or staff member of the sponsoring organization is probably more aware than an external consultant of these factors and of the political climate and organizational culture. Nevertheless, a needs assessor committed to a rational, systematic approach to NA may neglect to account for such factors in the plan. Implicit in many of the recommendations we propose for Phase 1 is the recognition of political factors. The main features are to (a) identify the interests, concerns, and worries of the key decision makers, gatekeepers, and stakeholders; (b) work out a written agreement that spells out what is expected on both sides; (c) choose and work constructively with a NAC whose members are broadly representative of stakeholders, and who can be prepared to vouch for the authenticity of the results of the NA; and (d) provide feedback at appropriate times to those who need to know.

Some experts on public involvement suggest that the NAC include people with divergent views of the problem, including some who might be critics or opponents of a policy or program in question. We advise exercising caution on this point. People with very strong and irreconcilable opinions may hamstring a committee and polarize the members into positions that impede further progress. On the other hand, the NAC will be strengthened by including people with contrasting opinions, but who are also open-minded and capable of conflict resolution.

Experience teaches that the area most likely for disagreement is that of solutions to the problem, not the nature of the needs. Disagreements may also arise at the point that decisions must be made about relative criticality of needs, all of which appear to have high priority. In part, this is because the matter of priorities is related to allocation of resources for programs and services. Chapter 4 offers some guidelines on which to base decisions on priorities, including both qualitative and quantitative methods.

Designing an Evaluation Plan
for the Needs Assessment

The purpose of an evaluation plan is accountability: How well did the NA meet its stated goals? An evaluation also gives information useful for future NAs. If the NA is to occur over an extended period of time, it is wise to do a *formative evaluation*—that is, monitor the project to be sure that tasks are being accomplished in a timely fashion and take corrective action if problems should arise. A *summative evaluation*, to answer the question of how well the NA met its goals, is embodied in the final report.

We recommend that the needs assessor and NAC construct a *success map* of the NA, showing how you envision the project to take place. The map also serves as a guide for the NAC, the NA staff, and other interested persons to follow projected events and as a monitoring device. If the NA is complex and subject to potential internal or external risks, you may wish to use some simple predictive devices for potential failures. Chapter 10 describes success mapping and several techniques for decreasing the likelihood of failure and maximizing success.

Some points to consider are (a) the degree to which NA tasks are accomplished in a timely and substantive manner in accord with the memorandum of agreement, (b) the ability to modify NA activities as warranted, (c) the completeness of the data collected, (d) the quality of the data in terms of identifying and explaining the nature of needs, (e) the degree to which the NA data are useful in developing action plans, (f) the quality of action plans (feasibility, acceptance, delineation of options), and (g) the level and nature of communications with key decision makers and stakeholders.

Most of the formative evaluation can be informal, setting aside time at NAC meetings to discuss the nature of these criteria and the extent to which they are being attained. Another option is to use an independent panel of three to five persons, similar in makeup to the NAC, to review periodically the progress and outcomes of the NA.

Needs and Solutions in Perspective:
The Case of the Pokey Elevators—A Cautionary Tale[2]

The manager of a 20-story office building was besieged by complaints from the tenants that the elevators were too slow. The elevators were positioned in a row on one side of a central corridor, with offices on both sides and on the opposite side of the corridor. To rectify the problem, the manager called in a prestigious engineering firm. After an exhaustive study with traffic flow charts and stopwatches, the engineers proposed installing two newer and faster elevators in the existing shafts. For $100,000, this solution would shave an average of 20 seconds off the waiting time on each floor.

The manager thought that the cost was pretty high for so little return. He called in another consultant, who proposed leaving the existing elevators but adding two new elevators at the ends of the central corridor. This solution would cost $150,000, but it would save the tenants an average of 35 seconds of waiting time per floor.

Knowing that the owners of the building would not put up $100,000 or more to solve the problem, in desperation the manager located someone who called himself a "problem consultant." This gentleman wandered around the building for 2 days, and on the third, slouched into a chair in the manager's office.

"Well," he began, "you told me that your problem was slow elevators, and that the solution was faster elevators. But that isn't really your problem. What those folks were trying to tell you is that they are bored stiff while waiting for the elevators. That's your real problem."

And for less than $1,000, the manager had mirrors installed beside the elevators on every floor. Women straightened their hair, and men their ties. There were no more complaints.

The moral of the story is: Don't jump to a solution without analyzing the need. In any phase of a needs assessment, one of the most difficult points to get across is the difference between a need and a solution. This story can be used to alert the NAC about the dangers of prematurely discussing or advocating solutions before adequately exploring the nature of the needs. A good warm-up exercise for the first meeting of the NAC, after introducing the NA project, is to have the group supply examples of their own needs and of "incorrect" solutions that occurred because of incomplete or faulty analysis of a problem.

SUMMARY

The purpose of Phase 1, Preassessment, is to explore what is already known about needs in the system or community and to do some preliminary investigation of existing records and other data before designing the main NA. The needs assessor works with an advisory or steering group called the NAC, which is broadly representative of the stakeholders. Two written agreements guide the work: (a) a preliminary agreement for conducting the NA, with a contingency clause permitting modification on the basis of the outcomes of Phase 1; and (b) a document that outlines the work to be accomplished in Phase 2, specifies the mutual obligations of the principal parties to the agreement, and obtains the commitment of top decision makers to support the NA and use its results in an action plan.

The chapter also addresses political and contextual factors to anticipate in Phase 2 and suggests a simple plan for evaluating the NA itself.

Notes

1. The Templeton study occurred in 1979 through 1981. Since then, the concern about oral proficiency in modern foreign languages has been expressed nationwide and addressed by professional organizations such as the American Council on the Teaching of Foreign Languages (J. N. Eastmond, Jr., personal communication, December 1994).

2. Adapted from Davis and McCallon (1974).

※

THREE

Phase 2—Assessment

In the preassessment phase, the needs assessor and NAC set the direction of the NA. They determined the focus and target groups, delineated the scope, and gathered preliminary data on the issues, concerns, and problems (the needs) that will be addressed in the formal assessment, Phase 2.

Tasks for Implementing Phase 2

The task of the assessment phase is to document the status, the "what is" of the issues, to compare the status with the vision of "what should be," and to determine the magnitude of the needs and their causes. The major output from Phase 2 is a set of need statements in tentative order of priority, based on criticality of the need, and their causes.

Figure 3.1 shows the flow of events for Phase 2, the formal assessment. Some of the information may have already been gathered in Phase 1 and reflected in the action plan for Phase 2. If so, the next task is to collect information as required and to perform appropriate analyses at the different points in the formal assessment of need.

The following section contains a brief overview of each step. Subsequent sections contain more detailed explanations on gathering, analyzing, and interpreting data.

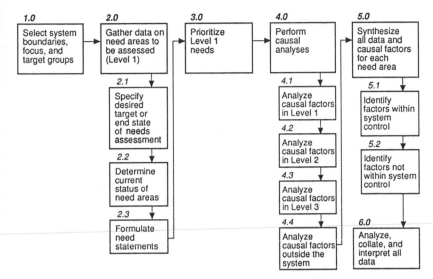

Figure 3.1. Flow of Events for Phase 2—Tasks for Implementation

1.0 Select system boundaries, focus, and target group(s).

2.0 Gather data in need areas to be assessed (Level 1). Each need is defined by determination of discrepancies between an initial state (what is) and a desired target state (what should be).

2.1 Specify a desired target or end state based on the system's vision, values, and goals and on societal values and goals.

2.2 Determine the current or initial state of the Level 1 target population in relation to desired end states.

2.3 Formulate need statements based on discrepancies between current states and desired target states.

3.0 Prioritize Level 1 needs.

4.0 Perform causal analyses.

4.1 Analyze causal factors residing in Level 1 (the service receivers).

4.2 Analyze causal factors residing in Level 2 (service providers).

4.3 Analyze causal factors relating to Level 3 (resources in the system).

4.4 Analyze factors outside the system—social, economic, environmental—that may be contributing to the persistence of the need.

5.0 Synthesize all data on needs and causal and contributing factors for each need area.

5.1 Identify causal factors that can be controlled within the system.

5.2 Identify causal factors outside the control of the system.

6.0 Analyze, collate, and interpret all data.

Explanation of Steps 1 Through 5

With regard to Step 1.0, the system or subsystem(s) to be assessed comes from the preassessment work. The boundaries of the system are, to a certain extent, arbitrary. Whether you do an NA of an entire system (school district, health organization, corporation) or of a subsystem (a school program, a particular target group of students, a unit in an organization) depends on many factors. Some factors to consider are the reason for the assessment, the context, and the kinds of decisions that are contemplated on the basis of NA results.

The specification of target groups differs with the kind of system or organization conducting the NA. Sometimes the target groups are part of the system itself: members of professional organizations, students in a school district or university, officers and enlisted personnel in a military unit, members of a health maintenance organization (HMO) that serves an identified group of patients. In many situations, however, the target groups are outside the system. Examples are customers of retail stores, library patrons, adults who might be interested in distance education,[1] users of public facilities such as transportation or parks, people with mental health problems, and families seeking homes.

When target groups are part of a system (a "closed" group), the needs assessor can get specific information on demographics and other background data of interest. When they are outside the system, they constitute "fuzzy" groups. That is, their characteristics might be known in general, but specifics are lacking. Thus, a community college system seeking to identify needs of people in a region for distance education does not have a readily identifiable group to survey or otherwise study.

In Phase 2, one goal is to specify the target group(s) and the boundaries of the system as clearly as possible. This provides a more precise focus and scope for data gathering and analysis, which were at least partially determined during Phase 1.

Step 2.0 (more specifically, Step 2.1—*specify target state*) is generally a matter of expert judgment, based on experience and arrived at by consensus of the NAC. Some target states have been determined scientifically, such as measures of blood pressure, weight, and heart function, but even in those areas a range is tolerable. Sometimes groups other than the needs assessors have set standards of performance or knowledge. Thus, most state departments of education have set minimal competency standards for high school graduation, which could be drawn on to specify target states for an NA. Likewise, many entry-level jobs set standards to be met by applicants, such as skills necessary for hand finishing a manufactured product.

In many cases, however, the desired states must be formulated by the NAC. Sometimes such states are expressed qualitatively. At other times they are expressed in terms of the percentage of the target population that should reach a certain level (e.g., of skill, acquisition of knowledge) in a specified period of time. Statements of desired states must be clear enough so that when a program is implemented to meet needs, evaluators can judge the degree to which the target population reaches the criterion.

For Step 2.2, at least some of the information regarding *current status* might have been gathered during preassessment. If more is needed, follow the data-gathering plan that the NAC outlined at the end of Phase 1. Data gathering is discussed later in this chapter, and Chapters 5 through 9 describe numerous data-gathering techniques in detail.

Step 2.3, *determining discrepancies,* can be accomplished in various ways. The method devised by the Templeton district, whose NA was described in Chapter 2, was implemented uniformly across departments and is easily adaptable to other contexts. The department heads who planned the NA decided to set two levels of standards for determining discrepancies in each need area—one for *adequacy* and one for *excellence.* The reasoning behind the two levels was based on evidence that many students with high levels of ability were not achieving their potential and that it was important to identify needs related to excellence as well as to adequacy or minimum levels of performance. The following is an example of an issue with two levels of standards from the physical education department. Issues, posed as questions, were used to identify potential areas of need.

Issue: Do students take responsibility for their own health and physical fitness?

Standards: An excellent program exists if:

1. At the end of the second year of physical education, 60% of the students voluntarily participate in a regular program of physical activity outside of school.
2. At the end of the fourth year, 60% of the students voluntarily participate in a regular program of physical activity outside of school.
3. Five years after high school graduation, 50% of the students voluntarily participate in a regular program of physical activity.

An *adequate* program had the same type of standards, except that the percentages of students needing to meet the criteria fell to 40%, 40%, and 30% for criteria 1, 2, and 3, respectively.

Criteria for a need (inadequate program) were stated: "A problem may exist if, at the end of the second year of physical education, less than 40% of the students voluntarily participate in a regular program of physical activity outside of school." Similar statements were made for the other two criteria. The criticality of need was determined by the magnitude of the discrepancy between observed student behavior (present status) and the criteria for standards (desired status).

If the current status of students for a given issue or need met the adequacy criterion, the department might direct resources to raise performance to the standard of excellence. If an area met the excellence standard, further action was predicated on maintaining that level.

In *prioritizing Level 1 needs* (Step 3.0), the priorities set are the foundation for the action plan that will be developed in Phase 3 (Chapter 4) to meet the needs. Consider specifying two levels of priorities. The first level is the more general one of goals or concerns, which are ranked in order of importance. At the second level, each goal area is analyzed and the needs or concerns within each one are separately ranked.

For example, a school district found that out of 16 general goals the greatest concerns were in academic achievement, citizenship, and personal fitness. Within the academic achievement goal at the subgoal level, the most critical needs were in reading difficult material, oral communication skills, and basic math concepts. The NAC also identified needs in subgoal areas for citizenship and personal fitness. The NAC decided to set priorities on the needs within each goal area separately to avoid problems of trying to compare noncomparable needs.

It is also desirable to set priorities not only for current needs but also for future needs (see the Delphi technique in Chapter 8 or the future-oriented NA techniques in Chapter 9).

Step 4.0 deals with *causal analysis of needs*. Why have the needs occurred or persisted? One of the most useful steps to undertake in an NA is to determine general and specific causes of high-priority needs. This section discusses some general considerations for analyzing causes. Chapter 10 contains a more detailed treatment of causal analysis and descriptions of three special methods.

The principal task is to analyze factors contributing to the presence or maintenance, or both, of each of the high-priority needs. Why does the need exist? Were any previous attempts made to meet the need? What were they? Why did they fail? What barriers did and do exist to prevent the need from being met? This analysis can be further subdivided.

For Step 4.1, *analyzing causes of Level 1 needs*, what are the characteristics of the target population? Consider personal, demographic, and other factors that might have contributed to the need in individuals and groups. For Step 4.2, *analyzing causes of Level 2 needs*, what characteristics of service providers might be contributing to the existence or maintenance of a Level 1 need? For example, a large department store was receiving an increasing number of complaints from customers who stated that their needs for finding what they wanted were not being met. One causal factor lay with certain sales personnel, who had inadequate knowledge of the stock, were indifferent to customers, and lacked good communication skills.

For Step 4.3, *analyzing Level 3 needs*, factors such as large class sizes, outdated textbooks, inadequate lab facilities, and noisy environments are often cited as contributing to poor student achievement. The presence and criticality of such factors should be determined for the local context, however. What inadequate system resources are causal factors in the school district in question?

For Step 4.4, *factors outside the system* (social, economic, environmental) may be contributing to the maintenance of the need. Causes of low academic achievement might be poverty, poor nutrition in the home, racial or ethnic discrimination, or less importance placed on formal education by members of a particular culture. Such conditions as environmental pollution from toxic wastes and a large incidence of single-parent families may also contribute to a variety of social and academic needs.

For *causal factors that can be controlled within the system,* Step 5.1, determine which of the Level 2 and Level 3 contributing factors are potentially responsive to action within the system. Are some of the factors related to training or attitudes of staff? Are there environmental factors within the control of the organization? For Step 5.2, *causal factors outside the control of the system,* consider such variables as family background; personal disabilities that cannot be compensated for; budgets that are controlled by external agencies, thus limiting resources; legal barriers; and so forth.

A caution regarding causal analysis: This should by no means become an exercise in laying blame on individuals or on policies or programs that have not worked in the past. The needs assessor has a great responsibility to keep the discussion of causal factors on as objective a plane as possible. We have found that using such methods as *fishboning* and *fault tree analysis* (see Chapter 10) in tracing causes through a system helps the NAC maintain a sense of the complexity of systems and the interrelatedness of causal factors. The object is to come up with useful information about the nature of the needs, not to point a finger.

Gathering Data

One of the major outputs of Phase 1 was a document that specified the kinds of data to be gathered in Phase 2, especially for current status and, to a certain extent, for desired end states. Here we describe some general methods for gathering data and criteria for their selection.

TYPES AND SOURCES OF DATA

Data for NAs are of two general kinds: opinions and facts. By facts, we mean statements that can be verified independently of the views or previous conceptions of individuals. The distinction between fact and opinion is not always recognized. The statement, "Students in the West Valley School District are receiving a poor education," is an opinion. It might or might not be supported by such facts as 7% of the most recent graduating class won National Merit Awards, 38% of students in Grade 5 are reading at the 45th percentile on state tests, and 125 junior high students received an honorable mention or better at the recent state science fair.

When people are asked to participate in an NA, they often have strong opinions that they confuse with facts. Sorting out the differences is an important task for the needs assessor. The job is made easier by a clear understanding of the kinds of information that are most useful in determining present and desired states and by choosing appropriate processes for obtaining the information.

METHODS OF GATHERING DATA

Table 3.1 presents an overview of three types of data sources for NA: *archival, communication processes,* and *analytic processes.*

Archival material (see Chapter 5) refers to data that have already been gathered for other purposes, such as social indicators, organizational or agency records, demographic data, census data, results of educational assessments, and program evaluation reports. Archival material is useful in establishing past and present conditions related to need areas or issues, the "what is" dimension. Another type is the information necessary for doing trend analysis (see Chapter 9). Archival material can be very helpful, but individual data items by themselves are meaningless unless they are put into a context. Existing records are most useful in NA as indicators pointing to avenues for further exploration rather than as facts in themselves.

A second general category of data gathering uses methods for seeking information directly from people rather than from examination of records. These are communication processes, which are widely used to solicit opinions about issues and need areas or to get information about which respondents have direct knowledge. There are two kinds of communication processes: *noninteractive* and *interactive.* In noninteractive processes, data are conveyed from individual respondents to the needs assessor or interviewer with little or no personal interaction. This is the domain of the survey questionnaire, the individual interview, the critical incident technique (CIT), the mailed Delphi, and the instrument used for cross-impact analysis (see Chapters 6 and 9). A national study (Witkin, 1994) found that the mailed questionnaire requesting opinions on needs is the method most widely used in NA and is often the only source of data—a practice that we do not recommend.

TABLE 3.1 An Overview of Data-Gathering Methods for
            Needs Assessment

Data Sources	Description	Information Produced

ARCHIVAL
Records, logs
Social indicators
Demographic data
Census data
Epidemiological studies
Rates-under-treatment
  (RUT)
Data from assessment
  programs
	Existing data usually
	found in records of
	organizations, agencies,
	or government bureaus;
	some are statistical or
	other demographic in-
	dicators of subgroups
	in the population; the
	needs assessor can also
	generate new records
	as databases for future
	NAs
		Quantitative data that
		help determine the status
		("what is") factors of a
		target group in regard to
		a need area; the data may
		also furnish information
		on causal or contributing
		factors of needs

COMMUNICATION
Noninteractive
  Written question-
    naires
  Key informant inter-
    views
  Critical incident tech-
    nique
  Mailed Delphi survey
	These techniques use
	structured forms or
	protocols that employ
	a variety of scales and
	response modes
		Mainly qualitative—
		values, perceptions,
		opinions, judgments of
		importance, observations,
		information from personal
		observations

Interactive
  Public hearings
  Community group
    forums
  Nominal group tech-
    nique (NGT)
  Focus group inter-
    view (FGI)
  DACUM process
  Futures scenarios
	These techniques involve
	large or small groups of
	stakeholders in varying
	degrees of interaction
		Mainly qualitative—
		opinions, expert judgments
		
		Group perceptions and per-
		spectives—values, inci-
		dence, or importance of
		needs
		
		Consensus on goals or
		  courses of action
		Information on causes
		Decisions on priorities

TABLE 3.1 (Continued)

Data Sources	Description	Information Produced
Analytic		
Fishboning	These use various kinds	Causal and contributing
Cause and conse-	of group processes to	factors
quence analysis	examine archival or other	
Success mapping	data, apply analytic	Consequences if a need is
Fault tree analysis	techniques, and produce	not met
(FTA)	graphic displays for de-	
Task analysis	cision making in vari-	Data can be combined with
Risk assessment	ous stages of the NA	other information to
Trend analysis		set priorities or criteria for
Cross-impact analysis		action planning
Force field analysis		
		FTA can be used
		for predictive purposes
		Success maps and FTA can
		be used in the
		NA evaluation plan

In contrast, group discussion processes seek a wide range of viewpoints, and sometimes consensus, through more or less interactive techniques (Chapters 7 and 8). Groups may meet in public forums, work in small group sessions (nominal groups, focus groups), or interact with others through a modified Delphi and other techniques. Group processes used to generate futures scenarios and future wheels are described in Chapter 9.

A third category combines data gathering with analysis. Analytic techniques, such as task analysis, trend analysis, force field analysis, and cross-impact analysis, use special methods of analyzing data gathered from archives or through communication processes. Other analytical techniques are methods of causal analysis, such as fishboning, cause and consequence analysis, and fault tree analysis (see Chapter 10). They are used to identify and analyze factors that may have contributed to the presence of the need or that have prevented it from being resolved in the past. Fault tree analysis is also a powerful tool for predicting the likelihood of certain outcomes in the future and for serving as a component of the evaluation of the NA plan.

CRITERIA FOR SELECTING METHODS

In a sense, there are no pure methods, and selection depends on the context of the NA (see the last section of this chapter), the kinds of decisions to be made on the basis of the findings, and necessary trade-offs in time, costs, and comprehensiveness. The main point is to ask, "What are the best means of getting useful information and perceptions?"

1. Consider characteristics of *target* and *respondent* groups. The target group is the one whose needs are being assessed, and the respondents are those who can give information about the needs. Sometimes they are the same people; for example, adults with chronic back pain, secondary school or university students, or homeless people using public shelters can respond about their own needs. But often the two groups are different. For a target group of preschool children with severe physical disabilities, the respondents could be parents or caretakers, orthopedic physicians and other specialists, and occupational therapists. Sometimes there is a combination: A technical school seeking to meet the future needs of adults in a region might want responses from present students, a sample of the community at large, and owners of businesses and factories that employ people in technical positions.

A particular data-gathering method might be constrained by certain characteristics of target groups. Primary school children or older children with reading disabilities are rarely involved in an NA with a written survey. Yet successful NAs have been conducted using oral questions (read by the teacher or recorded on audiotape) to which the children respond by marking cartoon-like pictures in a multiple choice format—a smiling face for "yes," a frowning face for "no," and a face with a "?" in it for "don't know." Table 3.2 gives some examples of data-gathering methods and item content appropriate for selected target and respondent groups at all three levels in different kinds of systems.

2. Choose a combination of methods that will yield different types of information. Each type has its constraints and limitations and each results in different types of information. A questionnaire may yield very different indicators of need than a focus group interview or critical incident technique. In fact, some NA studies have found that different methods produce contradictory data.

TABLE 3.2 Data-Gathering Methods and Item Content Appropriate for Selected Target and Respondent Groups

Target Group	Respondents	Sample Content
Service receivers (Level 1) Students, patients, customers	Service receivers students, patients, customers	Attitudes about school or services, self-reports of problems, felt needs, opinions on achievement of personal objectives, goals
	Service providers Teachers, counselors, specialists, medical personnel, salespersons	Direct observation about student achievement, patient health, requests from customers
	Stakeholders Parents, spouses, employers, community residents	Observation of target group's need areas, problems, achievements, barriers to reaching goals
Service providers (Level 2) Staff of school, agency, or organization	Service receivers Students, patients, customers	Perceptions of quality of teaching, services, interactions with clients, availability
	Service providers	Self-reports of needs in relation to needs of Level 1 target
	Stakeholders	Reports of observations of quality of teaching, service, health care
System (Level 3) Policies, system climate, availability and use of resources	Service receivers	Satisfaction with organization's facilities, climate, user-friendliness, adequacy for the job
	Service providers	Satisfaction with system in regard to how well it serves the primary target groups, and the working environment for service providers

An interesting study conducted by Demarest, Holey, and Leather-man (1984) looked at three different methods to determine educational needs for the nursing staff of a hospital. The methods included specialized surveys asking about educational needs and concerns, interviews with staff, and an examination of records. Random sampling without replacement was employed so that individuals interviewed did not also receive surveys. A major finding was that the three data collection mechanisms did not yield the same information and therefore did not identify the same needs. The authors concluded that having additional information from multiple sources, even though more costly to develop, collect, and analyze, helped them to better understand and interpret the results than any of the individual sources by themselves.[2]

3. Consider time, costs, and other constraints. How long will it take to construct and validate a questionnaire? How accessible are archival records? What are the costs of mailed surveys versus interviews or focus groups? (Note that the costs may be reduced through judicious sampling. A well-chosen sample can yield very similar results to a complete census of a population at a fraction of the cost. On the other hand, the public relations benefit of involving large numbers of stakeholders might be of importance to the NA.) Are there people available who are trained in facilitating groups? In view of the target and respondent populations to be involved, what difficulties might occur in gathering representatives for group sessions?

4. Consider the size of the system. Are the target groups and potential respondents at a single site, in a small geographic area, or spread over a large region or state?

5. Decide on the degree of interaction desired. Noninteractive methods, such as the written questionnaire, may be less costly and more efficient in use of time, but they have important limitations. Advantages and disadvantages of the written survey are discussed in detail in Chapter 6. A few advantages of written communication are that

- The NA can survey many people over a wide geographic area.
- Large amounts of data can be gathered in a relatively short time.
- Structured instruments can prevent sidetracking and irrelevant inputs.
- Noninteractive processes are relatively easy to manage.
- Survey data can usually be aggregated and analyzed by computer processing.

Interactive (group) communication processes are discussed in Chapter 7. Some advantages are that

- They involve people in thinking actively and creatively about issues and needs.
- Respondents can ask for clarification of questions and terms.
- Participants are more likely to feel that they have an important part to play in the NA and that the sponsoring organization cares what they think.
- Adjustments can be made in accordance with the communication styles of different ethnic and linguistic groups when such differences might affect the NA.

Interactive group processes are highly recommended for the exploratory (preassessment) phase of the NA—to define problems, identify areas of concern that warrant further analysis, and solicit support for planning and implementation from key groups. Noninteractive methods can then be used in the main assessment to validate issues, needs, and causes with representative samples of constituent groups.

CHOOSING RESPONDENTS

Respondents to written surveys and participants in group processes should be representative of the interests of the target groups and knowledgeable about the need areas under consideration. In Chapters 5 through 9, we provide recommendations on sampling strategies for specific NA techniques. In the following section we discuss some factors that should be considered no matter what techniques are used.

Sociolinguistic and Cultural Factors

Not all methods of collecting information work well with all groups. Some factors to consider are language, cultural and ethnic values, and individual differences.

LANGUAGE

It is not uncommon to find 50 or 60 different home languages in urban school districts; for instance, the Los Angeles school system has as many as 92. A large HMO in a metropolitan area, to which one of us belongs, posts all signs in clinics and hospital sites in 6 languages and furnishes interpreters when needed. School district question-naires directed to parents in an area with high recent immigration may need to be translated into Spanish, Mandarin, Vietnamese, and Rus-sian, for starters. Furthermore, the terminology, both in English and in other languages, must be as nontechnical and free from jargon as possible. (Try explaining "needs assessment" or "multicultural cur-riculum" in Spanish or Tagalog, as we had to do for NAs in the San Francisco Bay area.) It is also desirable to provide communication settings where clients or stakeholders with limited English profi-ciency can participate effectively in group NA processes.

CULTURAL AND ETHNIC
DIFFERENCES IN COMMUNICATION

"Rules" for social interaction and deliberation vary greatly among different ethnic and cultural groups. In some cultures, younger par-ticipants always defer to elders and lower status adults defer to those of higher status. Verbal and nonverbal factors include spatial relation-ships and distances that are tolerated between speakers, preferences for oral or written modes of expression, use of hyperbole or metaphors to express values, relations to authority figures, assertiveness or shy-ness in group deliberations, degree of eye contact, gestures, and willingness to challenge or defend points of view.

Two examples illustrate the perils of ignoring cultural differences when conducting an NA.

A regional education office convened a series of group meetings in five different sites within a state. Some of the groups included members of a minority that culturally was organized along strict hierarchical lines. In this group, younger people always deferred to elders, and adults deferred to those in authority. The NA relied heavily on semistructured group processes, where the facilitators hoped to get lively interchanges and clear expressions of need from the participants.

Each of the five groups was characterized by different geographic, economic, and educational backgrounds of the participants and their apparent needs. Yet when the researchers compared results of the NAs of the five groups, they found that the stated priorities were all in the same areas or were very similar. Probing uncovered the fact that the participants viewed the facilitators as authority figures and hesitated to express their own opinions. Unfortunately, the facilitators themselves had an agenda on what they considered the needs to be and were not skilled enough in overcoming their biases in leading the meetings and listening to the participants. Thus, cultural differences interacted with inept leadership so that the NA data were of little value.

Another example deals with more intangible factors: the way in which different cultures regard time, appropriate means of expression, and the sense of status.

Paul, a young lawyer skilled in mediation and group processes, was retained by a Native American tribe to assist with an NA and long-range planning. The issues necessitated working with a committee composed of tribal members and a few citizens from a town bordering the tribal lands. Paul presented a preliminary plan that was apparently acceptable to the tribe.

He soon encountered some barriers that puzzled him. There was little communication between the tribal members and the towns-people. The tribal chief repeatedly postponed actions that he and the elders had previously agreed on. Meetings always started late, and it was difficult to achieve closure. Target dates that seemed firm kept getting extended. After several frustrating months, Paul left the project and someone else stepped in and implemented his proposal, but in a revised form.

What had gone wrong? One of us knew Paul and discussed the situation with him while he was still actively engaged in the project. It soon became obvious that several cultural and communication factors of which he was unaware were affecting the situation:

- Paul had almost no insight into the cultural factors that were operative. It was suggested that he consult a cultural anthropologist at a nearby university who was also a consultant to Native American tribes in the area and who could give him some guidance as to how best to work with the group. By the time that Paul spoke with the professor, the project had badly deteriorated.

- Paul made the same kind of written and oral presentations to the group that he usually made to white, middle-class organizations accustomed to technical jargon. The committee received the presentations politely but largely ignored them.

- Paul was unaware of how important it was to clear everything with the tribe's elders before presenting ideas to the whole committee.

- He was also unaware that the concept of time in this setting was different from the one to which he was accustomed in the business and professional world. The more he pushed to get the committee to assemble at the stated time and to complete objectives by certain target dates, the less successful he was.

As a rule, white Americans, many western Europeans, and some Asian peoples adhere to rigid standards of time for business and social events, often with only a 5-minute leeway. Many Latin American peoples, as well as some other ethnic groups in the United States, place a different value on time. With them, arriving right on time is deemed to be either rude or of little importance. Guests might appear an hour or more after the scheduled time. In some cultures, it is also considered rude to plunge immediately into the business at hand without an extended period of ritual socializing.

This sense of time is a key factor in understanding cultures. One scientist asked people of different cultures how long "a while" was. African Americans saw it as 15 minutes, Koreans as 100 years.[3] Another powerful factor is gender differences, such as the expectation in many cultures that women should be submissive to men.[4] Other factors are attitudes toward clothing, badges, and outer gear, talk of successes, and what constitutes success. All cultures have certain rituals to which they adhere in solving problems. These include methods for achieving consensus as well as degrees of confrontation that are tolerated. In general, Americans are accustomed to taking adversarial positions. Japanese, on the other hand, value consensus much more highly.

An understanding of such differences helps the needs assessor avoid unproductive meetings and failure to achieve project goals. One way to prevent social bias or the use of inappropriate communication strategies is by seeking representatives of minority groups for the NAC. Another way is to consult a cultural anthropologist or ethnographer at the nearest university. Specialists and NAC members chosen from minority groups can give valuable advice not only on language and the more obvious cultural barriers but also on the best mix of interactive and noninteractive methods to ensure that the views of clients and stakeholders will be heard and taken into account in appraising needs.

INDIVIDUAL DIFFERENCES

Some factors of behavior in groups, such as shyness or aggressiveness, may be matters of individual differences and not necessarily cultural. NA data-gathering methods, whether by written survey or by group interaction, should also accommodate participants with limited mobility or with severely impaired vision or hearing.

If group processes are chosen, it is the responsibility of the needs assessor to make sure that the meeting sites are comfortable and easily accessible to all participants, and that the communication methods not only will encourage participation of all those present but also will not violate deeply held cultural norms that are different from those of the planners.

Analyzing, Collating,
and Interpreting the Data

Data analysis and interpretation in NA are often not clear-cut. It should be remembered that the reason for analysis and aggregation of data is to provide a sound basis for determining priorities of need and criteria for future action. Therefore, the analysis should reveal differences in magnitude of needs that are of practical value, not just of statistical significance.

The data-gathering methods discussed so far present the NAC with raw data. Information on current status has been derived from archival sources as well as perceptions of individuals and groups. Opinions on desired target states ("what should be") have been gathered from a variety of sources: from standards of performance, where they exist; from objectives for outputs, as in business; and from statements of desired levels of excellence, as in education.

Methods of aggregating data and ranking the results differ, depending partly on the data-gathering process used. In questionnaires, results can be reported in percentages of people choosing each answer option. Surveys using category scales are often analyzed for mean and standard deviation on each question, and the means placed in rank order. Similar analyses can be performed for whole subsections of the instrument.

Chapter 7 provides ways for analyzing data generated from group processes. With lists of goals, a number of analytic strategies might be used. Group members could order items by rank (keep the list short, 15 statements or less) and then average rankings could be calculated and placed in order. Or they could select the top third of the list and put those items in rank order. They might also select the bottom third as a rough check on group consistency in item selection.

Paired-Weighting Procedure (PWP). One method that we have found useful for deriving group judgments of relative importance of goals, needs, or other concepts is the PWP (Wickens, 1980). In this method, every item in a set is compared to every other item in a paired manner. For example, in a set of five, the first item is rated against the second item, then against the third, fourth, and fifth. Then the second item is rated against the third, fourth, and fifth items individually, and so on. PWP is not practical for more than 15 items because the raters must keep too much information in mind. We suggest that you double-check the wording of the items to be ranked or compared, to be sure that they are parallel in structure and in level of generality or abstraction. This reduces errors in the rankings and comparisons. Figure 3.2 illustrates the method of marking a PWP rating sheet and assigning weights to the paired comparisons.

Figure 3.2 shows how one respondent compared 10 items. The unmarked sheet originally displayed numerals in pairs along rows of horizontal lines, with no digits circled. Row 1, for the first issue, shows nine "1s" above the line and the numerals 2 through 10 below it. Row 2, for issue #2, shows eight "2s" above the line and the numerals 3 through 10 below—and so on. The rater circles the numeral of each pair that denotes which issue or need is more important than the other.

The PWP is best done as a group process. The facilitator reads aloud each pair of items and allows about 10 seconds for participants to mark their PWP sheets. In the example shown in Figure 3.2, the circled numerals indicate that this rater judged issue #1 as more important than the second, third, and fourth issues, but less important than issues #5 through #10. She ranked issue #2 as more important than issues #3, #7, #8, and #10, but less important than issues #4, #5, #6, and

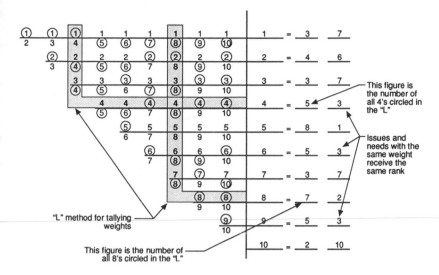

Figure 3.2. Aggregating Data From the Paired-Weighting Procedure
SOURCE: Wickens (1980). Used by permission.

#9 and so on. The figure also shows how two issues—#4 and #8—ranked in relation to the other eight. The L-shaped shaded area for issue #4 indicates that #4 was circled five times and therefore rated as more important than the other nine issues those five times (noted in the "weight" column); it ranked third in importance, as indicated in the "rank" column. Similarly, issue #8 was circled seven times, thus being rated as more important than the other issues seven times, and ranked second in importance. Participants record their weights for each issue on a master chart, and the facilitator aggregates the weighted comparisons across all respondents to arrive at the group ranking on the set of issues or needs.

Interpreting Data From Discrepancy Questionnaires. Needs assessors have often determined criticality of needs from a survey by obtaining rankings on two parameters at the same time, such as determining discrepancies between present and ideal states, calculating the differences, and ranking them in order. This works if the two parameters are stated in comparable terms, such as the current percentage of high school seniors in a district who graduate with an entry-level skill for the local job market compared with a desired percentage. Too often, however, comparisons are made on noncomparable items, such as importance of an objective versus perceived achievement.

Surveys such as the APEX questionnaires described in Chapter 6 lend themselves to scale comparisons on each question because the present and ideal states are stated in the same terms—that of performance. Therefore, the means and standard deviations of each question can be computed and the questions ranked in order of discrepancies. Figure 6.3 in Chapter 6 illustrates the method of comparison.

The following are some general rules for making decisions from NA data involving discrepancies:

- If you have discrepancy data for concerns related to different goals, don't compare them across goals. Compare only discrepancies for concerns of the same goal.
- As a rule, discrepancies regarding subgoal concerns of highly rated goal areas will be more important than subgoals for areas of less importance or value—but not always. Examine the items carefully.
- If two observed discrepancies are of equal magnitude, look at their values or ratings on the "what should be" part of the scale. The discrepancy with the higher "what should be" value is of greater importance.

The needs assessor and the NAC collaborate on merging the data from disparate sources, such as key informant interviews, nominal group processes, and a written questionnaire. The first task is to analyze the data from each source separately to identify the types and magnitude of discrepancies between present and ideal states as well as other information they provide. Are the data from all sources congruent? If not, why not? Discuss the differences, and use your best judgment to describe an understanding of needs as comprehensively as you can. Combine the results from the different sources to give a composite picture of discrepancies and their magnitudes. Make sure that the logic of how you developed the understandings and the composite picture is spelled out clearly.

Adding to the complexity of analysis is the fact that there are two other types of discrepancies in NA data. There are discrepancies among different respondent groups using the same method, such as in regard to perceptions of needs among students, teachers, and parents responding to the same questionnaire. In this case, two respondent groups might in fact have very different information about or understandings of the need area. If the discrepancies are large, the reasons might be discovered by means of interviews of a sample of respondents from the different groups.

There is also discrepant information gathered through two or more different methods, such as focus groups and questionnaires. In this case, the discrepancies might be attributed to noncomparable designs in the two methods—that is, the responses were constrained by the kinds of questions asked and the degree of allowance for probes. Such discrepancies may add to the richness or depth of information obtained about the needs, however, as noted in the Demarest et al. (1984) study described earlier.

Conducting Needs Assessments
in Different Contexts

As general background for Phase 2, it is helpful to be aware of the contexts in which NAs are conducted. One of the most common is that of an iterative program planning cycle. Figure 3.3 shows its major stages. NA precedes program-planning and is followed by implementation of the new program. Concurrently, the program is monitored and formative evaluation takes place. If necessary and feasible, revisions are made, the revised program is monitored, and, toward the end of the cycle, there is a summative evaluation. In turn, the data from the evaluation give information for a new stage of NA, which may lead to various outcomes: continuation of the program, continuation with radical modifications, termination, or branching programs.

Both planners and evaluators conduct NAs, but often from different viewpoints. This section discusses NA first in the context of planning, then of evaluation, and, finally, in three special contexts that have characteristics of both planning and evaluation: cyclical or iterative, Management Information Systems (MISs), and collaborative.

THE PLANNING CONTEXT

In planning, NA is the essential first step in documenting needs and developing programs or other strategies to meet them. It is assumed that the NA is the first step in forward planning, which is based on the system mission and goals (see Chapter 9 for a discussion of strategic planning). After gathering information on needs, the assessor

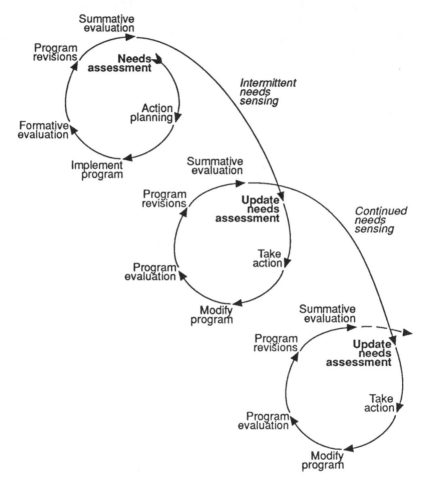

Awareness of System or Community Needs

Figure 3.3. Needs Assessment in an Iterative Program Planning-Evaluation Cycle

and NAC decide on priorities and develop an action plan for resolving needs. The scope of the plan and the timelines for completion depend on whether the NA is in the context of short-term or long-term planning.

The focus of planning may be a whole system, one or more subsystems, or specific program areas or target groups, to name a few. That is, a city might conduct a communitywide study to determine priorities of needs for the next 3 years or it might do an NA on its library services and recreational facilities. A business organization might conduct an NA as part of a reexamination of its total mission and goals in the context of organizational renewal or it might limit the NA to one department, such as marketing.

As an example of NA in the planning context of a whole system, the customer service department of Tri-Met, a three-county transportation system centered in Portland, Oregon, conducts an NA survey every September through November as part of its annual service-planning process. It solicits input from neighborhood associations and community groups throughout the region, then works with local jurisdictions and coalitions to gain a sense of the community's priorities. It also gets additional input on high-priority need areas through newspaper surveys and community workshops during February and March of the following year (the Tri-Met budget allocation survey is described in Chapter 6).

In organizational planning, the target population for NA is usually within the system and is therefore fairly well-known, or its characteristics can be fairly easily determined. As noted earlier, however, in many situations, the target population is outside the system and therefore fuzzy; that is, their characteristics and needs are harder to determine (see schemas A and B in Figure 1.1, Chapter 1). In the latter case, the strategies for conducting an NA and the types of data to gather differ from methods used in organizational planning. The following is an example of an NA with a fuzzy target population.

A planner on the staff of the Commission on Parks and Recreation of a western state is charged with the responsibility of designing parks in accordance with the mission statement of the commission. In this case, the state has acquired a 100-acre site, 50 miles from the nearest town, in a wooded area by a river. The planner's questions are, How do you assess the needs of potential users of the park? What kinds of facilities should be built? How many campsites should be developed? Should there be facilities for recreational vehicles? What kind? How many? What about nature trails? How many years can this plan be expected to remain in effect?

This example illustrates the desire for a Level 3 NA of a particular type, although no assessment has been done to determine the need for such a park. In fact, until Theodore Roosevelt established the first national park in the United States (Yellowstone), there was no concept of needs that could be met by the milieu of a national or state park. However, there is now a long history of such recreational areas, and the commission already has specific goals based on societal values, past experience, and the concept of public merit. Federal and state funds have been set aside. The main question is, What is the best use of this particular piece of land in order to meet (largely unexpressed) needs of potential users (Level 1)? What kinds of information are needed, and what are the best sources?

The potential users are a fuzzy group. They are out there somewhere, possibly in the nearest towns, but they could also be visitors from other states and other countries. How does one find a representative group that could articulate the needs?

As in other NAs, begin with what is known. At least four kinds of data are available to the needs assessor: (a) the characteristics of the site itself, (b) design of parks with similar physical characteristics in this state and elsewhere, (c) types of users and patterns of use in similar sites, and (d) information on what would not work on the site or what has gone wrong at other sites with similar characteristics.

1. *Characteristics of the site.* What are the natural features on and near the site? Is it flat or hilly? Are the woods dense or sparse? What are the sources of water? What kinds of development would the site sustain with minimum damage to the environment? Are there specific natural features, such as unusual species of birds, that would attract certain types of people? What about access roads? What about potential fire hazards?

2. *Design of similar sites.* What are the design characteristics of sites with similar physical features? What are some common characteristics? What are some unique facilities?

3. *Types and patterns of use at similar sites.* What kinds of people have been attracted to similar sites? What has worked elsewhere? What kinds of activities were the most popular? What age groups used them most?

4. *Failure analysis.* What kinds of problems have arisen at similar sites? What were the contributing factors? What barriers might exist for people with physical disabilities?

This type of NA does not usually lend itself well to a general survey. What seems to work fairly well is to use key informants as an advisory or steering committee form of the NAC. The key informants would represent various interest and stakeholder groups as described in Chapter 2. It could also include some neighbors of the site.

Unlike our previously discussed NAC whose purpose was mainly to help set direction for the NA and to monitor data gathering and analysis, NAs of fuzzy groups have a steering committee form of NAC that is itself the principal source of data on needs. It is representative of diverse groups of users in order to give breadth to the assessment.

THE EVALUATION CONTEXT

The main job of evaluators is to help managers and staff determine the merit and worth of particular programs and to decide the extent to which a program has been successful in meeting its goals. Evaluators also conduct NAs to identify goals, problems, or conditions that should be addressed in future program planning. Experienced evaluators note the following:

> Many requests for "evaluation" actually require a needs assessment. By probing, the evaluator might discover that the aim of the evaluation is neither to decide between continuing or dropping a program— summative evaluation—nor to help develop detailed, specific activities to improve a program—formative evaluation. Rather, the sponsor wants to discover weaknesses or problem areas in the current situation which can eventually be remedied or to project future conditions to which the program will need to adjust. (Herman, Morris, & Fitz-Gibbon, 1987, p. 15)

In many instances, a summative evaluation of a program turns out to be an NA, as when a sponsor calls for evaluating a nursing program or food services in an institution. Herman et al. (1987) point out that an NA is frequently used to make implicit goals public or to examine and critique existing goals.

As depicted earlier in Figure 3.3, information on needs also grows out of formative and summative evaluation in an iterative planning-implementation-evaluation cycle. Evaluation of goals, programs, and services may occur annually or at other stated times in the life of an organization, and data from the evaluation become important inputs to NAs.

In either planning or evaluation contexts, decisions following the NA involve determining priorities for allocation of resources, such as money or effort. Herman et al. (1987) state the following:

> Note that needs assessment can be rather similar to formative evaluation but formally differs in the typical size or scope of the program under investigation, and more particularly in the fact that formative evaluators often follow up the identification of weaknesses. They may work with the staff to attempt improvements during the course of the evaluation. In a needs assessment, on the other hand, the survey of needs itself is the end product. (p. 16)

We agree with this paragraph except for the last sentence. It is true that many needs assessors believe that NA equals a survey, and that once the survey is reported, the job is done. But the ultimate purpose of an NA is not just to gather data, but to make decisions about priorities and about actions to meet the needs. The three-phase framework we advocate, especially Phase 3, is intended to ensure that the organization or agency takes appropriate action on the basis of the NA.

Some evaluators also appear to regard a need as the discrepancy between a current state and a desired state in terms of *products,* such as the need for a specific reading method, cars that use fuel more efficiently, or a drug-prevention program. We caution against this approach. The best NA is conducted without preconceived ideas about solutions, and the criteria for appropriate solutions should arise from the analysis of the needs and their causes.

THE CYCLICAL NA CONTEXT

Large organizations frequently conduct specially focused NAs on a regular basis, such as every 1 or 2 years. An example is the facilities NA conducted yearly by a large cooperative HMO, which has clinics, urgent care centers, and hospitals in a multicounty region. Its NA plan is depicted in Figure 3.4. The figure shows the flow of events for a single facility operated by the HMO. The data from each facility in the scheduled review are assembled in notebooks, project summaries are reviewed by the planning team, and priorities are set for projects by region, by the entire cooperative system, and by projected costs (a) greater than $50,000 but less than $250,000 and (b) greater than $250,000.

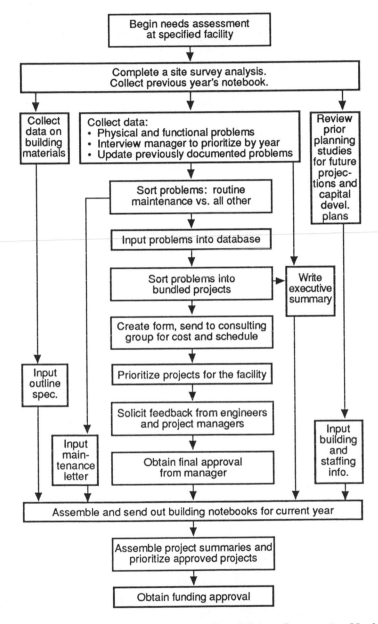

Figure 3.4. Facilities Needs Assessment (Level 3) in a Cooperative Health Maintenance Organization

This is a Level 3 NA, but the priorities for action are predicated on the needs of the HMO's clients (Level 1). It also takes into account criteria for communication and economy of movement of medical staff (Level 2) in order to conserve energy and to serve the patients more effectively. In other words, the concern for careful maintenance of facilities is closely related to the mission and goals of the organization, as well as to societal goals regarding the provision of health care in an efficient and cost-effective manner.

The NA is generally conducted in September. Data are analyzed, priorities are set, and any subsequent maintenance or simple repair work is expected to be finished early in the following year. Major renovation or construction of new facilities is subject to customary planning processes.

The NA may operate in both a planning and cyclical context in the organization. The annual facilities NA conducted by this HMO is also part of an overall strategic planning flow for regional governance, termed "The Ideal Process Flow." It was developed cooperatively by the board of trustees elected by the HMO members, management, medical staff, and consumer leadership. They first set the HMO's mission and vision, then develop strategies based on the mission, and finally establish goals and budget accordingly. This flow is a departure from previous planning in the HMO when managers worked out their budgets prior to the organization's specifying its annual goals. The current process sets goals first, then develops budgets. NAs fit into this general framework to guide planning and budgeting.

The Templeton NA described in Chapter 2 is an example of another kind of cyclical NA, projecting a 3-year cycle. NAs would be conducted yearly, with about one third of the departments in the high schools participating fully each year; those departments that were previously assessed would update their database on what they considered high-priority issues.

NA FOR A MANAGEMENT INFORMATION
SYSTEM (MIS)—ONGOING

With the advent of large capacity computers and the availability of data-based management systems, it is now possible to set up plans for continuous, ongoing NA. A school district, for example, can enter both qualitative and quantitative data on needs of its students, as well as a system of "red flags" or indicators to alert planners and administrators of changes in magnitude or trends of the needs. Health and social service agencies can set up systems for tracking the demands for certain types of service and the demographics of groups with varying needs.

The Templeton district not only instituted a cyclical departmental NA system but also began an MIS for schoolwide and districtwide issues and needs. Both qualitative and quantitative data were gathered by departments to put into an MIS. The requirements of the MIS were that planners and decision makers at the classroom, departmental, and schoolwide levels do the following:

1. Identify major unmet needs of students and support systems
2. Identify the criticality of those needs and set priorities for action
3. Sense when previously identified needs are being met (and to what extent) and when new ones are emerging
4. Use a rational and defensible method of weighing the merits of competing needs so that resources can be allocated where they most effectively maintain and enhance the educational quality of the school

Specifications for the MIS included

1. Processes for communication and interaction to promote a sense of ownership of the NA and responsibility for taking appropriate action on the basis of the data
2. The requirement that the data on needs be well defined and systematically collected over time
3. Provision of methods for determining potential consequences, both risks and payoffs, (a) if the critical needs are not met and (b) if critical needs are met—that is, results of interaction with other needs or with other parts of the system

The MIS was designed to contain not only crucial indicators but also information on implementation of the solution strategies from both formative and summative evaluation. Thus, the data from program evaluations also became part of the expanded database.

THE COLLABORATIVE (INTERAGENCY) NA

A collaborative NA is conducted jointly by two or more agencies or organizations, such as a city and the school district within its boundaries. Collaborative NAs are not common even though they offer some advantages over single-agency studies, particularly when a target population served by both organizations shows signs of increasing critical needs at the same time that resources to address the needs are shrinking.

The overview shown in Table 3.3 is based on an NA that involved four public agencies: a city, a school district, a county schools office, and another county agency that worked with cities on behalf of the national Community Services Agency. The two county agencies served as consultants and facilitators to the city council and school board. The four jointly designed the NA, held meetings, gathered information, and set priorities for action to meet critical needs.

Prior to the NA, the city council and school board had never held a joint meeting. The first step, to identify areas of mutual concern, was accomplished in an advertised evening meeting open to the public, at which the two boards engaged in brainstorming and other group processes. Interested members of the community attended as observers; they also answered a brief questionnaire related to their concerns.

Following the joint meeting, the project staff from the two county offices spent about 6 months in data collection (through interviews, questionnaires, inspection of social indicators and other archival material, and meetings with the NAC and community groups), causal analysis, and data synthesis. At a second meeting of the two boards, the consultants displayed the data on wall charts, explained the implications of the analyses, and described the strategic paths shown on the fault trees (see Chapter 10). The members of the two boards then divided into three working groups and set priorities for solutions in which the school district, the city government, and a group of business leaders would develop programs to meet the most critical needs.

Collaborative NAs and planning often meet with opposition or fail due to unintended consequences or to factors beyond the control of the planners. In the foregoing example, one problem was that important elected officials and decision makers were replaced in both the city and school district before the NA was completed. No countervailing measures were possible. Other problems often encountered are failure to identify a clear-cut mission and achievable goals for the NA, defense of an agency's "turf," and lack of commitment or involvement at the highest decision-making levels in each organization.

Joint effort is not always labeled NA. The mayor of a large urban city recently wrote an article in a major newspaper in which he called

TABLE 3.3 Interagency Needs Assessment

Steps	Procedures/Sources	Outputs
Identify major areas of joint concern	Nominal group process	List of joint concerns
Collect data on "what is," related to each area of concern	Social indicators, key informant interviews	Social indicator report; summary of interviews (report 1)
Collect perceptions of "what should be"	Interviews, survey, community meetings	Report collating perceptions (report 2)
Identify resources available in each area of concern	Service directories, other agency sources	Updated directory of services, if necessary
Do causal analysis on major concern areas	Fault tree analysis	Fault trees showing strategic paths, and explanatory narrative (report 3)
Synthesize data	Analysis of data from reports 1, 2, and 3 for each concern area; comparison of resources needed with resources available; set criteria for dealing with major causal factors (from strategic paths)	Executive summaries of data from each major concern/need area
Set priorities for joint action	Group processes with joint meeting of the two boards	Specific statements of proposed actions in one or more areas, with objectives and time lines
Evaluate the needs assessment	Interviews with key informants on both processes and outputs	Report to joint board with recommendations for the future

for a joint city-school district "summit" to address educational and family problems in the city—in effect, an NA. Limited but often effective collaboration occurs when different agencies and organizations develop consortia to deal with a specific problem, such as requirements for new and different standards of performance to accommodate emerging high technology developments in the workplace.

The probability of success of collaborative NA will be enhanced by keeping in mind the following recommendations (see Banathy, 1978; Witkin, 1984):

- The organizations involved should have a stable governance structure, with continuity of top and middle management.
- Staff should be assigned specifically to NA tasks, including helping to analyze the data. This presupposes that the organization is large enough so that the NA tasks will not add a burden to the workload of individuals. If possible, two kinds of staff should be involved: one for data collection and technical aspects of NA, and the other to facilitate meetings and planning processes. Technical and facilitator roles are very different, and it is best to use people who are trained for each task.
- Interorganizational linkages should be established on at least three levels: (a) elected officials in public agencies, or boards of trustees; (b) top management; and (c) lower-level staff in permanent positions. Although the actual work is usually accomplished at the third level, it is essential to get official support and active involvement at the other two levels.
- In joint NAs involving city or regional governments, identify and involve the informal power brokers to support interagency efforts. They are people with standing in the community who often operate behind the scenes. They can find resources and help or hinder the NA effort.
- If the collaborating agencies have never before worked together, focus the NA on specific, easily definable need areas amenable to solutions that can be quickly implemented and show discernible results in a year or less. Early results reinforce a good feeling about joint planning. After a few experiences of this kind, the agencies will be more agreeable to considering NA for longer-range planning on larger issues. Try to have a visible product as early as possible to maintain interest.

One happy outcome of the joint school district-city NA described earlier was that the city funded the development of a minipark and athletic field next to the high school, which had no facilities of its own. The facility was planned and operated jointly by the city and the district.

- Success is more likely if the impetus for joint NA comes from the primary partners, rather than from an external source. In the city-school district NA, the prime movers and data gatherers were from the two county offices because the other two partners were too small to have staff who could work on the NA. Although the NAC was broadly representative of the community, the elected officials and staffs of the city and district did not have the same sense of ownership of the NA that they might have had if the decision to collaborate had come from themselves.

- Involve community and grassroots groups as early as possible and keep them interested. Experts disagree as to whether community groups can or should assist with technical questions, data collection, and analysis, or whether they are most effective in providing communication linkages and general community support for an NA. Community members, however, often have certain types of expertise that can be called on when needed.

SUMMARY

The main portion of the NA occurs in Phase 2. Based on the preliminary searches from the preassessment phase, the needs assessor and NAC set the boundaries and focus of the NA, identify needs, set preliminary priorities, and perform causal analysis. The chapter discusses methods of gathering data, criteria for selecting methods, linguistic and cultural factors to consider, and methods for analyzing data. Five contexts for NA are described: planning, evaluation, cyclical, a Management Information System, and collaborative.

Notes

1. "The organizational framework and process of providing instruction at a distance." Distance education takes place when the teacher and student(s) are physically separated and technology (i.e., audio, video, computers, print) is used to bridge the instructional gap (Willis, 1994, p. 295).

2. Using three data collection methods is similar to the concept of triangulation in navigation and is widely accepted in social science research. In the original meaning, the third sighting provides an estimate of the size of error from the other two fixes, which is what the Demarest et al. study did (J. N. Eastmond, Jr., personal communication, Utah State University, December 1994).

3. Personal communication from Gerald M. Phillips, professor emeritus, Pennsylvania State University, July 20, 1994.

4. The late Dr. Gerald Phillips also commented as follows:

> I am currently working with people who are setting up mobile field hospitals for migrant laborers. They want to train the nurse practitioners

and practitioner assistants, and the few doctors, in "cultural" differences so they can communicate. The head of the project is a female, Mexican native, but she dares not appear despite having an MD and an MPH, because a project headed by a woman is suspect.

⊗

FOUR

Phase 3—Postassessment

In Chapter 1, we stated that a major purpose of NA is to collect information for setting priorities on needs in order to provide a rational
basis for allocating resources. We cannot emphasize too strongly that
an NA is not complete unless plans are made to use the information
in a practical way. Phase 3 is crucial to the success of the NA. It
answers important questions: What needs are the most critical? Why
haven't they been resolved before this? What are some possible solution strategies? How can we choose the best one(s)? The postassessment phase has been designed to help you and the organization
answer such questions.

Many NAs, however, do not include such a phase. Of 125 NAs
reported since 1981, fewer than half gave any attention to priorities
(Witkin, 1994). Other studies have found that many organizations fail
to use the results of an NA in any way at all. It is not uncommon for
the final report of an NA to languish on a shelf, with nothing concrete
done to meet the needs that were discovered.

Phase 3 is the bridge from analysis to action—to the use of the NA
findings. Decisions growing out of postassessment lead to important
changes in the system, such as new or revised programs, modification
of the system as part of long-range planning, reversal of previous
practices, and rearranging of priorities, to name a few. The activities
that we include under Phase 3 are not the norm for the practice of NA.
We assume that provisions for them have been built into the overall

plan developed at the end of Phase 1. They do require what we see as very worthwhile expenditures of additional time and resources.

Phase 3 brings important but subtle changes in the relationships of the NAC and the needs assessor to the top decision makers in the system and the managers who will direct the implementation of any changes. The role of the needs assessor and NAC becomes that of facilitating discussions about priorities and solutions and giving information and technical advice regarding the NA to those who will make the decisions about use. It is not the responsibility of the needs assessor and the NAC to make final decisions about system changes. Rather, they interpret findings and suggest alternative ways to address the needs. In Phase 3, the decision makers join the process by considering findings and weighing alternate solution strategies, thus fulfilling their previous commitment to take constructive action based on the NA.

Phase 3 has five major tasks, as shown in Figure 4.1.

The rest of this chapter is divided into two major sections. The first discusses what should be accomplished in each of the five steps. The second describes some techniques and processes that are applicable to one or more of the steps.

Major Tasks for Phase 3

1.0 SET PRIORITIES ON NEEDS

The assessment, clarification, and preliminary prioritization occurred in Phase 2. Now it is time for the needs assessor and NAC to set more rigorous priorities on needs, as shown in Step 1.0 in Figure 4.1. They first establish more in-depth criteria for determining which needs should be addressed. They then place them in order, determining which ones merit immediate action and which should be part of a longer-term plan.

Factors That Influence Priorities

Criteria for assigning priorities among needs are based on several factors:
- The magnitude of discrepancies between current and target states
- Causes and contributing factors to the needs

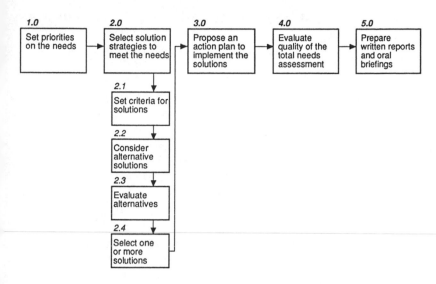

Figure 4.1. Major Tasks for Phase 3

- The degree of difficulty in addressing the needs
- Risk assessment—the consequences of ignoring the needs
- The effect on other parts of the system or other needs if a specific need is or is not met
- The costs of implementing solutions
- Political and other factors that might affect efforts to solve the need, including community values, local and national priorities, and public expectations

Organizing Priorities in Two Stages

As noted in Chapter 3, it is advisable to set priorities in two stages: (a) first, for broad areas, such as goals, concerns, issues, or target groups; and (b) second, on critical needs within each area. For example, in a mental health NA for a local area, the needs assessors identified three high-risk target groups: the elderly, numbers of dysfunctional families, and teenagers. In the last group, the NAC could set priorities on several identified critical needs: for persons with personality disorders, learning problems, and substance abuse, and incidence of teen suicides. Priorities for the elderly and for families would be determined separately. The two stages produce different categories of need.

Priorities are set first on needs at Level 1 and then at Levels 2 and 3, as in the following example.

> The HMO whose annual NA of facilities was described in Chapter 3 was studying the needs of its members with cardiac problems. It found two major Level 1 need areas that were not being adequately addressed: preventive care and nonsurgical management of cardiac problems. Associated Level 2 needs related to knowledge of prevention and management on the part of health professionals—primary care physicians, consulting nurses, and support staff for rehabilitation. Level 3 needs related to facilities for diagnostic procedures such as angiograms, which could be done on an outpatient basis without hospitalization. Decisions regarding critical needs at Levels 2 and 3 grew out of analysis of Level 1 needs.

The managers of the Level 3 (facilities) NA of this HMO also had a set of nine criteria to be used consistently by all regions engaged in the annual NA process. The first three were considered nonnegotiable criteria for priority funding: safety of patients and staff, urgent or threatening building system failures, and regulatory requirements with a potential for penalty. The order of the next six, although it was agreed on by the planning group, was subject to negotiation based on departmental priorities: prudent repair and replacement of facilities, operational cost savings, ongoing commitments, responsiveness to increased capacity because of membership growth, improved service or quality of care, and support or expansion of new initiatives.

Some NAs require that criteria for priorities be derived from the special circumstances of the situation. In cyclical or MIS NAs, however, general criteria for priorities can be established based on experience with the first round and later modified as circumstances change. Broad priorities related to major goals in a school system might remain stable for a time, but criteria for priorities in subgoal or special need areas might be subject to change. A further consideration is whether the priorities are being established in a short- or long-term frame.

Deriving Priorities From Several Data Sources

In Chapter 3, we stated that different methods of gathering NA data (surveys, analysis of archival sources, focus groups, etc.) might yield discrepant information on needs. Differing priorities may also appear from the same method used with different groups—for example, a survey of mental health patients, counselors, and family members of the patients, regarding needs of the patients.

When such discrepancies occur, the NAC may want to reexamine the instruments used in the NA and interview a few key informants from each respondent group to probe for reasons of the differences. If two or more distinct sets or rankings of priorities emerge, the NAC and key decision makers decide on a compromise ranking.

Aggregating data from different sources to determine priorities is ultimately a matter for discussion and expert judgment. Each method discussed in Chapters 5 through 9 has information on analyzing data and interpreting results.

Setting Priorities in an MIS

When an organization maintains an ongoing management information system, alert planners or research and development staff can often spot a critical need without conducting an elaborate NA.

One of the largest developers of software for computers receives more than 30,000 calls for help daily. The company has begun a new project, applying techniques from research on artificial intelligence to its software support system. The staff is learning from patterns in the calls and will program solutions into its software that will enable it to respond to frequent queries.

In this case, the company identified a critical client need (e.g., technical assistance) and is marshaling resources to meet it. It is not enough to recognize that the need exists, however. The information crucial to setting criteria for the solution lies in the patterns of the calls. As any organization aggregates data of interest for its MIS, patterns emerge that can be analyzed for critical needs. Whether the need area becomes a priority for action depends on other factors, such as competing needs and resources available for problem resolution.

Cutting-Edge Priorities

Sensing emerging needs via an MIS may run into opposition in some situations. Research and development or public service organizations are often aware of problems before they are perceived as needs by others. Yet an organization may encounter resistance in resolving such problems from those who would have to implement solutions. Meeting needs of handicapped adults is one example. For many years, groups representing such individuals advocated accessible public facilities, access to job training programs, and elimination of discriminatory practices. Not until the U.S. Congress passed the Americans With Disabilities Act (1990), however, did programs to meet these needs become a societal priority.

On the other hand, sometimes the appearance of new technology (a Level 3 phenomenon) is a catalyst for an awareness of needs and new priorities that had not previously existed. Such is the case with the rapidly growing electronic information superhighway, which is changing the way in which libraries think about information needs. In fact, the concept of a library has changed dramatically in the past 30 years, moving from print holdings (books, newspapers, magazines, card catalogs), supplemented by graphics (some large libraries loan out paintings), to the concept of information storage and retrieval via both print and nonprint media (audio- and videotapes), then to computerized access to sources, and, as this is written, to linkups with worldwide information and communication through Internet.

The existence of the technology has triggered a felt need in library users for access to the electronic superhighway and to sources of information on CD-ROMs. The recognition of this trend in the changing needs of clients (present and potential library patrons) has sparked NAs at Level 2 (training of library staff) and Level 3 (analysis of the libraries' potential for storage and retrieval of information). Once the priorities have been established, library systems have embarked on training staff and holding brief workshops to teach patrons how to use new computer stations. Note that the basic client needs for information and entertainment have not changed, but the delivery system and expected turnaround time have changed.

Furthermore, computers have not replaced print holdings. Card catalogs are still retained as a backup source, and shelves are still full of books. In fact, a whole new category of books, magazines, and newsletters on how to cruise the information superhighway has appeared.

Priorities Without Resources

In Phase 3, the NAC might set a high priority on a need for which there are no apparent resources to meet it. The priority-setting process should certainly consider present resources when selecting need areas for immediate attention, but long-range planning might incorporate methods for acquiring additional resources to address high-priority needs.

Problems of Turf in Large Agencies

In a citywide or regional NA, in which many departments or bureaus compete for resources, there may be clashes among managers (not necessarily expressed overtly) regarding the relative importance of the different departments and therefore the weight that should be given to priorities among them. Additional problems arise when the administrator or other person who is facilitating the meetings is inept at allocating reasonable amounts of time to each department, and when decisions are made on the basis of opinions rather than facts.

The Community Services Administration for a medium-sized city in a metropolitan area held several meetings to set priorities for the coming year for each department. The priorities were requested first from middle managers. The director of the library system, who was a top level manager in respect to his own system, was considered a middle manager in relationship to the Human Services Department, which included the library as well as other services.

Over a period of 3 months, there were numerous meetings totaling about 60 hours. Many of the middle managers came with lists of preferences, but no background of facts. At the final meeting, toward the end of the day, a person in charge of a department with a $10,000 budget took 30 minutes to advocate for his priorities. The library director, with a $400,000 budget, was given only a few minutes to present his priorities and the factual basis for them. Time ran out, people began to leave, and the director and others were left considering the needs assessment process a farce.

In such situations, we advocate the use of carefully planned and structured meetings as described throughout this guide. Ground rules for participation should be established in advance and department heads instructed to bring facts to support their arguments, both in writing and for oral presentation.

Setting Priorities for Level 2 NAs

We have discussed guidelines for Level 1 NAs as well as how Level 3 NAs should be derived from an understanding of needs at Levels 1 and 2. We have also alluded to the fact that assessments of training needs of Level 2 personnel should be grounded in their relationships as service providers with receivers inside or outside the system. Priorities of training needs may also be derived from the magnitude of discrepancies between current and desired levels of skill in making a product or performing a technical task.

Beyond those general considerations, are there more specific guidelines available for designing Level 2 NAs and deriving priorities from them to guide training? Several methods are commonly used: surveys asking personnel what kinds of training they want or think that they need; observation of on-the-job performance; analysis of data from personnel evaluations; and analysis of technical or knowledge requirements for jobs using new technology, such as online computers and electronic search services being installed in public libraries, among others. In addition, there are specialized techniques for analyzing job requirements in detail, such as DACUM (see Chapter 8). Such specific job analyses can form the basis for reducing discrepancies between current job performance and a required level.

Instructional designers have raised the question of whether potential trainees have sufficient insight into their own needs to provide a basis for setting priorities on the content of instruction. One model of NA represents an employee-centered approach that uses more than one dimension on which to base priorities for training needs. It is the multicomponent R-C-D model (Misanchuk, 1984). The three components are *relevance* of a task or skill to the job role of the individual, *competence* of the individual to perform the task, and *desire* of the individual to undergo training in the task.

Schwier (1986) extended Misanchuk's R-C-D model to extract implications for training needs. Although employees should, in general, be able to identify which tasks are most relevant to their job roles, there are situations in which there is a disparity between the organization's and the employee's perspectives of job relevance—the "what should be" dimension of NA. Schwier's model uses three levels for each scale, with training implications for each. The levels from high to low on the R scale are relevance, irrelevance, and interference. Levels on the C scale are competence, benign incompetence, and perceived lack of aptitude. And levels on the D scale are desire, apathy, and subversion.

From the three scales, Schwier shows how any employee's ratings can be depicted graphically in three dimensions—low-high relevance, low-high competence, and low-high desire. The different possible configurations hold implications both for priorities of training needs and for the design of the training to best meet the needs. Employees with low competence, low perception of relevance, and low desire would require different training from those with low ratings on competence but high on relevance and desire.

Schwier (1986) emphasizes that the multicomponent NA "is conducted within the context of organizational objectives. . . . The needs assessment is preceded by a thorough task analysis, and, regardless of the outcome of the assessment, the organizational objectives do not change" (p. 92). For example, regardless of employees' perceptions of relevance of training in emergency radiation treatment in a uranium mining operation, the organization would continue to include the safety of its employees in its objectives.

2.0 SELECT SOLUTION STRATEGIES

2.1 Set Criteria for Solutions

In Chapter 3, we discussed setting criteria for determining priorities. In this section we consider criteria or standards for judging the merits of alternative solution strategies, corresponding to Step 2.1 of Figure 4.1. At a minimum, proposals should meet criteria of *feasibility, acceptability,* and *effect on the causes.* Will the solution work, and will people who have the need accept it? Will service providers and managers accept it? Does it fit with societal goals as well as organizational goals and policies? What causes or contributing factors will the solution address?

The feasibility criterion also involves resources. Are resources available for the solution requirements, and if not, can they be acquired? Feasibility, however, should not be the overriding criterion. Sometimes needs assessors prematurely constrain the process of prioritizing by focusing only on those areas where a solution seems feasible. The feasibility question can be dealt with in the Level 3 analysis, where resources required are matched against resources available or possible.

In setting criteria for solutions, the NAC considers both parameters and constraints. The HMO facilities NA discussed earlier had three nonnegotiable parameters—safety of patients and staff, urgent or threatening building system failures, and requirements of regulatory bodies. Constraints related mainly to costs.

Criteria in themselves do not describe a solution. For example, a car manufacturer decides to design a new car to meet the needs of a certain segment of the population. Some criteria parameters might be that (a) the car will get at least 30 miles per gallon of gas in city driving, (b) emissions will meet standards of the Environmental Protection Agency, (c) the front and rear bumpers will withstand impacts at 30 miles per hour, and (d) the finish will be rustproof. Constraints would be such matters as the cost of such a car and the existence of technology to meet the design specifications.

These criteria do not describe the car's engineering features or the design of the chassis, but when various designs are suggested, they can be compared with the criteria for a match. The manufacturer can also weight the criteria—that is, the ability to withstand impacts might rate twice as high as the rustproof factor.

The tasks of analyzing needs, setting priorities, and determining criteria for solutions are integrally related. Sork (1982) developed a generic model that provides a conceptual framework for the process. The model is presented in the discussion of techniques later in the chapter.

2.2 Consider Alternative Solutions for Each Critical Need

In earlier stages of the NA, the NAC and others involved in data gathering may have prematurely suggested solutions instead of focusing on needs. Ideally, they were noted and put aside for future consideration. The NA has now reached the stage for the NAC to consider those solutions and generate and examine additional solution strategies.

First comes the proposal of a number of alternative solutions for each need area separately, without evaluating their merits. Next, the solutions in each need area are clustered into categories reflecting the three levels of targets. Assuming that the target group with the needs is at Level 1 (students, clients, people with specified health or mental health problems), the solution strategies might occur at one or more levels.

A school district has identified a need regarding elementary school children who exhibit a constellation of problems, including hyperactivity, very short attention span, and severe underachievement academically, in spite of their having average or higher intelligence. The district has data on the number of children who exhibit the syndrome, the effect of their behavior on classmates and teachers, possible causes of the problem, and steps that teachers and parents have previously taken to deal with the problem. Interventions based on the needs data take place at all three levels: prescribed medication for some of the children (Level 1), special training for teachers in classroom management with heterogeneous groups (Level 2), and finding money in the budget to reduce class size (Level 3). The district rejects other solutions—such as putting the children into special classes—because of opposition from parents and recent federal and state legislation that mandates education for all children "in the least restrictive environment."

Generally, we recommend that criteria for evaluating alternative solutions take into account both the criticality of need and the likelihood that the chosen solution will address causal or contributing factors. In this example, the two overriding factors were criticality of the need and acceptability to teachers and parents. The solutions did not address causal factors—they dealt only with management of the symptoms. Sometimes that is all that can be expected for short-term solutions. Moreover, dealing with the causes was really beyond the control of the school.

2.3 Evaluate Alternatives on the Basis of the Criteria

Consider each alternative solution separately in the light of feasibility, acceptability, effect on causes, and other criteria set forth in Step 2.1. Comparisons among alternatives can then be made by summarizing the important features of each in relation to each criterion, using a form such as the one shown in Figure 4.2.

After discussing the merits of each proposal in the light of the criteria, the NAC weights each solution as to the degree to which it meets each criterion: high, medium, or low. Some points in favor of a

Criteria	Solution 1	Solution 2	Solution 3
1			
	_____	_____	_____
2			
	_____	_____	_____
3			
	_____	_____	_____
4			
	_____	_____	_____

Figure 4.2. Form for Comparing Alternate Solution Strategies

solution might exist that do not fit any of the criteria, and those can be noted as well.

After the weighting process, the NAC should go one step further and consider each of the high-ranking solutions in regard to the forces that drive toward the contemplated change, and those that push in the opposite direction, restraining change. One of the most productive and enjoyable methods for doing this is through force field analysis (FFA), which is described in detail later in this chapter.

2.4 Select Solutions to Implement

Up to this point, the NAC has considered alternative solutions separately. On the basis of all the information, including advantages and disadvantages generated in the FFA, one or more solutions are selected for each need area. Certain questions will arise; for example, Is it better to choose a solution that can be quickly implemented with high visibility of results, or one that may have more effect in the long run, but that will take more time to design and install?

Sometimes it is desirable to focus first on short-term strategies that can be easily implemented and that will give positive reinforcement to the organization and the community, such as the minipark that resulted from the collaborative city-school district NA described in Chapter 3. Such solutions make a visible link between NA activities and actions taken later. At the same time, it is desirable to outline longer-range plans, perhaps with provisions to implement the solutions in stages—such as the three-way partnership (school district, city, and business community), which formulated long-range plans for career preparation and job enhancement for youth in their area.

3.0 PROPOSE AN ACTION PLAN

Decisions about solutions must generally be approved by a governing board or other decision-making body. The needs assessor acts as an adviser to decision makers regarding an action plan to guide installation and implementation of one or more solutions (see Figure 4.1). The plan should include descriptions of the solutions, rationale, proposed timelines, human and physical resources required, and an estimated budget.

4.0 EVALUATE THE QUALITY OF THE NEEDS ASSESSMENT

Step 4.0, the evaluation of the NA, is like the evaluation of any project. The main questions to answer are, How well did the NA meet its goals? What were its strengths? What problems were encountered? If the system were to hold a similar NA in the future, what changes in methods or other factors would you recommend? Were there some unexpected results?

In Chapter 2, we suggested that the evaluation plan might be based in part on a success map and some analysis of potential problems in the plan through fault tree analysis (FTA) or other causal techniques (see Chapter 10). If the needs assessor used FTA in predicting possible failures in the NA process, review that analysis. Did any of the predicted failures occur? Why? Could they have been prevented? What actions were taken that prevented other problems from occurring? If possible, the evaluation should weigh the effect that the NA process had on the various participants and the probable effect of recommended actions on service receivers and providers, other stakeholders, and the organization or the community itself.

5.0 PREPARE REPORTS AND BRIEFINGS

It is helpful to think of those who assess needs, those whose needs are being assessed, and those who have the power to make decisions about programs to meet the needs as being linked in an information network. Each of the groups requires different types of information in a timely manner, and preparing these is the task of Step 5.0.

Most needs assessors are aware that frequent communication with decision makers and key individuals is important for the success of all NA activities. Nevertheless, we underscore the necessity of clear and frequent communication, not only to top management and policymakers but to important stakeholder groups as well.

The first written document, perhaps accompanied by an oral briefing, was the NA plan or memorandum of agreement submitted to the governing board for approval at the end of Phase 1. If appropriate, the needs assessor has continued to furnish brief reports, oral briefings, or both during the assessment phase, especially if the data gathering and analysis take more than a month or two. At the end of Phase 3, the needs assessor prepares final reports to decision makers and policymakers to communicate the results of the NA. They include the salient features of the NA plan, the major outcomes, priorities and their criteria, the action plan with the criteria used to arrive at the solution strategies, and recommendations for future NAs based on the evaluation.

One of the most important things to do to promote use of the results of an NA is to write reports that are understandable to your audiences, eliminating technical jargon as much as possible.[1] We recommend the following approaches: Vary the reports as needed for different audiences, such as a policy board, top decision makers, managers, and staff who will implement solutions. Include graphic displays—simple charts, tables, and illustrations—to clarify the narrative. Use appropriate visual displays as well for oral reports to groups. If the NA was the first comprehensive one done in the system, it is important to include copies of survey instruments, interview protocols, data analysis methods, and the like for archives for future use by planners and needs assessors (see Smith, 1982, for alternative strategies for communicating project results).

We have emphasized the importance of including a broad base of stakeholders in the NA process. Their involvement, and indeed their sense of ownership (and empowerment), is essential to the acceptance of the NA process and results. Their active support is vital for the implementation of action plans. Therefore, the needs assessor must make sure that all participants in the NA process are sent reports or invited to final meetings.

Techniques for Phase 3

In this section, we describe four concepts or techniques that were referred to in the earlier discussion of the major tasks of Phase 3. They are *risk assessment*, a generic model for dealing with priorities, a group process for the Phase 3 decision making, and *force field analysis* (FFA). In addition, we present a case study of an organization in which FFA was an essential element of the NA.

RISK ASSESSMENT[2]

Traditionally, priorities for action in NA have been based on the magnitude of discrepancies—the larger the discrepancy between a desired or ideal state and the present state, the higher the priority for action on a need. (We have also discussed other methods for assigning priorities on needs, as in the HMO facilities NA discussed earlier.) Now we recommend that the determination of priorities be made in part on the basis of magnitude of the risk if the need is not met, not just on the magnitude of discrepancies. When combining data from Level 1 priorities and causal analyses, decide what is the potential risk of not taking action to meet the needs, rather than focusing primarily on needs with the largest discrepancies.

Instead of asking, What are the needs? (which usually leads to people listing wants and desires), the question to ask is, What are the inhibiting factors, obstacles, barriers, risks, and potential failures? Now the data on critical Level 1 needs can be viewed in the light of the risk assessment. A cause and consequence analysis (see Chapter 10) may be useful here. Are there any changes in criticality of the needs? The highest priorities go to the areas of greatest danger.

The concept of risk assessment in NA has been used with school systems, government entities, and regulatory agencies concerned with water pollution, among others. One of the difficulties in using risk assessment to set priorities, however, is that there is often disagreement between researchers and stakeholders as to the nature and magnitude of the risks. Also, perceptions of degree of risk might not be in accord with facts. Therefore, it is essential that the NA be based not only on perceptions of risk by various publics but on hard data as well, as the following case illustrates.

> A New Hampshire toxic-waste dump was cleaned up to the point that children could eat small amounts of dirt for 70 days a year without being harmed.
>
> But the government insisted that $9.3 million be spent to burn the soil to remove the remaining 10% of toxic chemicals, so that children could eat small amounts of dirt for 245 days a year.
>
> Breyer [a prominent jurist] said cleaning up the last 10% would be a waste of money because the area is a swamp, no dirt-eating children were on the premises, they weren't likely to be there in the future, and at least half of the chemicals would be expected to evaporate by 2000. He also criticized government regulators for failing to study all risks and give the highest priorities to the greatest dangers. (Epstein, 1994)[3]

The needs assessor and NAC should be alert to the possibility that needs having high visibility or severe social or economic impact may be subject to myths and distortions, often communicated\through the media. The skilled needs assessor can enhance the validity of risk assessment through careful examination of archival data, working with key informants, and employing trend analysis.

A GENERIC PROCESS FOR DETERMINING PRIORITIES

The following steps are adapted from the work of Sork (1982), who developed a model for determining priority of need in community adult education. Most of the needs in that effort come from economic and social indicators of well-being.

Select Appropriate Criteria

The model suggests two general categories: *importance* and *feasibility*. Importance includes the number of people affected, the degree to which meeting the need would contribute to organizational goals, immediacy, and the magnitude of the discrepancy between current and target states. Feasibility criteria include educational efficacy (the degree to which an educational intervention or program can contrib-

ute to eliminating the need), availability of resources, and commitment to change.

Assign Relative Importance to Each Criterion

All criteria can be weighted equally. Or they can be assigned any
value from 1 to 10: First, identify the criterion that carries the least
weight in decisions about priorities and assign it a value of 1. Then
assign values to the remaining criteria; a factor of 2 carries twice the
weight of a factor of 1 in the final decision, and a factor of 10 carries
10 times the weight.

Apply Each Criterion to Each Need

Applying each criterion to each need results in a weighting of each
separate need for each of the two categories (importance and feasibility) and their subcategories. Express the weights in the same units,
either numerical values or descriptors (e.g., high, medium, and low).

Combine Individual Values to
Yield a Total Priority Value for Each Need

To achieve a total priority value for each need, two different techniques can be employed: plotting judgments of importance and feasibility on a quadrant chart or using an additive aggregation rule to
combine weighted ranks into a mean rank for each need.

Arrange Needs From Highest to Lowest Total
Priority Value and Indicate How Priorities Will Be Used

By ranking the needs by total priority value, the NAC decides and
clearly states how the resources will be allocated to meet specific
needs. Sork (1982) suggests alternatives and adds a caution:

> For example, will the organization begin work simultaneously on the
> "top" group of needs, or will [it] work on meeting one need at a time,
> beginning at the top, until available resources are exhausted? Will a
> group of needs at the "low" end of the list be ignored, or will some
> attempt be made to address all identified needs? And how will newly

identified high-priority needs affect the allocation of resources to established, ongoing programs?

Be forewarned—procedures for determining priorities can be manipulated to produce a result that supports someone's personal priorities. Safeguards should be employed to reduce the chances of individuals using the priority-setting process as a means of furthering their own self-interests at the expense of others in the organization or community. Open communication and involvement in decision making are two factors that should reduce the chances that the process will be abused. (p. 9)

A GROUP PROCESS FOR PHASE 3 DECISION MAKING

A method that has considerable value in making the transition from Phase 2 to Phase 3 involves the NAC, along with additional stakeholders, in a highly structured three-session group process (Wickens, 1980). It works well with a group of about 12 to 15 people. All should have some information about the general need area but few or no preconceived ideas about solutions. All three sessions are fast-paced, tightly structured, and highly oriented to completing tasks and producing specific outcomes.

The following illustration is based on an educational NA. The group generated four kinds of ideas: concerns about the educational program, needs for program improvement, resources currently being used in relation to needs, and resources that could be used or that should be obtained.

Session 1

In Session 1, the participants identify what students in a school or district are doing well and what they are not doing well and cluster each set of statements into categories. The categories are reviewed during a period in which group members advocate for categories that they believe to be significant. After advocacy, members vote individually, and those categories with the highest votes are selected to be used in Session 2.

Session 1 lasts about 2 hours and includes the following eight activities and time allotments:

1. Introduction to the three sessions—the agenda and time allocations for activities, and the roles to be played by the facilitator and participants. (10 minutes)
2. Brainstorming what students in this school are doing well and recording the ideas generated by the total group. (20 minutes)
3. Brainstorming what students in this school are not doing well and recording the ideas generated by the total group. (20 minutes)
4. Clustering the ideas into 10 or fewer categories and posting the categories for large group review.
5. Presenting and approving categories with regard to their clarity and wording. Total group must approve each category. (10 minutes)
6. Advocating for the importance (or unimportance) of individual categories by individuals in the group, with 30 seconds allowed per comment. (10 to 20 minutes)
7. Rating the importance of the categories using a paired-weighting procedure (PWP; see description in Chapter 3 and Figure 3.2) and summarizing the results from the group. (20 minutes)
8. Selecting the highest priority categories for Session 2 and quickly brainstorming likely sources of data regarding them. (10 minutes)

Each of the foregoing activities has a specific outcome—usually a list summarizing the main points agreed on. Each activity also has ground rules for participation (e.g., ideas from brainstorming activities are accepted without criticism or commentary, and the clusters are kept to a reasonable number to maintain group focus).

Interim Data Gathering

In the next 1 to 2 weeks, participants gather data for each high-priority cluster (task 8), for which they volunteered or took assignments in the last activity of Session 1.

Session 2

Using the information gathered in the interim, the large group divides into subgroups, each of which develops problem statements within a category and brainstorms potential causes of problems. Examples of problem statements might be, "Student achievement in mathematics is low compared with that in similar school districts," or "Increasing numbers of students in middle schools are smoking."

The whole group then reviews the work from the small groups, followed by a question and clarification period; the group then votes on the most important causes of each problem. Voting is based on the rule of three—each participant selects only the three most important causes of a problem. The outcome of Session 2 consists of lists of problems within categories and prioritized causes of those problems.

Session 3

The group engages in two brainstorming activities of 20 minutes each. In the first, the whole group identifies resources currently available; in the second, small groups identify resources currently unavailable but that could potentially be used for resolving a problem. Once the resources are identified, they are put in tabular form with three headings: *Problem, Resources Currently Available,* and *Resources Currently Unavailable.* The group reviews the table as well as the materials from all three sessions that will be included in the final outcome report: the list of categories (Session 1), the list of problems and causes (Session 2), and the list of available and potentially available resources (Session 3). Session 3 is designed to last approximately 90 minutes.

FORCE FIELD ANALYSIS

Force field analysis (FFA) is a technique developed by Kurt Lewin (1947) for diagnosing a situation by looking at both the driving and restraining forces that influence change in an organization. We recommend its use in NA as a way to analyze alternative solutions to a given need. It has qualitative and quantitative aspects. Figure 4.3 shows a simple diagram illustrating the concept.

The theory underlying FFA is that there is a point of equilibrium in any system, whether it refers to a state of productivity in a company or an area of need that calls for change. The NA has determined that there is a discrepancy between what is actually happening and what stakeholders would like to see happen in terms of results or outcomes. Reasons why the discrepancy exists have been analyzed, and a change strategy that looks as if it would meet the needs has been selected. The question now is, What are the forces that would support such a change, and what are the forces that would act against it? Hersey and Blanchard (1977) recount a case in which an FFA could have saved a new program. The following is a paraphrase of their report.

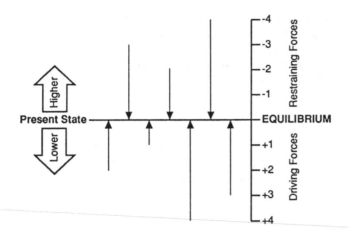

Figure 4.3. Generic Diagram for Force Field Analysis: Driving and Restraining Forces

An enthusiastic new superintendent of schools and his assistant took over a large suburban school district with the intent to "humanize" the schools by changing the prevailing teaching approach from teacher-centered (high task/low relationship style) to child-centered (high relationship/low task, or low relationship/low task style). In the second method, the students would play a significant role in determining what they should do.

The two administrators spent 15 to 18 hours a day working with and supporting teachers and administrators who wanted to use the new behaviors. Suddenly, six months after they had hired the superintendent, the school board called a special meeting and fired him. He and his assistant sued the school board, considered themselves educational martyrs, and went on lecture tours to talk about the evils of schools.

At that point, one of the administrators became familiar with FFA. When asked to think about the driving and restraining forces for the new plan, this is what he discovered:

Driving forces: The principal ones were the enthusiasm and commitment of the top administrators and a small group of teachers and students.

Restraining forces: The superintendent and his assistant had never had a good relationship with the mayor, chief of police, or editor of the local paper, who were important opinion makers in the community; the new administrators were viewed as encouraging permissiveness in the schools; the teachers' association felt that the new programs asked the teachers to assume responsibilities outside their contract; parents were concerned about discipline; and the superintendent, who had been hired by a 5-to-4 vote of the board, lost some of his supporters when they were defeated in an election.

In sum, the forces against change were overwhelmingly more powerful than the forces for change. If the superintendent had done an FFA at the beginning, he would have seen that his change strategy was doomed unless he took steps to work with key people who represented the restraining forces. (Hersey & Blanchard, 1977, pp. 277-280)

Using FFA to analyze two kinds of forces—those pushing for and those restraining change—and then deciding on strategies to overcome the restraining forces is somewhat analogous to success and failure mapping, which is explained in Chapter 10 under fault tree analysis. The tendency on the part of managers or program innovators who are enthusiastic about the changes they propose is to plan only for success. That is, they focus on what they feel is necessary to accomplish the objective.

Many times, however, a "successful" plan can crash because the proponents did not analyze potential failures. Similarly, an FFA brings to consciousness those forces that might support or undermine a proposed solution to a need.

What can be done to deal with opposing or countervailing forces to a plan? The decision makers may decide to reject the plan, to modify it to make it more feasible or acceptable, or to go ahead and confront the opposing forces directly and seek to change them to supporting forces. Often, the best strategy is not to try to expand the helping forces, but rather to minimize the opposing forces. In some cases, as illustrated in the case history that follows, further research uncovers facts that turn a supposed negative force (such as cost) into a positive one.

A NEEDS ASSESSMENT USING FORCE FIELD ANALYSIS

The Purchasing Directors' Association (PDA), a nonprofit organization that supplies equipment to all school districts in the state, from pencils to computers to school buses, did an NA to analyze how they could better serve their clients—the purchasing agents of the 254 school districts. The goal was to determine the districts' needs with respect to products, services, and procedures when purchasing from PDA. The main questions were, How have changes in areas of education affected purchasing decisions and choices? and How can PDA be more responsive to existing needs and proactive in anticipating future client needs?

The NA was conducted by an external consultant who was skilled in facilitating organizational change. The product of the NA was to be a set of recommendations from a customer base to the PDA board so that the organization could implement new programs and procedures. The management team that made the recommendations was composed of key personnel who headed the five departments: warehousing, customer service (which produced the catalog), accounting, purchasing, and distribution. There was also a task force of 15 purchasing agents representing the customers. The NA was divided into two phases:

Phase 1. The consultant surveyed all the customers regarding their needs and degree of satisfaction with the services. The task force interpreted the results and also developed a set of recommendations to PDA.

Phase 2. The management team reviewed the task force recommendations in light of organizational and operational factors. They also did an FFA, analyzing each recommendation separately for positive and negative factors, and suggested criteria and solutions to eliminate negative factors and to maximize positive ones.

Each department's problems and recommendations were analyzed independently. The FFA showed that the most critical problem was the catalog, which was essential for ordering items. The catalog was antiquated in design, poorly organized, and not updated in a timely fashion. The task force recommended that PDA issue a reorganized color catalog, to be updated yearly. The management team considered the forces for and against changing the catalog. Figure 4.4 shows the FFA.

Forces against change were a possible increased cost due to restructuring and use of color, difficulty of publishing on a yearly basis, doubt about in-house capability to redesign the catalog, doubt whether the

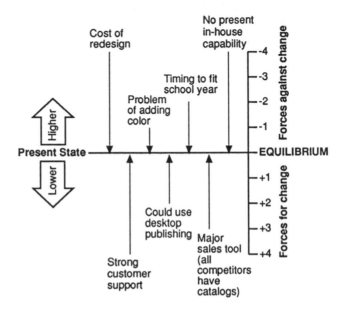

Figure 4.4. Force Field Analysis of Catalog Recommendation in a Purchasing Directors' Agency

timing of publication would fit in with the school year, and questioning whether there would be enough lead time each year to issue an update.

Forces supporting change were that a previous survey showed that customers wanted a new catalog, that the catalog itself was a major tool for keeping customers, and that the PDA's new desktop publishing capability with graphics support made it more feasible than their old labor-intensive method in which graphic artists were employed to draw hundreds of separate illustrations.

Each manager researched the problem in his area to find information related to the positive and negative forces. For example, the warehouse had been relying on a private parcel delivery service for delivery of items. The suggested solution was for PDA to do its own delivery and, therefore, have total control. Although the solution at first appeared too costly, the warehouse manager came back a month later with information on costs of trucks and drivers, a preliminary distribution plan, and a schedule—all of which indicated that the solution was feasible and cost-effective. Accordingly, the management team recommended that PDA implement a pilot distribution program, in a limited geographic area, for 4 months.

Both the task force and management team were delighted to be involved in the NA, liked the FFA, and found that after research and analysis, some of the factors that were on the negative side had moved over to the positive side. Costs of certain changes turned out not to be as high as had been feared, and, due to new technology, the PDA was able to implement in-house solutions that simplified much of the work and made it more cost-effective.

SUMMARY

Phase 4, Postassessment, is essential to the use of NA findings. The needs assessor, NAC, and key decision makers examine the NA data and causal analyses to set priorities on needs, suggest alternative solutions, select one or more solutions in each need area according to a set of criteria, propose an action plan to implement the recommendations, evaluate the NA, and communicate the results of the whole NA by means of written reports and oral briefings to policymakers, stakeholders, and other interested parties.

Techniques presented for the postassessment phase are risk assessment as a concept in setting priorities; a group decision process for generating needs, causes, priorities, and analysis of resources; a generic model for identifying priorities; and force field analysis as a method of evaluating proposed solutions.

Notes

1. One of us learned the hard way about the importance of doing an audience analysis before presenting an unfamiliar idea. The occasion was an oral briefing to top level school administrators about the application of systems analysis (a brand new concept in education at the time) to planning an innovative and complex project. When the presentation, complete with graphic displays, was over, there was a long pause. Finally, the county superintendent—a courtly gentleman—said kindly, "Dr. Witkin, I haven't the faintest notion what you were talking about."

2. The brief description of risk assessment in this chapter owes its genesis to a discussion with Kent Stephens, President of CEO Sciences, Springville, Utah, held on May 24, 1994.

3. Reprinted by permission of Tribune Media Services.

PART II

Methods for
Conducting a Needs Assessment

FIVE

Records and Social Indicators

In Phase 1, your preassessment explorations probably uncovered the fact that many indicators of needs, issues, and concerns were already available in existing files, reports, or organizational records. But archival data of all kinds are valuable for the Phase 2 assessment as well. Many kinds of records provide information on the current status of target groups—characteristics of people in Levels 1 and 2, and information on resources at Level 3, as well as what services are being provided, to whom, and in what quantities. Social indicators are variables that describe conditions or states of a population. They are helpful in assessing needs, and they can be accessed through or derived from records.

In this chapter, we describe general considerations for using records (archived sources) and social indicators and then follow with a closer look at specific methods. They include unobtrusive observations, the use of existing records, the modification or creation of record keeping systems, rates-under-treatment (RUT), using data from existing data banks, and two special techniques—mapping and indirect estimation.

The use of existing records is generally cheaper and requires less time than creating new data sets. On the other hand, such records are rarely designed expressly for the purpose of needs assessment; consequently, needs must be inferred from them, with inferences subject to value judgments and questions of interpretation and validity.

For example, high divorce rates might be an indication of the need for family counseling services within a metropolitan area. The divorce rate, from this perspective, represents the symptom of a deficiency or a problem that might require professional assistance or other support. But a rise in the divorce rate may, in part, merely reflect the fact that divorces are easier to obtain and carry less social stigma than in the past. As a needs assessor, it is important to be alert constantly for alternative explanations of data in existing sources. In this example, estimating the magnitude of the need for services in a given geographic area might require additional data, such as the incidence of poverty in single-parent families and other data regarding problems of children in families in which parents are divorced.

Social Indicators

Social indicators are variables representing important characteristics of a group or social situation, which agencies usually keep track of over a period of years. They are used individually or as combined indices to describe and analyze social situations and the needs relevant to them. They also allow us to examine trends over time, that is, persistence of needs (see Chapter 9 for a description of trend analysis).

Although qualitative data are valid as social indicators, quantitative data predominate. Depending on which indicators are selected, they can be used to assess each of the three levels of needs—service recipients, service providers, and resources at the system level.

Social indicators provide three types of information useful for needs assessment. First, they contain facts about the current status (the "what is" condition) of a group or the delivery of services to the group. Second, implied or actual standards or norms are inherent in some social indicators, so that discrepancies between current and desired statuses can be deduced. One example is the norms of standardized testing programs used by schools. Another is in the field of health, where norms have been established for vision and hearing, heart and lung functioning, and the like.

Third, social indicators can also provide information on which to base predictions about possible future needs, as in epidemiologic studies of health care services. In the case of AIDS, for example, epidemiologists count the number of individuals with the disease (prevalence—the "what is" status); they estimate from records the number of individuals who will become HIV positive in the near future (incidence—the "what will be" situation); and they determine the current number of individuals receiving counseling and medical services. From these data, health professionals and policymakers better understand the dimensions of the problem and the assistance that might be required. In this situation, the magnitude of the need is estimated not from the difference between what is and what should be, but between what is and what might be if the disease proceeds unchecked at the current rate. The same reasoning could apply to NA in education, city planning, and other fields.

SOURCES OF SOCIAL INDICATORS

The following are typical social indicators and their sources that are obtainable for education, social services, and government.

Education. The results of school, district, state, and nationwide assessment programs; data from previously completed needs assessments; program evaluations related to the need area of interest; accreditation reports; school records dealing with student absenteeism, health, behavioral problems, and episodes of violence; records of teacher absences; demographic data; census data regarding a school district; and classroom observations.

Social Services. Demographic characteristics of clients served; previous needs assessments or evaluation reports of programs; documentation from intake records; use of services within catchment areas; client satisfaction data; information from scales of adjustment to jobs and social situations; census data regarding age, ethnicity, income, divorce, and separation; rates-under-treatment (RUT—see following section for explanation).

City, Region, or Government Units. A variety of census or demographic data (housing patterns, age, ethnicity, income, level of educational attainment, poverty, unemployment, homelessness); use of government services (health care, public transportation, parks, recreational centers); transportation patterns; results from previous needs assessments or specialized studies of the governmental unit; judicial and legal records; estimates of the projected growth of the unit.

For all three fields, the types of data can also be categorized according to their sources. The three major types are (a) existing agency or institution records (archival sources) that are routinely maintained, (b) census or other specialized data banks, and (c) evaluations of a particular program or specialized NA studies focused on a particular area of concern. An additional source, not frequently included in NA, is unobtrusive records, measures, and observations.

KEY QUESTIONS TO ASK BEFORE
USING RECORDS AND SOCIAL INDICATORS

To use existing records, social indicators, or both, the needs assessor and the NAC should consider a number of questions prior to accessing, collecting, analyzing, interpreting, and reporting results. These are some examples:

1. What do we currently know about the need area and what kinds of data do we have that support our knowledge and understanding?
2. What more would we like to know; would existing sources of data be helpful in this regard?
3. What kinds of data are contained in existing sources? Can we obtain access to them?
4. How closely do these data fit our informational needs and what types of inferences might we have to make?
5. How have these data been obtained and maintained? (i.e., What is their quality? This is an especially important question about agency or institutional records.)
6. What kinds of safeguards should we observe to guarantee the confidentiality of records?
7. If available records do not fit our informational needs, is it possible to modify the current record-keeping system, or should we develop and implement a new one?
8. Do current agency and institutional records contain qualitative as well as quantitative data? What is their nature and value?
9. How do regionally or nationally collected data relate to our local situation? Do the trends in such data apply to the parameters we see locally?

Unobtrusive Measures and Observations

DESCRIPTION OF THE MEASURES

An unobtrusive measure is an observation of a situation or event of interest, usually without the people observed being aware of the observation, that furnishes information beyond the observation itself. A classic example of an unobtrusive measure is the weighing of food thrown away by students who eat in the school cafeteria. The technique has been used as a before-and-after measure to evaluate the acceptance of a revised menu; it might be used as a substitute for a questionnaire, and repeated weighings over several months would indicate whether the change had long-term consequences. The unobtrusive measure, then, is an indirect method of getting information.

Most discussions of records and social indicators do not include reference to unobtrusive measures as a source of information for identifying and understanding needs, yet they can be excellent sources of information. For example, to understand the need for certain types of vocational preparation, the needs assessor might seek information directly from records provided by national, state, and regional agencies. On the other hand, the need might be inferred by counting want ads in local or regional newspapers (the "help-wanted" index) and comparing jobs advertised to current training programs. Want ads could be monitored over time (monthly or yearly) to identify emerging trends in regard to vocational training. This type of data, which was never intended for NA purposes, is valuable for analyzing needs.

Other kinds of unobtrusive measures are also available. The number of applicants for certain types of jobs may be an indication of labor force supply or demand. Attendance and discussion at school board meetings could reveal the degree of community concern about schools, understanding of school problems and issues, and worry about taxes. Community concerns also surface at zoning meetings, open board meetings for public agencies, and other community meetings. Complaints about services might be signs of inadequacies in their delivery, quality, or abundance. The "Letters to the Editor" columns in local newspapers often reflect trends in a community's concerns about some aspect of government or government services.

ADVANTAGES AND DISADVANTAGES
OF UNOBTRUSIVE MEASURES

The use of unobtrusive measures for NA has many advantages.

1. Such indicators as want ads and job applications are unbiased because they were not created expressly for an NA purpose.
2. The data already exist and are generally accessible with a small investment of time or staff.
3. Unobtrusive measures and observations may be indicators of a need or the concerns of the population or of a specific group.
4. They are a unique source, different from other NA data sources.
5. They can be a valuable complement to other sources of data.

On the other hand, using unobtrusive measures in NA has several disadvantages. First, inferences must be made from variables that are not direct measures of a need. Letters to the editor may indicate issues that are important only to a small but vocal group of individuals, not to the population at large. The number of applicants for a job or for admission to a prestigious university could be misleading in terms of need. In both cases, it is likely that the applicants have applied for more than one position or university opening. Lack of knowledge of multiple applications could result in overestimating need.

Second, unobtrusive approaches may not yield indicators that are representative. They could be valid indications of the concerns of one particular group but not of the general population. The old adage—that the squeaky wheel gets the grease—applies, and the needs assessor must be aware of self-selection, especially when interpreting results from unobtrusive data.

Third, deciding which unobtrusive measures to select and use is problematic. For example, complaints about work could be observed over time in the workplace and taken as an indication of need. However, complaining about work may be part of the American psyche and not necessarily related to need. Records of productivity and attendance, in this instance, may be better indicators of need. Finally, some kinds of repeated observations, such as in a school or workplace, may become obvious to those being observed, who may then seek to manipulate the situation—in which case the measures are no longer unobtrusive.

Given their advantages and disadvantages, we advocate the use of unobtrusive sources as part of the NA process, but only in conjunction with other techniques and data sources. The following illustrates how the use of existing records in combination with unobtrusive observations helped a mental health agency understand a need (Patton, 1990).

Data from intake records showed that the numbers of individuals seeking counseling at a mental health center were fewer than anticipated. The results were puzzling inasmuch as the center had been strategically located to serve a much larger number of people. No cause could be determined from existing records for this situation. Direct observation of the entrance to the center, however, led to an understanding of the problem and a simple resolution. The center had posted a large sign saying "Mental Health Center— Intake" at the corner of a very busy street. The high visibility, intended to attract clients, led to avoidance instead. The observer recommended that the sign be moved around the corner to a side street, so that clients who felt a stigma was attached to seeking mental health treatment would feel more comfortable entering the center. The solution worked, and intake numbers increased.

Qualitative (unobtrusive observations) and quantitative (agency records) data together were more powerful than either source individually.

Use of Existing Agency or Institution Records

SOURCES OF RECORDS

Many agencies and institutions maintain records in the normal course of business, some of which are useful sources of NA data. Mental health agencies, health services, insurance companies, social service agencies, public services, schools, libraries, public corporations, and businesses routinely keep a variety of records. Records are necessary for understanding the clientele served by and the nature of services available through organizations. How is the clientele changing? What is the quality of service or goods provided? How do new or altered programs and services affect clientele and perceptions of quality?

For NA purposes, records provide extremely valuable information. Agencies, institutions, and businesses often issue yearly reports containing trends and analyses of key indicators that come from existing records.

Records are based on forms or standard mechanisms for collecting intake, process, and outcome data. As individuals enter a system (e.g., a mental health center or medical office), they or a staff member complete a form requesting age, gender, address, nature of the problem, and other relevant information. As they move through the system, more records are generated for services provided and the nature of the process involving the client (i.e., attendance and degree of progress). Outcome measures at the end of involvement are collected, and, in some instances, follow-up data are obtained.

The result, if all of these types of information are recorded and maintained, is a set of systematic input, process, and outcome data that have great potential for analyzing, understanding, and resolving needs. In places that maintain a computerized management information system (MIS), the requisite data might well be logged onto a computerized database.

USING EXISTING RECORDS

To access and use existing records in the NA, we recommend the following steps, adapted from King, Morris, and Fitz-Gibbon (1987):

1. Develop a list of characteristics or indicators that you feel are helpful in understanding the nature of the need or area of concern.
2. Find out what kinds of data and information have routinely been kept by the agency. Sample a few records to see what has been kept and the quality of record keeping.
3. Compare Steps 1 and 2 to determine the extent of fit.
4. Prepare a strategy for obtaining data from the records. Consider access to records, computer transfer, confidentiality, sampling of records if desirable, manual transfer, and so on.
5. Access records with as little inconvenience to agency staff as possible.

As we mentioned in Chapter 2 in the description of the two-session preassessment process, one of the main steps is to assemble indicators of the problem, then examine the records to find actual data regarding the concern. Table 2.2 in Chapter 2 shows a form for compiling such data, which applies to the foregoing steps. For example, discussion about a lack of student motivation in the high schools of a school district might result in a list of indicators such as incidence and patterns of absenteeism, single-period cuts, failures to turn in homework on time, class disruptions requiring some action, suspensions of students, and discussions by teachers in staff meetings. Sources for the data pertaining to each indicator might be records kept in the principals' and vice-principals' files, minutes or other records of staff meetings, reports by teachers and counselors, and the like. Each school would have a different set of sources. Access to such records would be worked out through the school secretary with approval by the principal.

CAVEATS REGARDING EXISTING RECORDS

Some caveats, however, are in order. First, do not assume that records have been maintained at a reasonably high level of quality. Both their reliability and validity may be suspect, varying with the clarity of forms, level of understanding required of individuals completing forms, truthfulness of individuals, degree to which all questions have been answered, time when process information has been recorded (during, immediately after, or long after an intervention, program, or treatment), and completeness of process information.

Second, in many circumstances and for a variety of reasons, individuals may provide little or no information about themselves or others. Perhaps they are unwilling to make judgments about others, or they may be considering self-preservation. Teachers or counselors dealing with sensitive topics and issues may feel uncomfortable about judging others and consequently enter only the "softest" of statements and notes into records. Or they may be concerned with the legal consequences of their statements and reluctant to place themselves in possible jeopardy. Therefore, they avoid recording certain types of sensitive information.

Consider the case of the needs assessor who is examining records to understand the nature of teacher referrals of students for disciplinary reasons. Do the records overstate or understate the nature of the problem? Are causes of the problems fully clear? If there are a large number of referrals, could teachers be using them as a way of not dealing with problems in their classrooms? Would the records reflect this situation? Is it possible that the number of referrals and the rationale for them would tend to overemphasize the problem and its dimensions?

Third, records are generally weakest in terms of process variables, that is, the degree to which the process (of treatment, a program, or an intervention) is either adequately described or described at all. Keeping such records requires the use of qualitative data (notes, observations, interviews), which tend to be difficult to enter and work with in a record-keeping system. As a consequence, input and outcome records in education and mental health may be more reliable and adequate than those for processes. Moreover, in a complete system of records it would be necessary to integrate dramatically different types of data, which is more easily said than done.

Fourth, some observers have concluded that there may be good organizational reasons for incomplete or poorly kept records—that bureaucrats may want to prevent the kind of thorough audit of records that can place blame (e.g., Garfinkel, 1967, pp. 186-207).[1]

A fifth concern with records is the degree to which outcome measures are fully representative of the effects of processes or treatments to which individuals have been exposed. In education, for example, it is well recognized that standardized tests capture only part of the outcomes of the educational process and generally do not include measures representative of the total curriculum. Standardized tests also tend to focus on areas that are more easily assessed quantitatively (mathematics, science) and focus less on such qualitative areas as attitudes and value formation.

Analogously, in mental health, client satisfaction or adjustment is difficult to measure and may not be indicative of a full range of subtle behavioral changes. In addition, most systems do not have provisions for the collection of long-term follow-up data that would demonstrate effects over time and that are fully sensitive to processes, treatments, or both.

Finally, remember that in accessing records, you are dealing with the work of others. In other words, to have access, you must invade someone else's turf. It is important to do this as unobtrusively and with as little disruption as possible.

We raise these cautions not to discourage or disparage the use of existing records but, rather, to ensure that interpretations of the data are screened through an understanding of what has gone into their generation. Clearly, they are of greatest value when combined with other sources of data.

SOME APPLICATIONS TO NA

A common form of record keeping arises from achievement-testing programs in schools. Because of accountability legislation, nearly all states require school districts to measure the performance of students. Inherent in testing programs are standards—norms or preassessment competency levels—that permit comparisons of student performance to the standards, and of schools and districts to each other in regard to standards. In many states, the ability of students to meet standards is a part of graduation requirements and is linked to the type of diploma a student will receive. It may also be viewed as an indicator of the educational quality of the school system.

The comparative features of testing programs allow for the identification of deficiencies (i.e., needs) for individual students as well as school systems. Because testing information is in the public domain and schools can be compared to each other, the term "high stakes testing" is often used to characterize these programs. Programs for keeping test scores are among the largest and most public forms of record-keeping systems in existence.

Among the assumptions that underlie the use of testing programs are the following:

1. Goals or outcomes are agreed on, with either an implied or an a priori standard to be attained.
2. Tests in areas such as math, reading, citizenship, and writing are accepted as indicators of educational performance. Their use, however, does not rule out adding other indicators of quality—numbers of graduates going to college, percentages of graduates who vote, labor market participation rates for graduates, and the like.
3. Students who fall below expectations will be helped to raise their level of performance.

In Ohio, for example, students are required to pass tests in the four areas noted in Step 2 to graduate. They take the tests each year, starting in the ninth grade, and have up to four opportunities to pass all four.

TABLE 5.1 Data for State Proficiency Test Results

Percentage of Ninth-Grade Students Who Passed the Proficiency Test(s)

District	Math	Reading	Citizens	Writing	All Four[a]
1	75	98	84	94	67
2	54	90	81	82	50
3	21	63	38	71	16
4	72	89	76	85	57
5	61	92	79	88	52
6	74	92	77	82	58
7	38	71	50	84	30
8	30	71	47	74	21
9	53	80	60	86	42
10	70	89	72	93	59
11	61	94	81	89	54
12	56	85	82	94	55
13	50	83	60	84	41
14	38	78	54	81	29
15	84	96	93	99	79
16	57	86	66	90	46
17	35	73	47	78	27
18	74	90	80	92	65
State average	43	78	55	76	33

SOURCE: Adapted from Stephens (1991). Used by permission of the Columbus Dispatch.
a. The percentages in this column are not an average of the previous four columns; rather, they represent the percentage of ninth-grade students who passed all four proficiency tests on the first try.

Table 5.1 displays data for results of proficiency tests administered to students in the 18 school districts of one county. The table was adapted from one published in a local metropolitan newspaper (Stephens, 1991). District results are shown for ninth graders taking the tests for the first time. At a glance, the comparison of districts' high stakes testing is readily apparent. There are a variety of other ways of comparing results to standards: normal curve equivalents, derived scores, numbers of students per quartile, and comparisons to national norms or those of schools of similar socioeconomic status. Besides tests and other records mentioned previously, schools have used results of student satisfaction and attitude surveys in their records.

In a different context, Table 5.2 (McKillip, 1987) shows how data collected by an agency are combined with information from the census to determine the degree to which the mental health needs of different constituencies were served. Several ways of estimating the number to be served are shown in the table. Such estimates help the

TABLE 5.2 Agency and Census Data Related to Mental Health Service Needs

	1 Target Population	2 Percentage of Population	3 Unduplicated Count of Agency Admissions	4 Percentage of Agency Admissions	5 Expected Admissions[a]	6 Expected Admissions[b, c]	7 Over or (Under) Admissions[d]
Men	31,905	51.86	495	52.77	486	486	9
Women	29,617	48.14	443	47.23	452	452	(9)
0-14 years	10,089	16.40	79	8.42	153	154	(75) or (76)
15-24 years	21,704	35.28	229	24.41	331	331	(102)
25-44 years	15,234	24.76	473	50.43	232	232	271
45-64 years	8,485	13.79	122	13.01	129	129	(7)
65+ years	6,010	9.77	35	3.73	91	92	(56) or (57)
Total	61,522	100	938	100	938	938	—

SOURCE: Adapted from McKillip (1987). Used by permission of Sage Publications.
a. Column 2 figures × 938.
b. Column 1 figures × .01525.
c. Target population from census of 61,522 divided into 938 = .01525 gives the proportion of the target population that has been served.
d. Column 3 figures compared to Column 5 or Column 6.

needs assessor examine the adequacy of service as related to a particular stratum within a population. For example, from Table 5.2, it appears that men were slightly overrepresented and women underrepresented among those served by the agency, and that both the very young and the elderly were greatly underrepresented whereas those aged 25 through 44 were greatly overrepresented compared to expectations derived from census data. Again, we emphasize that other information would be necessary to establish whether or not a need is truly in evidence, perhaps including causal analysis to establish factors contributing to the levels of service of differing demographic groups (see Chapter 10). In addition, estimates of numbers to be potentially served do not necessarily translate into demand for or interest in the service being provided.

Some records do not yield sufficient data or data in as comprehensive a form as needs assessors might wish. In addition, several studies have shown that existing records yield different information from data collected by surveys or interviews and may indicate different needs.

Using Records in Cyclical Needs Assessments and Management Information Systems

Records also play a valuable role in promoting the ability of an organization to conduct NAs on a cyclical basis. Periodic summaries on a yearly or biennial schedule are very useful for understanding needs and emerging trends within an organization. We strongly encourage developing such summaries and placing them on the agenda of governing boards for review and analysis. Summarized data used in this fashion facilitate groups in reviewing needs at all three levels as well as keeping their focus on needs-related priorities. Records that are updated periodically, using the same categories of data, provide a perspective on whether a given need is increasing, decreasing, or remaining at the same level.

Closely related to cyclical NA is the use of MISs for continuous, ongoing sensing of needs. An organization with computers of large storage capacity can set up an MIS that includes databases with relevant need indicators, which can be monitored frequently for trends. If indicators are built into the record-keeping system, they help the needs assessor spot problems almost as soon they occur. A clear example is in health, where flu epidemics are rapidly identified through school absence rates. To carry the flu example a bit further, a work slowdown caused by the so-called "blue flu" is directly observable through records in an MIS.

It is important to keep in mind that both cyclical NAs and MIS approaches to NA are based on records. They are subject to the strengths and weaknesses of any record keeping and will tend to be weakest in terms of information about processes.

Modification or Creation of Record-Keeping Systems

In a program evaluation context, King et al. (1987) noted the value of modifying or creating record-keeping systems. In many instances, available data may not or may only tangentially fit the need or concern under consideration. In such situations, it is necessary either to modify the existing system so that it more closely fits the kinds of data required or to design a new one that permits a more appropriate analysis of need. If the organization intends to do ongoing or cyclical NAs and to set up an MIS for this purpose, the records would need to be tailored to the specific context (see Chapter 3).

To do so, we recommend the following steps (Steps 1 through 3 are identical to those for existing records, referred to earlier) based on the work of King et al. (1987).

1. Develop a list of characteristics or indicators that you feel are helpful in understanding the nature of the need or area of concern.
2. Find out what kinds of data and information have routinely been kept by the agency. Sample a few records to see what was kept and the quality of record keeping.
3. Compare Steps 1 and 2 to determine the extent of fit.
4. If the fit is not good, consider the possibility of modifying or adding to the record-keeping system.
5. If the fit is poor, consider the possibility of creating a new record-keeping system.
6. Think about ways of making changes in the record-keeping system that are as limited in disruptions to staff as possible.
7. Think about benefits to the staff as a way of motivating them to adopt the changes.

Most of the steps are self-explanatory. In Step 4, modifications might be as simple as changing or adding a few questions to an existing form. Another option, if the need for more or different information is pressing, would be to add a page or so of new questions to the original form, thus not affecting what was already being collected. Make sure that you consult with staff so that they understand why you are doing this, why the supplemental information is needed, and how it will benefit the organization.

Consider this example.

A large school district, which planned to conduct a new opinion and attitude survey of students in all 12 high schools, set up a new record system. Over a period of time, the survey results were intended to serve as a record- or pulse-keeping source of data about student and school needs. At a reasonably low cost, space was left on the survey form for individual schools to place questions pertinent to their specific situations. The district's research office agreed to analyze and report results from those additional questions to individual schools. Such an approach increased ownership of, interest in, and perceptions of the value of the survey on the part of the different schools. The flexible stance of the research office definitely enhanced acceptance of the new survey.

This example highlights the importance of observing Steps 6 and 7 in the list recommended by King et al. (1987) for creating a new record-keeping system. The willingness of the research office to work with other staff made them feel that their ideas were of consequence and incorporated into the system. Providing a sense of ownership in the records reinforces the likelihood that the new system will be implemented as planned.

Rates-Under-Treatment (RUT)

RUT is the use of agency or institutional records together with census data from one area to understand the potential need for services in another location. In its simplest sense, agency records (e.g., in mental health) are examined to determine the nature of clients being served and the needs that are being treated. Then, those needs and client characteristics are compared with other areas of similar demographic make-up to estimate what types of needs should be expected and services provided. For example, if an area has a decline in school enrollment, an aging population, and an emerging caseload of more counseling for the elderly, it might be anticipated that other areas undergoing comparable transitions would experience a similar type of service needs.

RUT is a logical approach to needs assessment and is particularly useful for planning purposes. But because it relies extensively on the use of existing records, it has all the disadvantages of existing records as well as their advantages. One disadvantage may concern agency characteristics that are not readily apparent. As an illustration, an agency may be predisposed to focus on treating family problems, due to the qualifications of its staff and its procedures for selecting staff members. Thus, it may not be fully attentive to problems associated with other groups, such as the elderly. An RUT bias could exist in current records that would be misleading if it were the only measure applied to the analysis of needs.

Using Existing Databases

THE CENSUS AND OTHER LARGE DATABASES

Census Data

In certain fields, needs assessors rely heavily on large data banks or databases, particularly those produced by the U.S. census. Aside from enumerating the population and describing many of its characteristics every 10 years, the U.S. Bureau of the Census conducts a number of specialized studies of social indicators and other features of the population (such as retail and wholesale trades) in the decade between censuses. Other similar and accessible databases are available from government agencies such as the Bureau of Labor and the National Center for Educational Statistics. In addition, industries such as banking and insurance have collected masses of information regarding such matters as the level of household indebtedness pinpointed to specific geographic areas, life expectancies of different population groups, patterns of health-related behaviors, and the prevalence of crime.

Social indicators from such bases are used separately or combined with others to create composite indexes for small and large geographic areas, depending on the focus of interest. Multivariate statistical techniques as well as simple z *score* averaging are employed to come up with the composite. For example, the needs assessor might combine information on the quality of housing, crime, income, education, and other indicators when examining the needs for police services within an area. Multiple correlation techniques could be used to predict needs. Prevalence rates determined from databases could be monitored over time and would be helpful in predicting the potential incidence of health or mental health needs in the future.

There are important features of the census to note when using reports and information derived from it. First, the census is based on the premise of complete enumeration or as complete enumeration as possible. Whereas some cases may not be counted or difficult to count (the homeless), census error is different from that of a survey based on random sampling, and the error may be systematic rather than random for some subgroups within the population. Second, the fact that the census employs self-reports calls into question the accuracy of such social indicators as race, income, level of education, and age. Third, some social indicators such as poverty are indirect or composite indicators, derived from a combination of other variables included in the census.

Fourth, the census is an enumeration of the entire population, not just citizens. It also takes into account individuals living in a variety of institutional circumstances. Thus, the census data might be regarded as more complete than surveys that sample populations.

With regard to the last point, it should be recognized that the census is subject to potential errors, such as undercounting some segments of the population such as the homeless and illegal immigrants. Moreover, the size of certain minority racial and ethnic groups may be considerably overstated or understated in the census. This is due to several factors: the ambiguous nature of racial and ethnic categories in the census, the prevalence of people of mixed race or ethnic origin, and the perception on the part of census respondents of the advantages or disadvantages of being counted as part of a given group. Such discrepancies, although minor from a statistical point of view, do have major import for federal resource allocations and for estimating the dimensions of need.

Data from the census are available in a variety of geographically related formats, such as blocks within a census tract, census tracts, counties, metropolitan statistical areas (MSAs), and consolidated metropolitan statistical areas (CMSAs). Obviously tracts, blocks, and counties in rural areas are less densely populated than those in urban areas. MSAs are at least one county in size—for example, the Greater Louisville MSA. CMSAs consist of two metropolitan areas that are close together and that also can stand alone as separate entities—for example, the San-Francisco-Oakland CMSA and the Minneapolis-St. Paul CMSA.

For easier access to census data and other reports, the U.S. Bureau of the Census is organized into nine regional offices that can easily be contacted and that help to facilitate the use of available information (U.S. Department of Commerce, 1990). The U.S. Bureau of the Census also provides a list of many national clearinghouse organizations that offer a wide variety of data services and sources of information.

The needs assessor can have access to data through formats that are attuned to the needs and level of computer skills of different users. Traditional approaches such as printed publications, computer tapes, and microfiches are part of an expanded set of options that have recently become available. They are supplemented by on-line information systems, laser disks (CD-ROM, compact disk-read only memory), and flexible diskettes for microcomputers. The U.S. Bureau of the Census provides many files for users, such as TIGER/Line, as well as numerous specialized supplementary tape files—known as stf's. The files have many applications such as mapping information and relating data to ZIP codes.

Geocoding

Geocode analysis aggregates individual data over a geographic area by using codes for street addresses or census tract numbers to denote geographic locations. The needs assessor can link data available by geographic service areas—such as school enrollments, community mental health centers, or incidence of crime related to law enforcement resources—to the geographic codes, thus generating data available for comparison across geographic areas. Geocoding can use linked databases with mapping techniques (see the following section) to develop a close look at an array of demographics and social indicators for specific areas. If an aspect of needs assessment is to understand characteristics of those who receive services, then geocoding can save a great deal of time and effort.

As an example of the use of geocoding, consider the case of a large university that recently noted changes occurring in its enrollment pattern, with larger numbers of older students matriculating (Jagtiani, 1994). To interpret these changes, the university could either conduct a survey of current students to understand what was happening or sample their ZIP codes. Then using geocoding, other databases could be brought in so that a comprehensive picture of current students is developed. Their general financial status, the educational level of their parents, how they are funding their education, their parents' employment, and other related variables could be studied. Such data would be incorporated into a comprehensive NA strategy for examining the background of students, where they are coming from, what types of students are currently underrepresented in the student body, and a host of other variables.

By using the data from geocoding, a needs assessor at the university could avoid the cost of a survey (money, development, resources, nonresponse and nonreturn rates) and at the same time probably obtain more in-depth data. The one shortcoming is that the data are limited to what is in the databases and would not deal with personal reasons and expectations for students being at the university.

Epidemiology

Existing databases are also commonly used in epidemiologic studies, especially in health and mental health. *The Incidence and Prevalence of Conditions in Children: A Sourcebook of Rates and State-Specific Estimates for DHHS Region IV* (Freeman & Farel, 1990) is a good illustration of such usage. Freeman and Farel cited the following sources as being of value in deriving prevalence and incidence rates of diseases in children: national population surveys; surveillance systems; reporting of notifiable diseases; regional, statewide, or county surveys; hospital-based or other provider-based case series; specialist providers; service reports; the U.S. census; and state vital statistics reports. They noted, however, that there are difficulties in calculating such rates depending on varying definitions used for reporting diseases, the severity of reported problems, and how the data for some problems were obtained (i.e., laboratory examination vs. data supplied by physicians).

Two terms are important in epidemiologic studies: *prevalence*, the number of existing cases of a disease in a given population at a specific time, and *incidence*, the number of new cases in a population over a period of time. Rates are calculated for a given population. In conjunction with these rates, the needs assessor describes the number of cases that are receiving treatment and compares prevalence, incidence, and treatment rates. Freeman and Farel (1990) used an example from national data in which they found the rate or prevalence of bronchial plexus palsy (BPP) to be 200 per 100,000 births. Then, taking live births across all children in Alabama in 1989 (60,718) as an example, and applying the ratio of 200:100,000 to it, the incidence or estimated number of babies with BPP would be 200:100,000 × 60,718, or 121.4 cases. This calculation assumes that the general population in Alabama is similar to the national group from which the incidence was calculated.

That assumption is not always accurate, as Freeman and Farel found in another study that demonstrated that serious errors could arise from applying national data to predictions at the state level. For example, the estimated incidence of a disease in a geographic area, based only on national rates in the total population, can be erroneous if subpopulations are not taken into account. Table 5.3 contains data estimating the incidence of asthma, using national rates, for the South Carolina population of children aged 3 to 17. The top part of the table shows that for all children in South Carolina, not taking race into account, the estimated number of asthma cases would be 53,265. But using data related to race (the bottom part of the table), they produced a total number of expected cases of 58,210—4,945 more than in the previous estimate.

Applying the epidemiologic method to education, Taite (1990) determined the prevalence of dropouts in a school district and then the degree to which a priori criteria specified by legislators were predictive of the dropout rate of students at risk. She found that the state-mandated standards designed to identify students with below-standard academic performance were unsuccessful in identifying imminent dropouts (only 40%), but that alternative criteria derived from her study of actual dropouts accurately located 73%. Her report includes a model for projecting dropout rates.

TABLE 5.3 Comparison of Overall Incidence and Race-Specific Incidence of Asthma in South Carolina

	National Rate		South Carolina 3-17 Population		Estimated South Carolina Cases
All children 3-17 years	6,700/100,000	×	795,000	=	53,265
White children 3-17 years	6,200/100,000	×	(795,000 × .62)	=	30,560
Nonwhite children 3-17 years	9,400/100,000	×	(795,000 × .37)	=	27,650
Total					58,210

SOURCE: Adapted from Freeman and Farel (1990). Used by permission.

Mapping and Indirect Estimation

MAPPING

One methodological approach of importance to needs assessors is combining social indicator data with mapping techniques. This allows the demonstration of results in a powerful manner for decision makers and users of NA findings. The work of Hall and Royse (1987) in mental health is a good illustration of the combination of the two methodologies. They examined the ability of six social indicators from the 1980 census to predict admissions to public mental hospitals in Ohio over a 6-year period. The admission rates were gathered on a county-by-county basis. Using multiple regression methods, the authors found a strong relationship ($R = .784$) between those variables and the admission rates.

There appeared to be two critical factors affecting the high level of prediction attained. One was the creation of a more sensitive measure of employment status and the other was the elimination from the regression analysis of counties with state hospitals. Those counties tended to bias the prediction due to the relative ease of geographic accessibility to service.

Hall and Royse then predicted admissions for each of the other counties within the state. The results were portrayed in a table as well as on a state map that included county designations. Various degrees of shading were used to portray the admission rates per county.

Although both ways of presenting data are acceptable, the combination of the map with the table of predicted rates puts all of the results visually and comparatively in front of the reader (data user) at one time. In our judgment, the two techniques combine for dramatic effect.

One can envision other combinations of these two techniques for NA. For example, predictions of the incidence of mental health problems derived from various indicators could be combined with maps of transportation systems and population density in a geographic area. Then, planning algorithms might be applied to determine the best locations for mental health facilities.

Theiss, Anderson, and Gideon (1991) present a strong case for maps as a way of representing NA data. They stress the communicative value of maps and how they convey findings quickly and clearly. They suggest that, in mental health in particular, maps help decision makers and planners focus on the equity and accessibility of services and even the efficiency of service delivery. The authors describe different types of mapping formats and furnish examples of maps used by the Texas Department of Human Services.

INDIRECT ESTIMATION

After considering methods used in epidemiology and mapping, the needs assessor might ask, How well will prediction formulas derived from national or statewide data and indicators apply to my specific county or location within the state? This question reflects what has been termed the *ecological fallacy* or *level of analysis* problem. It was most clearly displayed in the South Carolina asthma example described by Freeman and Farel (1990), where using national data without taking into account local variations would lead to a sizable underestimation of need.

This problem is compounded by the multiplicity of ways to estimate incidence depending on the particular social indicators selected as predictor variables. One significant aspect of the Hall and Royse (1987) study was the suggestion that better estimates of admissions could be made through the use of two indicators with improved or modified definitions. Several methods for deriving incidence rates in mental health and social services have been developed, but their validity and general applicability have not been established.

Tweed and Ciarlo (1992) compared the predictive quality of seven different methods that use social indicators for indirectly assessing or estimating mental health service needs. Their description included key characteristics of each model along with their strengths and weaknesses. Then, using the models, they predicted the mental service needs in the state of Colorado.

Assumptions underlying indirect estimation are that (a) there is actual, nonrandom difference or variation in prevalence rates for the need for services across geographic locations within a state; and (b) the variation is a function of characteristics of the people living within an area and the conditions under which they live as indicated by social indicators. The results of the Tweed and Ciarlo (1992) study suggested that although all seven models have advantages and disadvantages, the Slem Linear Regression model tends to be better for predictive purposes than the others, especially when predictions are compared to actual service use data. The Slem model is as follows:

$$\text{Predicted } R'_{subarea} = \beta_0 + \beta_1 X_1 + \beta_2 X_2,$$

where

> X_1 = Percentage of households composed of one person
> X_2 = Percentage of separated or divorced males (aged 15 years or over)
> β_0 through β_2 are specified parameter weights

The original model was calibrated using service use data.

Given the findings of Tweed and Ciarlo, local conditions and the choice of predictive model are important considerations with regard to prediction. Therefore, we recommend selecting predictive models by the nature of the particular need or problem and examination of the advantages and disadvantages of specific features of each model.

Considerations for the Needs Assessor

The discussion in this chapter of general types of existing records, as well as specialized sources and techniques for analysis such as geocoding, mapping, and epidemiology, is intended to give you, the reader, an overview of what is available. Their usefulness will depend a good deal on the area of concern being dealt with as well as individual expertise in using statistical and other analytic methods.

Education, social services, and health services all tend to have preferences for certain kinds of data. Until recently, we have thought of epidemiology as primarily relevant to understanding patterns of disease. But as Taite (1990) demonstrated, the technique can be applied to educational needs as well.

The main point is to begin the needs assessment by finding out what is already known about the need in general and the local context in particular. This means that national or regional data should be translated into estimates applicable to the geographic context of a specific NA. By doing a preliminary investigation into existing records and databases, the needs assessor and NAC will have a better handle on what further information they should gather to document the needs and where they are likely to find it.

SUMMARY

This chapter describes how data from social indicators, unobtrusive measures and observations, agency or organizational records, and existing databases (especially the census) can be used in NA. Coupled with techniques such as mapping and indirect estimation, existing data can offer a powerful set of tools for the assessment of need. The needs assessor and NAC may also recommend the creation of new or revised databases for an organization to set up or add to an MIS for ongoing or cyclical NAs. Existing data are particularly useful in the exploratory stages of NA and for identifying current states with respect to a need area, but in some cases they have predictive value as well. Such data are best used in conjunction with other NA methods and with causal analysis to get a broader understanding of the needs as well as to provide validity checks.

Note

1. We are indebted to Professor J. N. Eastmond Jr., for bringing this point to our attention. The fields of ethnography and ethnomethodology are excellent sources for methods of observation of social phenomena.

⊗

SIX

Surveys, Interviews, and
the Critical Incident Technique

Surveys, especially in the form of written questionnaires, are the most frequently used means of gathering data in NA, either alone or in conjunction with other methods. This chapter provides guidelines for three kinds of survey methods appropriate for a comprehensive NA: the written questionnaire, the interview, and the critical incident technique (CIT).

Questionnaires

Reports of hundreds of NAs conducted since 1980 indicate that many needs assessors consider the written questionnaire synonymous with NA (Witkin, 1994). We do not agree with this point of view. Instead, we recommend that questionnaires compose but one part of a NA strategy and that they be used to gather specific kinds of data. Moreover, we suggest that questionnaires be implemented only after other more exploratory methods have been employed.

Constructing surveys properly is an exacting task, and entire organizations have been formed to conduct opinion polls via surveys. This chapter will focus on issues, as well as survey types, that are particularly appropriate for NA. For a better understanding of the organizational survey process and survey design, see Rosenfeld, Edwards, and Thomas (1993). Other helpful general sources are Alteck and Settle (1985), Bradburn and Sudman (1988), Edwards and Thomas (1993), Henry (1990), Orlich (1978), and Sudman and Bradburn (1982).

ADVANTAGES

- The written survey is relatively easy to administer.
- It can be administered to either small or large groups, and respondents do not have to be in the presence of the needs assessor.
- The structured instrument offers less opportunity for sidetracking and irrelevant information than do group interactive processes.
- It may be less expensive than other methods of data gathering.
- A great deal of data can be gathered in a relatively short period of time and can generally be aggregated and analyzed by computer processing.

DISADVANTAGES

Despite the advantages, some experts note that "the survey process is complex, time-consuming, and expensive" (Edwards & Thomas, 1993, p. 419). Many steps for developing surveys require specialized knowledge and skills, and some organizations may be too small or without the means for constructing a valid and reliable survey. In addition, we have observed the following problems with NA surveys:

- Needs assessors often expect the survey to provide information for which the method is unsuitable.
- The questionnaire may use too broad a brush. If the survey is too short, it is usually too general to be useful. If it is too long, it may be too costly to develop and administer, and respondents may not want to take the time to answer.
- It is usually not an appropriate vehicle for directly determining discrepancies, that is, by seeking responses simultaneously to "what is" and "what should be" questions (for an exception to this point, see the discussion of the APEX survey that follows).
- The NA survey is often used incorrectly to elicit people's wish lists, rather than as a means of determining needs.
- NA surveys are rarely evaluated for validity and reliability.
- Mailed surveys have become so common that many people discard them without responding.

In the past, many school systems and other organizations used surveys that had been constructed and validated by research groups or that had been developed and made available by other school systems or agencies, sometimes with the help of expert consultants. Although such questionnaires might have validity and reliability estimates, a disadvantage is that the questions are often too general or not applicable to the local situation.

APPROPRIATE USES OF SURVEYS FOR NA

Before designing the survey, first ask, What is the problem or need area for which we need information? Then determine if the data are already available from other sources, such as existing records, census data, test scores, primary source reports, or direct observation (see Chapter 5). The survey should be focused on information regarding a specific need or set of needs, issues, or concerns that cannot be gathered in any other way.

Even though NA surveys often look like public opinion polls or questionnaires, they differ in important ways in both purpose and formal features. Needs surveys furnish data for system-specific, time-based decisions about priorities for planning, resource allocation, or program evaluation. The survey format and methods of data analysis should allow inferences to be drawn about priorities and the criticality of needs.

The usual opinion poll on issues such as education, health care, or crime often yields contradictory results that furnish little in the way of guidelines for public policy making. For example, researchers from two major universities found that nearly all Californians were dissatisfied with the school system in general, yet the majority were not really unhappy with their own local schools, as evidenced by the fact that a third of the respondents gave their local schools high marks (Tang, 1993). The poll seemed to reflect the respondents' discontent with ills of society—such as the existence of gangs, youth violence, and unemployment—which they blamed on bad schools. Other studies have shown that the public's perception of the seriousness of certain types of crime appears to rise and fall with the amount of exposure given to the crimes by the media.

The most effective type of survey for NA asks respondents for informed opinions based on personal experience, background, expertise, or knowledge, or for facts about themselves and others about which they have direct knowledge. As a general rule, we recommend that respondents not be asked to make global judgments about the adequacy of community services or student achievement unless they have more than hearsay knowledge about the community or school system.

Planning the Survey Questionnaire

There are seven main elements to consider in planning the survey: target population, sampling, method of distribution, questionnaire design, item content, item formats and scales, and data analysis.

SELECTING TARGET POPULATION AND LEVEL OF NEED

Whose needs are you studying (Level 1, 2, 3, or a combination)? For example, determine the Level 1 population that is the target of the NA (e.g., cardiac patients, students, or single parents on welfare). Or, if Level 2 is your concern, consider what group of service providers is the target population (nurses, teachers, counselors, or others).

Depending on the information or opinions that you seek, the survey may be directed at the Level 1 population (e.g., high school students), service providers at Level 2 (parents and teachers of those same students), or both. Table 3.2 in Chapter 3 displays examples of item content appropriate for different target and respondent groups.

SELECTING THE SAMPLE

The NAC determines whether all or a portion of the target population should be surveyed. For example, if high school students are the target, it might be possible to administer the survey to all the students in a school. But a well-chosen sample, either random or systematic, can also give reliable information. Typical sample sizes (S) for different group sizes (N) are: $N = 100$, $S = 80$; $N = 400$, $S = 196$; $N = 700$, $S = 248$; and $N = 1000$, $S = 278$. In general, the smaller the total group, the larger the proportion drawn for the sample.

In a *random* sample, each person in the population theoretically has an equal chance to be chosen. There are tables of random numbers that can be used for selection purposes. In a *systematic* sample, every *n*th person is chosen, such as from an alphabetized class list. Also consider the use of stratified random sampling or purposive sampling if it is warranted in your situation. In any case, be sure that the sample is representative of the population to be surveyed.

DETERMINING APPROPRIATE
CONTENT AND TYPES OF ITEMS

Content for items can be derived from many sources: input from the NAC, key informant interviews, focus group interviews (see Chapter 7), previous NAs or program evaluations in the organization, or data from existing records. Items may also be suggested by information from broad social indicators or the results of NAs done for research purposes, such as accessibility needs of handicapped persons or learning needs of children with attention deficit disorder.

The best content for NA surveys is information or opinions about aspects of the program under consideration or an area of concern about which the respondents have personal knowledge or experience. A postoperative patient might be asked specific questions about her course of recovery, tolerance for medication, and ability to perform certain tasks before and after surgery. Types of content are the following:

- The degree of agreement with a set of goals, conditions, or behaviors
- The frequency with which some condition or behavior occurs
- The degree of satisfaction with services, courses, programs, communication channels, or any other features or processes in the system
- The level of difficulty that the respondent has with specific tasks. (The respondent might also estimate the level for someone else who has been closely observed, for example, parent for a child, teacher for a student, nurse for a patient.)
- Perceptions about barriers that may have prevented the need from being met in the past

Some pitfalls to avoid are the following:

- Global statements or questions about adequacy of services of programs
- Questions asking for direct statements of needs
- Wording questions in such a way as to elicit lists of solutions

DETERMINING METHODS OF DISTRIBUTION

The survey format and types of questions chosen depend in part on how the survey will be distributed and administered. For example, if the survey is to be administered to a group in a meeting, the NAC may want to use more complex question or response formats that the administrator can clarify if necessary. Whereas if the survey is to be mailed, it must be designed so that the directions leave no ambiguity in the reader's mind as to what is wanted.

The choice of methods for distributing and administering the questionnaire is important to ensure the highest rate of return consistent with time and budget constraints. For a replicated strategy for attaining high return rates from mailed questionnaires, see Altschuld et al. (1992). Frequently used methods for distributing questionnaires are the following:

- The U.S. mail, for communitywide citizen surveys
- Surveys in school systems administered to students and staff during class time or at meetings designated for the purpose
- Surveys for parents that are sent home with students
- Brief surveys, published in local newspapers, that seek public reaction to or support for such matters as recreation, educational goals, or transportation needs (see Tri-Met example later in this chapter)
- Surveys of specific populations that receive regular newsletters, such as from a city recreation department or a Health Maintenance Organization, can be included in the newsletter

A hospital collecting data for a longitudinal study of postoperative cardiac patients uses a two-pronged approach. In the first phase, a social worker administers the questionnaire personally to the patient in the hospital, clarifies questions, and explains that there will be two follow-up surveys. The same questionnaire is mailed to the patient 6 months later, and again after a year, with a stamped, self-addressed envelope enclosed.

Decisions regarding the method of distribution to use are based on time, cost, ease of reaching the target population, and estimated rate of return. Mailed surveys usually require follow-up telephone calls or postcards to boost the return rate. Surveys that are published in newspapers or organization newsletters have two drawbacks: a potentially low rate of return and a self-selected sample of respondents who may not be representative of the target population.

Extensive research shows that return rates of mailed surveys increase if a stamped, self-addressed envelope is enclosed. The survey should be introduced with a cover letter that explains its purpose, the type of people who are being surveyed, how the data will be used, and a requested date of return. If possible, show how the survey will benefit the respondents and when they might know the results. The main rule is to make it as easy as possible for respondents to complete and return the survey.

In recent years, the problem of nonreturn of mailed surveys has become so acute that some organizations have offered special incentives. A shoe manufacturer offered to donate $1.00 (to a maximum of $2,500) to one of three suggested charities for every respondent who completed the questionnaire; teachers have been paid to gather data about their students; and one company mailed a hot apple cider mix with the questionnaire![1]

DESIGNING THE QUESTIONNAIRE

Construction of the instrument begins with involvement of the NAC, which should identify the following:

1. How does the survey fit with other NA data collection methods?
2. What kinds of questions need to be asked, based on the preassessment?
3. What types of decisions will be made from the collected data?
4. What kinds of questions or items will elicit usable data?
5. How will the data be analyzed and collated with other NA data to establish priorities?

In the preassessment phase, the NAC sets general aims for the use of the survey. Now, the NAC helps determine who the respondents will be and whether the questions will be addressed to their own needs or to those of others. For example, a questionnaire could be answered by teachers in a school system (Level 2), but the questions might pertain to needs of students (Level 1), the respondents' own needs (Level 2), or needs of the system (Level 3).

Choose a general format and layout that is easy for the user. Then decide whether to employ separate machine-scorable answer sheets;

if not, encode the response choice for data processing. Also, build in methods of protecting the identity of respondents. If necessary, have the survey translated into other languages.

Questionnaires can be used with young children if appropriate formats are employed. One NA survey for elementary school children provided questions on audiotape, and the child marked pictures on multiple-choice response sheets (Witkin, 1979). The only reading required was to recognize the numbers on the rows of responses. A brief slide-and-tape presentation was furnished for the teacher to show the class before administering the survey. A caution when doing NAs with students or any youngsters is to assure them that the NA is not a test, that there are no right or wrong answers, and that their opinions are important.[2]

DESIGNING ITEM FORMATS AND SCALES

Each item consists of a stem and a format for response. Here are typical response formats for NA:

Open-Ended. The survey provides questions that the respondent answers in a few phrases or sentences.

Multiple Choice. The question is followed by several statements or items among which the respondent chooses.

Category Scales. These are usually five-point scales with descriptions (anchors) at each end of the scale. Questions may be asked about frequency (never-always, rarely-most of the time), amount (least-most), or satisfaction (not at all-very much). Alternatively, one may use adjectives for each point on the scale: almost never, occasionally, some of the time, frequently, almost always. Four-point or six-point scales can be used to prevent artificial clustering around a midpoint. Figure 6.1 shows a frequency scale that uses both qualitative adjectives and percentages of time.

Category scales may also determine the strength or intensity of judgment regarding satisfaction with services, courses, programs, communication types or channels, or other features or processes in the system. However, a problem frequently occurs with category scales, especially when they are used to rate importance. Ratings of importance of educational and societal goals that have high face

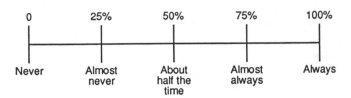

Figure 6.1. Frequency Scale With Anchors for Five Frequencies

validity and are socially desirable often cluster at the high end of the scale, making it very difficult to establish priorities. To avoid this problem, questionnaires may use other item response formats that force choices on the respondents. Some examples follow:

Rankings. Items are ranked in order of importance or preference, with only one rank assigned per item. This works best with 15 items or fewer.

Paired Comparisons. Items are presented in pairs, and the respondent chooses one from each pair. The items of interest are presented several times in different paired groupings.

Most and Least Important. The respondent chooses the three to five most important (or desirable) and the three to five least important from a list of statements.

BUDGET ALLOCATION METHOD

A variation of the forced-choice method is often used in community surveys to establish perceived importance of programs or services or priorities for action. Respondents allocate a fixed number of points, sometimes shown as dollars, among a set of items such as goals or services—for example, 100 points spread among 10 items. The number of points and the rules for allocation are set by the needs assessor, depending on the types of judgments desired. For example, one rule might be that some points must be given for every item or that the amounts among items must vary.

The following vignette illustrates a Level 3 survey using the budget-allocation method.

To get input for their yearly planning process for transportation improvements, the Tri-Met Customer Service of Portland, Oregon, published a survey in several regional community newspapers that asked readers for their highest priorities for the region's public transportation system. Thirteen options were listed in a column: closer service; more frequent service; later or earlier service; weekend service; faster trips; different destinations; more comfortable buses; more comfortable waiting areas; more safety and security; service for people with disabilities; more MAX (the metropolitan rapid transit system); measures to make it easy to bicycle, walk, and carpool; and other options that the respondent could specify. Instructions were as follows:

1. Assume you have 10 bundles of money.
2. Distribute these 10 "$" to the items listed by placing the number of dollars beside items that you think are important.
3. You may distribute them however you wish. The higher the priority, the more "$" you may wish to give that item.

Because there were more items than bundles of money, the respondents had to make real choices. They could distribute their dollars thinly—one or two to many services—or bunch them up by allocating most of the money to a few items of high priority. The survey page also listed 11 community workshops to be held at different locations during the month where the issues would be discussed.

Nearly 1,000 people returned the lists. The same set of services was used for priority setting in 11 community workshops in the Portland metropolitan area during March 1994, but participants were given only three dollars to allocate to their top priorities. Many people added other suggestions for improvements, however. The survey found a significant difference in opinions between current riders of Tri-Met and nonriders as to the importance of closer service. The information proved very useful for the 1994-1995 planning cycle. (Tri-Met, 1994)

A more complex variant has been used by other communities. The Palo Alto, California, school district conducted a community survey that listed services offered by the schools with a brief explanation of each (McCollough, 1975). Using a system of points to represent dollar expenditures in the budget, respondents made decisions on which services to reduce or eliminate, which to maintain, and which to expand or add. As a simulation of the decision-making process of a school board in setting budgetary priorities, the procedure clearly showed the relationships among district educational goals, the curriculum, support services, and expenditures.

An important feature of the survey was that it supplied specific information about what the schools were doing, such as the number of hours per week devoted to reading instruction in the primary grades, the ratio of counselors to students in the high schools, and the percentage of students who achieved above the mean on a statewide math test.

In NA surveys without the budget-allocation design, the questionnaire might supply brief factual statements about the present status of each item, thus giving respondents a basis for judgments regarding the adequacy and desirability of the amount of effort devoted to selected components of a program. This feature overcomes some of the drawbacks of asking for global judgments about the desirability of a set of goals or services.

The budget allocation design can be used by any organization that seeks opinions from staff or stakeholders regarding allocation of effort and resources to programs and services. It is particularly helpful for assessing needs in a time of retrenchment, when priorities are a real concern. But it is also useful when a system is considering improving or adding services, as in the Tri-Met example. It should be noted that the focus of the NA using the budget-allocation method is usually at Level 3 because it deals with preferences about resources.

Behaviorally Anchored Rating Scales

A major drawback to interpreting NA surveys that ask for global judgments of frequency or acceptability is that the scales may be ambiguous, or it may be difficult to infer what the respondents are really thinking. To overcome such drawbacks, NA surveys can use items based on the concept of behaviorally anchored rated scales (BARS). These scales define performance as carefully as possible, so that they leave little chance for misunderstanding. BARS have been used to assist businesses in measuring the competence of managers or performance of employees, selection and performance of pharmacists, motivation of engineers, the effectiveness of rehabilitation counseling, and student evaluation of pharmacy instruction (Grussing, Valuck, & Williams, 1994).

BARS go through several phases of development. The following steps are adapted and synthesized from several sources, business and elsewhere (see Witkin, 1984, pp. 79-86).

1. Gather a pool of *critical incidents,* or specific illustrations of effective and ineffective performance behavior, from persons with knowledge of the area to be investigated.
2. Determine the *performance dimensions* of the problem by clustering the critical incidents into a smaller set and establishing broad definitions of high, moderate, and low amounts of the trait.
3. Verify the dimensions and scales through *retranslation* with a different group of people to eliminate ambiguous terms and place the items in appropriate categories. Set a criterion—for example, that 70% of this group must assign an incident to the same dimension as the first group for it to be considered valid.
4. Convert the items into *scales* on each dimension. The scale must be anchored along its entire length and have high agreement from the group as to the scale values of the items.[3]
5. Construct the *final instrument,* which consists of a series of vertical scales, one for each dimension, anchored by the agreed-on incidents. The rating for each incident chosen in Step 4 determines its location on the scale. Incidents are not necessarily located at equal intervals.

For an example of BARS in NA, see Figure 6.2, which displays five questions from a survey suitable for students in grades 6 through 12. The survey uses a two-response discrepancy format with a five-point horizontal scale for each question. Each scale describes a behavior at three levels—least difficult, fairly difficult, and most difficult (the two intermediate levels were not provided in this version, although they could be added). The student gives two responses to each item: (a) the behavior that he or she *usually* exhibits, and (b) the behavior that he or she thinks students in that grade *should* exhibit.

This survey is part of the APEX survey (Witkin, Richardson, Sherman, & Lehnen, 1979), a package of questionnaires designed for students, their teachers, and their parents. The items were field-tested before the final version. The student survey elicits self-reports, the parent

Circle two answers for each item.   Example:

What you can do **now**   A Ⓑ C D E

What students in your grade **should** be doing   A B C Ⓓ E

25 In the library, I find books...	A only with someone's help.	B Between A and C	C by using the card catalog.	D Between C and E	E by using the card catalog and reference guides.	A B C D E

In the library, students in my grade should find books...   A B C D E

26 Information about different careers or jobs: I know...	A little or nothing about jobs or careers.	B Between A and C	C something about the skills required.	D Between C and E	E all about the rewards and requirements.	A B C D E

Information about different careers or jobs: Students in my grade should know...   A B C D E

27 Plans for future career and training: I have...	A no ideas for a career or training.	B Between A and C	C some ideas for careers and training.	D Between C and E	E a future career picked out; detailed plans for training.	A B C D E

Plans for future career and training: Students in my grade should have...   A B C D E

28 Consumer education: I know how to...	A open a checking account.	B Between A and C	C A, and cash checks using proper ID.	D Between C and E	E A, C, and balance a checkbook.	A B C D E

Consumer education: Students in my grade should know how to...   A B C D E

29 Foreign language class: I understand my teacher...	A only when teacher speaks English.	B Between A and C	C only when teacher speaks slowly, simply,	D Between C and E	E however quickly teacher speaks, no matter what is said.	A B C D E ☐ I don't take this subject.

Foreign language class: Students in this subject should understand their teacher...   A B C D E

Figure 6.2. Behaviorally Anchored Rating Scales (BARS) Using a Two-Response Discrepancy Format

SOURCE: Witkin, Richardson, Sherman, and Lehnen (1979). Used by permission.

NOTE: From the APEX Needs Assessment Survey for Secondary School Students.

survey requests observational data on the same behaviors for their own children, and the staff survey asks for judgments based on observations about the same students in their classes.

Part A of all three surveys contains scales on student performance, Part B on attitudes, knowledge, and health, and Part C (on the student and parent forms) on help for students. Part C for teachers is a self-report on help that they desire for themselves. Parts A and B, therefore, focus on Level 1 needs, and Part C on Level 2. The content of the scales was derived from educational literature related to school goals, and the behavioral items were based on expectations set forth in courses of study, state assessment programs, and frameworks for subject matter. Items were validated by groups of high school students and teachers and revised as needed to improve content and clarity of language.

The behaviors chosen for the least difficult end of each scale are typical of average students in middle or upper elementary grades. Those at the most difficult end could be exhibited by high school seniors. Schools can adapt the surveys to their own situation or construct items on the same model. (If we were revising the scales, we would probably specify behaviors at all five levels of difficulty, not just at three.) A similar format with appropriate anchors would work with groups in health, mental health, social service, and business settings. Some BARS scales use a format with a vertical line to show the range, with behaviors listed horizontally on both sides of the line. There can be more than five choices, and they do not have to be equidistant from each other.

Surveys using BARS fit several criteria for a good NA:

- The items are specific and relatively unambiguous. (They are quite different from questions that call for a global response, such as "How well do students in this school read?")
- They can be used with either a single-response or a two-response (discrepancy) format.
- They call for judgments made from personal experience or observation, not opinions received from others, such as reports in the media.
- They can be used for instructional as well as NA purposes. After responding to the APEX survey, students can review their own answer booklets and help aggregate the data to derive a class or school profile; then teachers and students can use the items to develop individual or group objectives for instructional improvement based on the identified

critical needs. Students can also compare their mean or median responses with those of their parents and teachers and discuss the implications if the discrepancies among the three groups are large.

- They give the NAC concrete information on which to base priorities of needs.

We do not usually recommend a two-response format for surveys (judging "what is" and "what should be" on the same instrument). But if BARS are used, as in APEX, the survey defines actual discrepancies based on a realistic comparison of the two-response items and, therefore, gives more information than surveys with typical category scales or forced choices.

Determining the Method
of Data Processing and Analysis

Planning for data processing and analysis of surveys involves coding items and responses and deciding how to aggregate the data. At this point, the analyst considers what types of descriptive and analytic statistics are most appropriate—means of item responses, percentages, rank orders, analyses of subgroups, analysis of variance, and so on (see Sudman & Bradburn, 1982, pp. 252-259).

Equally important for NAs is the way survey data are used, together with other information, to indicate priorities for constructive action. This matter was addressed in Chapter 4.

A special analysis is possible for two-response discrepancy formats, as in the APEX surveys (see Figure 6.2). Figure 6.3 displays results from an APEX survey administered to 156 students and 134 parents in a junior high school in California. The diagonally hatched lines are student responses and the solid black lines indicate parent responses. Each horizontal line shows the magnitude and direction of discrepancy between status and standards on a single item. The point at which the line begins on the left is the median response for status; the point at which the line ends on the right is the median response for standards. A line with an arrow pointing to the left indicates that the median response for that item was higher for status than for standards—in other words, the respondents felt that they were already performing at a higher level than that expected for students in their grade.

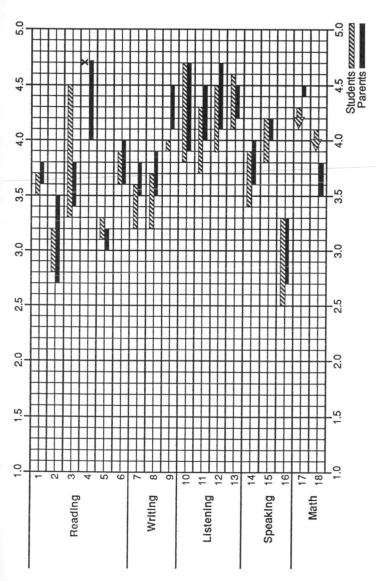

Figure 6.3. Analysis of BARS Data From APEX Survey, Part A, With a Two-Response Discrepancy Format

SOURCE: Witkin and Richardson (1983, pp. 22-23). Used by permission.
NOTE: Comparison of median scores fom student and parent questionnaires.

144

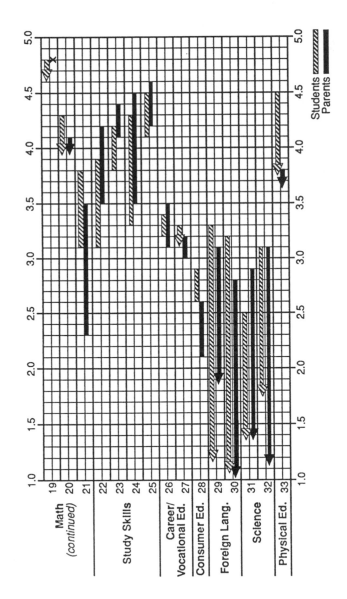

Figure 6.3. (Continued)

In this survey, there were six questions about reading skills, three on writing, four on listening, and so on. The graph is read as follows:

On item 3 (a question about what students do when finding an unknown word in a reading passage), the student median response on the five-point scale was 3.3 for their present level of skill (status), and 4.5 for what they thought students in their grade should be able to do (standards). On the same item, the median for responses by their parents (each of whom answered the questions for his or her own son or daughter), was 3.4 for status and 3.8 for standards. Apparently, parents had lower expectations for their children than the students had for themselves.

The graph also shows the relative weight given to different items in the same group of skills. In speaking, for example, item 14 (dealing with sentence structure and vocabulary) was deemed more important than item 16 (on participating in class discussion or giving a speech). Interestingly, the questions on consumer education, foreign language, and science all rated lower than the basic skills areas and showed higher medians on status than on standards. Such results would have to be interpreted with caution. The results may have been skewed because many students were not taking a foreign language or science class at that time.

Because the teachers answered the same questions regarding the students in their own classes, a further comparison could have been made between teacher responses and those of students and parents.

Analysis and interpretation of BARS data for NA does not end with compiling displays such as shown in Figure 6.3. As mentioned earlier, the survey questionnaires are excellent tools for discussion with respondent groups or with key informants who represent those groups. Such discussion could produce important insights into needs and their contributing factors.

The Interview

Individual interviews are an alternative or an adjunct to the written survey or used to elicit critical incidents (see the following section on the critical incident technique). The principal characteristic is that the interviewer asks the questions and records the answers. Interviews may be held face-to-face or by telephone. The following discussion draws on Orlich (1978) and Witkin (1984).

PLANNING FOR THE INTERVIEW

Planning includes determining the purpose of the interview and the types of information wanted, constructing the interview schedule, selecting the sample, and selecting and training the interviewers. Two important considerations are the time needed to schedule and conduct interviews, and the importance of interviewer training.

Determine the Purpose of the Interview. What information is desired and at what stage of the NA? Some sample uses of the interview in NA follow.

The open-ended interview is a good tool to use for exploring issues. In preassessment, interviews with key informants can identify broad areas to explore in depth later by other means: important issues, areas of unmet needs, organizational or system factors to consider, and information on existing records, previous NAs, or evaluations to examine. Open-ended interviews may also evoke critical incidents.

In the assessment phase, interviews with a sample of people who responded to a written questionnaire can validate or expand the implications of the written questions.

Key informants can supply information on barriers and factors that have contributed to the existence of the need or about previous programs or solutions that have failed to meet the need. This is important for assessment and postassessment.

Construct the Interview Schedule. The schedule or protocol includes the format and instructions for the interviewer as well as the way the answers will be recorded: either in writing or by recording. The two general formats are the *nondirected* (unstructured or open-ended) and the *directed* (tightly structured). The structured format generally contains specific questions of fact or opinion that can be answered with a simple yes or no, or by choosing from a multiple-choice set, or by responding to ratings on a category scale. Interviewers use a standard procedure so that all respondents are taken through the questions in the same order and in the same way. The protocol can include one or more questions of a general nature, leaving room for open-ended responses and opportunities for other comments.

For the nondirected or unstructured interview, the interviewer has a general guide that outlines a set of issues to be addressed. The interviewer asks the issue question, then follows with probes to clarify the respondent's meaning and to be sure that there is understanding on both sides.

Select the Sample. Respondents may be (a) key informants—individuals with specialized knowledge about the issues or needs, either because of their position in the organization or community or because of their expertise; (b) a random sample of the population of interest; or (c) a sample representative of major stakeholders in the NA, such as doctors, nurses, and patients or students, parents, and teachers. The size of the sample is considerably smaller than for mailed questionnaires.

Select and Train the Interviewers. Interviewers can come from a variety of sources: professional consultants; polling organizations; college students majoring in speech communication, public administration, or evaluation; or members of the public contacted through newspaper advertisements. Although it is preferable to use interviewers who do not have a personal stake in the outcome of the NA, some schools have successfully used parents, students, members of advisory boards and committees, or other stakeholders.

Researchers have found that the best results are obtained by interviewers with whom respondents can identify, especially when race, language, ethnicity or cultural background, gender, or age could make a difference in the responses. It is essential that the interviewer establish rapport with the respondent, especially in face-to-face interviews. In telephone interviews, the interviewer must be able to establish rapport and credibility through the voice alone. Obviously, for respondents with limited English, the interviewer should be fluent in the respondent's native language. We recognize that it may be impossible to find such interviewers in communities with a large influx of recent immigrants who speak many different languages and dialects.

For a survey of elderly people in publicly assisted housing, the interviewers were women in their late 50s or older who were retired or displaced homemakers. One of the most effective was 71 years old—the respondents trusted her and she was good with probes on open-ended questions.

It is essential to train interviewers. If the needs assessor does not have the requisite background or the agency doing the NA does not have a staff person trained in interview methods, various departments in a nearby university are often able to supply a faculty member or graduate student to train others. In one interagency NA, two interns from a regional commission on higher education were hired to develop interview protocols and to train local interviewers. The interns were given honoraria and received graduate credit through a state university.

The best training includes both practice and supervision. Interviewers for an NA conducted by the Institute on Aging at the University of Washington in Seattle had a 5-day training period that covered information on the aging process, the interviewing process, and the specific contents of the survey. The interviewers then practiced on each other and on older people in senior centers and nutrition centers. Key project staff were present every day at the building where the interviews were conducted to answer questions that might arise. Training sessions can also be videotaped and critiqued by both the trainers and the trainees.

Extensive training was also part of a large-scale epidemiologic catchment area survey used to determine the prevalence and incidence of mental health disorders in the United States (Eaton et al., 1984). Training in this study was absolutely essential because approximately 18,000 individuals were interviewed in five cities twice during a 6-month period.

CONDUCTING THE INTERVIEW

Interviewers set up their own schedules, including time and place, which should be at the convenience of the interviewee. Generally, the interview begins with a series of structured or simple fact questions, which are nonthreatening and enable the informant to be at ease. The interviewer also explains the purpose of the interview and how the results are to be used and assures the respondent of confidentiality.

It is important that all structured interviews be conducted in a standardized manner and that the interviewer not interject comments or add to the questions, except as provided for in probes. The interviewer may clarify the scales or categories used, if necessary, but must avoid biasing the questions with verbal or nonverbal responses.

For structured interviews, the interviewer usually records answers on an interview form. With unstructured protocols, the interviewer either writes down the responses immediately or tape-records them for later analysis. Tape-recording is preferable if responses are likely to be long and if there are many probes. It also frees the interviewer to listen carefully and to observe nonverbal behaviors.

The interviewer explains why the session is to be taped and obtains permission to do so. If the survey requires opinions on sensitive issues, it is necessary to assure the interviewee that the tape is only for purposes of analyzing and aggregating data and that no unauthorized persons will have access to it. The interviewer should be aware, however, that taping the interview may inhibit free expression, even with assurances of confidentiality. An added consideration is that listening to taped interviews is time consuming and could double the amount of time needed for the data-gathering phase. An alternative is to have a second person present at each interview to take notes on responses and nonverbal behaviors.

ADVANTAGES AND DISADVANTAGES OF THE FACE-TO-FACE INTERVIEW

Advantages

Personal interviews have some advantages over the written survey:

- The respondent is allowed opportunity for free expression and for revealing attitudes and feelings.
- The interviewer can add probes to the main questions and solicit information on causes or contributing factors to the need or issue.
- The interviewer can observe and record nonverbal behaviors.
- Interviews obtain a higher rate of participation than the mailed survey.
- Individuals with vision problems or who cannot read or write can participate fully.

Disadvantages

- Usually, not as many people can be contacted as in a mailed survey, and therefore the sample is smaller.
- The interview may be more expensive than a mailed survey because of time and costs of hiring and training interviewers, reimbursement for time spent in conducting the interview and writing reports, and transportation.
- The method is more time consuming, and scheduling may be difficult.
- Results of open-ended or unstructured interviews may be difficult to summarize and interpret. Collating and analyzing patterns of responses is a job for trained analysts; to increase reliability, two analysts are often used.

- Interview responses may be unwittingly biased due to the age, gender, race, or experience of the interviewer. Perceived differences in educational or socioeconomic levels between the interviewer and respondent may inhibit responses. Furthermore, respondents may not truthfully answer questions that they find embarrassing or sensitive and may be hesitant to reveal their true opinions or attitudes.

TELEPHONE INTERVIEWS

Another option for the needs assessor is to use telephone interviews. They can be conducted at reduced cost (no transportation), with more perceived anonymity, and possibly more validity, because persons often respond to telephone interviews freely once the interviewer establishes rapport. Structured protocols are generally preferable to unstructured ones. As in all interviews, it is important that the respondent not have to keep in mind a long question or a series of response options. Disadvantages are that the interviewer cannot observe nonverbal behaviors and it is difficult to conduct long or nonstructured interviews by telephone.

Critical Incident Technique

A survey may also use the critical incident technique (CIT), either in part or as the whole survey. CITs are direct observations or self-reports of specific behaviors that relate to performance in a given situation. The CIT is appropriate for identifying any of the three levels of need.

A common procedure is to ask respondents to recall specific events or conditions recently observed that illustrate that an organization or agency is doing an unsatisfactory job or that something about the system needs improving. They are also asked to recall incidents that show that the system is doing a satisfactory job. The survey can elicit critical incidents (CIs) from service receivers, service providers, and other stakeholders. Both positive and negative incidents are sorted according to program areas or issues, which are determined by the nature of the assessment.

CIT has been used to supply indicators or exemplars of goals that are difficult to measure using standardized testing procedures. One study identified behaviors such as self-management, initiative, responsibility, and resourcefulness on the part of students enrolled in a comprehensive system of individualized education.

CIT may be used as an exploratory method in the preassessment phase to identify need areas that should be explored in greater depth in Phase 2. It also may be a major element in Phase 2 to supply indicators of present status of a need area. The following example shows a specific application of CIT to the analysis of communication needs (Goldhaber & Richetto, 1977; for background details of the technique, see Goldhaber & Rogers, 1979).

A communication audit at a large midwestern university employed CIT to assess satisfactory and unsatisfactory staff communication. The 991 respondents reported a total of 566 incidents related to communication with immediate supervisors, subordinates, coworkers, and top management. CIs were analyzed for percentages of positive and negative incidents and divided into 35 subcategories, such as information adequacy, organizational roles, and interpersonal relationships. The analysis led to specific recommendations regarding communication needs of the organization as they existed among management, supervisors, and workers at different levels. The survey also identified strengths in communication.

The questionnaire had six sections related to sending, receiving, channels, sources, and so on. Each section requested a critical incident, or *communicative experience*. The respondent described the experience, the circumstances leading up to it, what the person did that made her or him an effective or ineffective communicator, and the results.

CIs must be both specific and recent. If the incidents are worded too generally (e.g., "Students in this school have no respect for authority"), the data are difficult to interpret. The best use is to collect a large number of specific CIs, categorize them, and make interpretations of need after consultation with key informants at different levels in the system or organization (for a bibliography on CIT, see Fivars, 1980).

General Issues for All Types of Surveys

As with any NA method, it is important to ensure that the respondents are the best qualified to know about the needs at issue. Not only should participants be representative of the stakeholders, but the survey must avoid the bias of noninclusion. In NAs for social services, for example, it may be advisable to include homeless people or migratory workers, a feature requiring interviews rather than mailed surveys. An NA survey could be designed with mailed questionnaires to stable, homogeneous populations and personal interviews with members of heterogeneous groups of lower socioeconomic status and from rural areas.

SUMMARY

When used appropriately, the survey is a significant part of a comprehensive NA. We recommend that it not be the sole means of gathering data, but that it be included as part of a larger data collection strategy. Key informant interviews can help in preassessment to identify issues and areas of need to explore later and to provide input to questionnaire content. Targeted written questionnaires can focus on identified need areas to get in-depth opinions or facts or to determine agreement with organizational objectives. The CIT is useful in detecting areas of strength and weakness in a system or program, identifying desirable skills or performance characteristics (for the "what should be" dimension), and supplying indicators of the attainment of goals that are difficult to measure in other ways.

The survey form is deceptive in that it often looks easier to construct than it is. Many NA surveys fail to obtain meaningful and reliable information because they are too general or have other design faults. If at all possible, pretest the question items and formats on a pilot sample of respondents.

Notes

1. We are indebted to Professor Nick Eastmond, Jr., for these examples of incentives.

2. The survey for children was part of an NA package for elementary schools, which also included questionnaires in English and Spanish for teachers and parents. The wide acceptance of the materials in several states for many years after initial development was probably due to the fact that early versions were pilot-tested and validated with over 100,000 people in school districts throughout California.

3. Barnes and Landy (1979) compared BARS to graphic rating scales, and concluded that the choice of an anchoring procedure—whether to use BARS or other kinds of scales—depends on the nature of the actual rating process.

꧁

SEVEN

Basic Group Processes

Aside from the survey, group processes are the most widely used method for gathering opinions and data for needs assessment. The processes can take different forms, but the salient feature is the opportunity for face-to-face interaction among those who have pertinent knowledge or a stake in the assessment. Depending on the context and the purpose of the NA, the groups may include service receivers, service providers, policymakers, key members of an organization, members of the community, or experts in a field. In addition, the needs assessment committee (NAC) itself is an ongoing group that engages in various types of discussion and decision-making activities in the course of its work.

Group processes are important to NA because they demonstrate the willingness and interest of the needs assessors to understand and take into consideration the views of stakeholders. People who participate have an opportunity to present and exchange views in a more fluid and livelier fashion than is possible with written questionnaires. As with any of the methods presented in this book, however, we recommend that group processes be used in conjunction with other data-gathering methods.

In this chapter, we discuss purposes and features of group discussion in general, followed by descriptions of three basic processes that have become popular for NA: the community group forum, the nominal group technique, and the focus group interview. The chapter concludes with a discussion of common problems in using group processes and tips for making them more effective.

Purposes of Group Processes in Needs Assessment

We make a distinction between the types and purposes of group processes used by the NAC and those used to collect data from other groups. The NAC is a specially constituted group that meets regularly as a working committee to achieve specific goals. For the NAC, group discussion is used mainly in the service of planning and implementing the NA and therefore to (a) clarify the focus and boundaries for the NA; (b) select the methodology for the assessment; (c) analyze, discuss, and interpret results; (d) determine causes of the need; and (e) prioritize results. The NAC also assists planners and managers in identifying and generating solution strategies and developing action plans. To achieve these purposes, the NAC engages in problem-solving discussion and other techniques as appropriate—games, brainstorming, lateral thinking, or simple scenarios.

Because the NAC is oriented toward purposeful action, the group usually seeks consensus rather than majority rule. We will have more to say on consensus techniques later.

The needs assessor may convene groups from the community for a few hours or a day to collect information and opinions about needs and use of the NA data in action planning. The main purposes are (a) to determine areas of concern to the community, (b) to identify frames of reference and perspectives held about needs, (c) to identify potential priorities of the community, and (d) to determine possible solutions and courses of action that might be acceptable to stakeholder groups. The group sessions usually result in a written product.

Although some groups may contribute knowledge as input for the NA—for example, information about current status related to the need area—the "data" are more likely to be opinions, values, perceptions, and preferences. Groups may also be valuable sources for historical or contextual information regarding the need area, determining causes of needs, and providing input to priorities for action.

The group processes can work reciprocally with other sources. For example, perceptions about a need area can later be verified by examining demographics, test scores, economic databases, or other existing hard data sources.

General Features of Effective Group Processes: The Needs Assessment Committee as a Task Group

In this section, we consider some general guidelines for the work of the NAC as an ongoing group committed to certain specific tasks. Because the NAC may work with the principal needs assessor for a period of weeks or months, it is essential that the members operate effectively and that the meetings be productive as well as enjoyable.

Scheidel and Crowell (1979) note that every discussion group can be viewed as a *task group* as well as a *team*, and that the discussion team is focused on its task by its leader. Success or failure of the group can be attributed to one or more of three factors: procedure, participation, and leadership.

In all likelihood, the leader at NAC meetings will be the principal needs assessor. It is the leader's responsibility to plan the meetings, help set goals and target dates, and facilitate the discussion. It is not the leader's job to take over the decision-making tasks of the group. An effective leader can help the NAC work as a team by setting procedures that will help the group reach its goals.

The Scheidel and Crowell (1979) book is an excellent desk guide for group leaders and members. We can recommend it for both the experienced group leader and the novice. The following are some features of group processes that apply to the NAC as well as to the three special methods discussed later.

STRUCTURING THE PROCESS

Group processes proceed through three major stages:

1.0 Planning
1.1 Establish clear purposes for the meeting. Specifying the purposes and outcomes to be achieved helps participants understand why their investment of time is important and what is expected of them. The purposes serve as guidelines for the content of the discussion.
1.2 Decide on sampling, meeting site, structure, procedures, and leadership.
1.3 Invite the participants.
2.0 Implementation. The steps are different for each type of process. See discussions in the following sections.
3.0 Follow-up

3.1 Analyze the data in light of the decisions to be made.

3.2 Use results appropriately and do any necessary follow-up.

3.3 Communicate the results in a timely fashion to key decision makers and stakeholders.

Attention to detail during the planning stage increases the likelihood that the group process will be productive. Aside from substantive concerns, planning includes choosing a comfortable and appropriate setting; arranging the room for optimum interaction according to the demands of the process; and providing refreshments, name cards or tags, handouts, pencils and paper, wall or flip charts, and equipment such as overhead or video projectors.

If all or most of the participants work at one site, it is often advisable to conduct meetings off-site to avoid interruptions. Room arrangements will depend on the type of group process. Large forums generally use a theater style. For small groups, seating can be around a table or in a semicircle or circle, depending on whether the group will need a writing surface. Comfortable chairs are important, too.

Planning also includes providing an agenda in which activities are allocated to reasonable blocks of time. For NAC meetings, the agenda focuses on specific objectives to be accomplished at each meeting or decisions to be made. For data-gathering processes with other groups, the agenda grows out of the reason for the meeting and the particular process employed. The plan should include at least one break for each 2 to 3 hours of work.

The budget for NAC meetings and other group processes will vary according to the type of process. It may include such items as rent of meeting rooms, cost of supplies and refreshments, secretarial help, paid newspaper announcements, preparation and duplication of materials, postage, fees for outside leaders, equipment rental, and honoraria for group participants. Some of the costs may be borne by the sponsoring organization or civic groups, which might donate meeting room space, equipment, secretarial time, and the like.

LEADERSHIP

Effective leadership is crucial to the success of group processes. Although some techniques have unique leadership requirements and special features, certain skills are requisite for all group processes.

The capable leader is good at listening, summarizing, moving the group along, sensing the mood of the group, knowing when to let the group stay on a productive tangent or move it off an unproductive line of thought, and establishing an atmosphere of cooperation and participation. The leader refrains from expressing bias, from trying to influence group thinking, and from interjecting personal opinions into the discussion. It helps if the leader is enthusiastic, positive, and task oriented, but not so much as to overwhelm the group.

The leader's tasks are mainly to facilitate and to encourage the participation of everyone, without letting one or more individuals dominate. In brainstorming activities, the leader must be able to get all ideas on the table from each individual, without criticism or interruption from others in the group.

INVOLVEMENT OF PARTICIPANTS

Participants must perceive that they are fully involved in the process. They want to feel free to express their opinions and ideas, and, in turn, they want those ideas to be honestly and democratically considered. They want to be valued and appreciated. They need to feel a sense of ownership in the process. The skilled group leader ensures that these needs are taken into account throughout the group process.

An essential key to effective participation is listening. Just as a good leader is a careful listener, so the group members should be as well. Lundy (1986, p. 92) lists nine levels of listening, going from complete inattention to full attention. Here are some of the common behavioral levels in ascending order of excellence:

- Being present physically, but not mentally
- Hearing the speaker, but doing something else at the same time
- Interrupting the speaker prematurely and frequently
- Allowing the speaker to finish but, meanwhile, intensely thinking of a counterargument or response
- Allowing the speaker to finish and then pausing, summarizing what was heard, and only then replying

Good listening is difficult, and most people have never learned effective listening strategies. One of the reasons that listeners find their minds wandering during discussion is that the rate of listening is about five times faster than the average rate of speaking. During this time, it is easy for attention to wander intermittently from the flow of speech. Group discussion members can take advantage of the differential between speaking and listening by focusing on the topic, ignoring external distractions, taking notes unobtrusively, and thinking about the ideas offered. When necessary, they can also ask for clarification of an idea. Scheidel and Crowell (1979) state the following:

> The member as listener must exert self-discipline enough to resist pleasurable tangents, to conquer the temptation to be reminded of that favorite story. The listener needs to interpret voice and gesture as sensitively and objectively as possible, and to listen responsibly because the listener's inner thought-line and the group-developed thought-line need to correspond as closely as possible. (p. 73)

ACHIEVING CONSENSUS

In the work of the NAC and other decision-making task groups, the objective is to achieve consensus on an issue—that is, to reach decisions that best reflect the thinking of all the group members. Reaching consensus means finding a proposal or statement that all members can support and that no member opposes. It does not mean that there must be a unanimous vote or even a majority one. It is probable that no one will be completely satisfied with the decision, but that everyone can live with it (Scholtes, 1990).

The day-to-day discussions of the NAC may use brainstorming and other techniques to reach consensus. Decisions that will have a major effect on the direction and methods of the NA should belong to the whole group and be supported by consensus. The nominal group technique (NGT) is a highly structured method of reaching consensus. It is not necessary that there be consensus from the discussions at a community forum or the focus group interview (FGI), unless the NAC establishes a specific goal that requires consensus on which to base future actions, such as setting priorities. Discussions of the NGT, FGI, and community forum follow shortly.

RECORDING GROUP IDEAS

Successful group processes have built-in procedures for capturing outcomes. They include tape or videotape recording where applicable, collection of work samples, designating one member of the group as recorder, having other facilitators present for observation purposes, and strategies for debriefing and comparing notes after the meeting is over. All group processes also include systematic methods for generating final reports of the meeting.

It is essential that careful records be kept of NAC meetings. Figure 7.1 shows a decision summary form that has proved highly useful. Rather than taking minutes of the meeting, a recorder writes down each decision made by the group, what action(s) will be taken as a result, who is assigned to each action, and a target date for completion of the task. The needs assessor then distributes copies of the summary to the NAC members with a red circle around the name of each person who has agreed to do a task, and records the date completed and other pertinent information on a master sheet. The summary form thus focuses the group on decisions and action rather than just talk, and serves as a reminder of progress in the work of the NAC and tasks to be accomplished, a monitoring tool, and an archive useful for interim and final reports.

FOLLOW-UP PROCEDURES

In our work, we always follow up group meetings with thank-you notes and summaries of findings sent to participants. We also present findings and recommendations to governing bodies both in writing and in formal oral debriefings (and sometimes informal ones). The goal is to maintain open communication channels throughout the three phases of NA.

Three Group Processes
Frequently Used in Needs Assessment

The foregoing discussion presented general guidelines for ensuring the effectiveness of any group discussion, particularly of the NAC as an ongoing group charged with a specific set of tasks. In the rest of this chapter, we describe three group processes that are frequently used in NA. They consist of a large-group technique, the community forum, and two small-group processes, the NGT and the FGI. In Chapter 8, we discuss four other specialized group processes: DACUM, the group or modified Delphi technique, electronic group

160

Date _____ Type of Meeting _____ Place _____

Attendees: _____
_____
_____
_____

Decision	Action to Take	By Whom	Target Date	Date Completed

Figure 7.1. Decision Summary Form

processes, and concept maps. Moore (1987) is a good source for more information on NGT, Delphi, and other special group processes.

Table 7.1 contains a summary of key features of the three group processes now under discussion: its structure; its purpose in NA; and its approximate size, sampling considerations, outcomes likely to be achieved, and some advantages and disadvantages.

The following sections describe aspects of planning, leadership, involvement of participants, and the like that are characteristic of each process.

The Community Forum

The community forum is a well-established procedure for NA. In general structure, it is analogous to the New England town meeting, in which a community is called together to discuss a pressing issue. In the NA context, the community forum (also sometimes called a public hearing, or community speak-up) is used to gather stakeholder concerns or perceptions of need areas, opinions about quality or delivery of services, information on causes of present needs, and exploration of community values.

The forum is most effective with a group of about 50, but if a general invitation is issued to the community, the size might be considerably larger. Some forums have attracted several hundreds, depending on the perceived urgency of the issue. The forum can be used by itself in the exploratory phase of the NA or in conjunction with other methods in Phase 2. Some large-scale NAs have followed the community forum with task force groups to investigate specific areas of concern. The forum can also be supplemented with key informant interviews or small-group processes.

The following are features of the three stages that are of particular relevance to the community forum.

PLANNING

One purpose for the forum might be a review of goals (desirable target states) that are being considered for inclusion in an NA process. In such a case, it is advantageous to provide participants with copies of the goals in advance of the meeting. The advance copies might contain a few questions guiding the examination of the goals. If the

TABLE 7.1 Key Features of Three Group Processes

Feature	Community Group Forum	Nominal Group Technique	Focus Group Interview
General structure	Large-group discussion format (many techniques may be used)	Small-group technique with limited interaction	Small-group interview with a limited set of questions
Purpose in NA	Obtaining ideas regarding various aspects of NA	Generation and prioritization of needs and concerns	Obtaining perceptions and views (not consensus) regarding an issue
Approximate size of group	50 or fewer	10 or fewer	8 to 12
Sampling concerns	Heterogeneous, but variations are possible	Heterogeneous, but variations are possible (don't mix super- and subordinates)	Usually homogeneous in accord with the area of concern
Outcomes	Ideas, views, worksheets, votes, depending on purpose and technique used	List of ideas and group views in order of priority	Individual and group perspectives on a focused area or theme
Pluses	Face-to-face discussion, multiple views, demonstrates interest in the community	Many ideas produced, priorities established and discussed, limited chance for dominance by one person	Perspectives on how an issue is viewed. Themes can be probed in depth
Minuses	Must make many arrangements in advance, possible dominance by one or two persons, possible conflicts in group	Ideas are produced on the spot rather than over time, rigorous enforcement of rules, limited ability to generalize from a small group	Requires expert leadership and more than one group for reliable results

forum is to develop preliminary goals for an NA process, then it is desirable to integrate small-group activities in which participants write and discuss goals. Small-group activities require the use of additional facilitators.

Other purposes for the forum might be reviewing the procedures and structure of a proposed NA, gaining publicity and public support for it, and setting priorities from the results of a completed NA. The forum might have a dual purpose: to give information to the attendees and to receive opinions and information in return.

Sampling in the community forum is a mechanism for involving and obtaining information from a defined community or population. Sampling is predicated on such questions as the following:

- Do you want a cross-section of the community represented?
- Are there specific groups in the community that will be involved?
- What do you hope to gain from their involvement? Would key inform-ants from those groups be best for the meeting? and if so,
- How should they be identified, selected, and contacted?

Our suggestion is that diversity in sampling is often the best course to follow, especially when generating a range of opinions and percep-tions about a need area.

Leadership of the forum is critical to its success. Leading large group meetings is both a skill and an art form. The leader must be able to get the group actively and enthusiastically engaged in the task before it. The leader must sense the pace—be able to know when to move forward so that the group work does not drag and know when to allot more time to a topic than had been planned.

Whether to select a leader internal or external to the system con-ducting the NA depends partly on the purpose of the forum and the availability of funds. Other factors are the degree of risk in the situ-ation (e.g., Is the topic highly controversial? Is there polarization of viewpoints in the community?) and the status of the individual. If the meeting deals with a sensitive issue, it is desirable to have an external, neutral individual to lead the meeting so that there is no perception of bias.

On the other hand, it may be important to have a leader who is knowledgeable about the organization and its areas of concern, and who understands how it operates. A forum leader chosen from the organization should be a well-respected individual with demonstrated leadership ability who strives to be as neutral as possible.

The structure, format, plans, and schedule for the forum should now be taking shape. Many options are available. For example, to generate ideas, a short, open-ended questionnaire can be given to the group near the start of the meeting. The whole forum could engage in brainstorming procedures, or the group could be broken into smaller groups and a nominal group process conducted with each. If the purpose is to examine solution strategies, a list of needs with potential solutions could be presented, followed by large-group discussion and voting. (Caution: Make clear to the group that such votes are advisory only and do not guarantee specific action.)

Once decisions about structure and format are made, an agenda is produced and the meeting is scheduled. In educational NAs, multiple community group forums are often held to accommodate a wide cross-section of the community and to provide replicated data.

Contacting the sample may be accomplished in several ways. In conducting forums open to the entire community, one school system publicized the activity in fliers sent home to parents and distributed to the community as well as in announcements in local newspapers. The forums were used as a mechanism to obtain community input regarding needs faced by the schools (rapid growth, changing population, enlarged district boundaries, technological and societal change) and potential building and program solutions. Despite the efforts to have a broad spectrum of the community represented at the meetings, attendance was still weighted toward parents with children in the schools.

In contrast, if a targeted group is desired, the needs assessor might contact specific organizations within the community (clubs, civic groups, key businesses) to provide the names of potential participants. This is a key-informant approach to sampling. Once identified, initial contact by phone or mail is followed by a second contact (most likely by phone) to confirm attendance at the meeting.

CONDUCTING THE FORUM

Most community forums are held in the evening, with about 2 hours allotted for the session. If the group is quite large, the audience is seated theater style and it may be necessary to have portable microphones available for both the leader and the participants. At the beginning, the leader explains the outcomes expected and ground rules for participation. For example, with a large group, it is best to limit the time for any one individual's comments so that others will have equal opportunity. Expressed forthrightly in a facilitative, supportive manner, ground rules become norms that groups accept and follow.

Among other leadership activities, a good leader encourages everyone to express views and comments, adheres to the schedule as closely as possible, and periodically summarizes the sense of the meeting so that the group sees progress and understands where it is in terms of the schedule.

The meeting should be taped and recorders assigned to observe and take notes. When the allotted time has run out, the leader brings the forum to a close, thanks the participants, and indicates when and how they will be notified of the results.

Some forums schedule a period in which participants can form into small groups to discuss an issue or generate ideas. Assuming that the hall does not have fixed seating, the groupings can be easily arranged by asking people in every other row to turn their chairs to face the people in the row behind them. If a community forum is to have more extensive input to the NA, it is effective to schedule the meeting for a half day or longer, divide the group into smaller task groups, and put them in separate rooms to accomplish the task.

FOLLOW-UP

To analyze results, make sure that all products (small-group assignments, completed surveys) are collected and any group votes on issues are recorded. Immediately after the forum, the leader and recorders debrief and compare perceptions of what transpired. They look for main themes; the degree of support for themes, issues, or points of contention; and the like. A summary of the meeting, its outcomes, and recommendations is completed as soon as possible after the session is concluded.

To publicize the results, the needs assessor can send a short synopsis of the final meeting report (under five pages) with a thank-you note to all participants. Additional publicity should be placed in local newspapers and newsletters. The NAC must be prepared to capitalize on the extensive investment of time, effort, and money in the community group forum process.

Here is an example of a community forum in action.

> In the mid-1980s, a suburb of a major Ohio city faced an unprecedented period of growth. Projections indicated that the school population could grow from approximately 6,000 to over 10,000 students, making the district one of the larger ones in Ohio. The district viewed the situation as an opportunity to proactively examine building and program needs for the long-term future. Various data collecting and planning activities were undertaken, summarized, and subsequently translated into building and program plans.
>
> Through public announcements, the district issued an open invitation to the entire community. More than 20 community forums were held in a 2-week period to communicate what had transpired in data collection, the needs facing the schools, and a series of action alternatives that the district was considering. Teacher leaders and key community members or well-known university faculty who resided in the area were identified and trained to conduct the forums, which were held in the homes of community members. Approximately 1,000 individuals (generally 30 to 50 in each session) participated. At the completion of each forum, attendees voted on alternatives using a form that had space to state any comments they had about the plans and the meeting.
>
> The forums were very successful in providing guidance to the district for its building program and the school curricula. The district reached large numbers of people who were then able to interact in smaller, more manageable groups.

The community forum is a flexible technique, easily tailored to local situations. One adaptation to the example given would have been to have half of the forums focused on the needs and how they were assessed, with the other half dealing with solution alternatives. Also, the self-selection of most community forum participants can be both an advantage and a drawback. In this example, the majority were people with a direct interest in the schools. A more representative sample of the population of the community at large could have been obtained by the use of key informants representing all sectors of the community.

The Nominal Group Technique

One of the most frequently used small-group techniques in NA is the nominal group technique (NGT). Generally, 6 to 10 people participate in a group whose main purpose is to produce a large number of ideas in a relatively short period of time. In this technique, the word "nominal" has a literal meaning. That is, the participants form a group in name only. For most of the session, the group members do not interact as they would in other group processes.

Moore (1987) notes the following:

[The NGT] is a method for structuring small-group meetings that allows individual judgments to be effectively pooled and used in situations in which uncertainty or disagreement exists about the nature of a problem and possible solutions. . . . [It] is helpful in identifying problems, exploring solutions, and establishing priorities. (p. 24)

The NGT follows specific rules at key points in the process, which are explained to participants at the start of the session. Failure to adhere to them compromises the special nature of the technique. The outcome of the NGT, prior to group discussion or advocacy, is an extensive list of brainstormed and rank-ordered ideas.

Like any other group process, NGT has three major phases or steps: planning, conducting it, and follow-up. In this section, we discuss only those aspects that are different from other group processes.

PLANNING

The purpose of the NGT is to produce and prioritize a large number of ideas regarding a topic. Most small groups will develop an extensive list of ideas about needs or solution strategies in a short time. Therefore, the number of areas for a group to explore must be limited prior to the meeting. The leader provides a specific statement or question, not a vague or general one. Examples in an educational NA context might be:

- What are the main problems we face in attending to the professional development needs of our members? (a Level 2 need for a school or a Level 1 need for a professional organization)

- Identify the factors or aspects of your work that lead to job satisfaction or dissatisfaction. (Level 2)
- What might be the major components or features of a system designed to address an already identified need? (Level 2 or 3)

A group of just 10 knowledgeable participants will generate many ideas, possibly 30 or more for each of the questions posed. Consequently, the NGT is restricted to one or two key questions or concerns. The NAC discusses, defines, and agrees on the concerns of greatest interest to the NA before using this technique. If a large number of concerns or needs must be addressed, plan to use three or four nominal groups, with each focusing on a different subset. To save time, convene a large group and divide them into subgroups, each with its own facilitator.

The sampling procedure differs from that for the community group forum. Instead of issuing a general invitation to the community, the NAC selects participants from specific constituencies, either chosen randomly from those groups or limited to key contacts or opinion leaders. In NA, the sample could be a cross-section of individuals broadly representing a community (parents, civic and business leaders, etc.), or it might be from a specific population with specialized knowledge (teachers, administrators). The NGT is a good method to use when people in a group do not know each other.

One caution is to avoid forming a group containing subordinates and superordinates within the same organization. The presence of higher-ups may curb the willingness of other group members to express their ideas. Some experts, however, note that the NGT is a good method to use when it is important to neutralize the effects of differences in status or dominance by one or two individuals (see Moore, 1987). Certainly, status has less effect in the NGT than it does in more highly interactive groups.

The skillfulness of the leader is critical to the success of the NGT. The leader must be knowledgeable about the process and ensure that its rules are fully observed. Prior experience with the technique is desirable. We suggest the use of an independent leader, external to the organization involved in the NA. Such an individual usually can establish and maintain rules more easily than an internal person.

To contact the sample, letters of invitation followed by phone calls to ensure attendance generally will suffice.

CONDUCTING THE NGT

In the NGT, there is much less latitude of allowable procedures than in other group processes, and following the rules for structuring the sessions is a major key to its success. Here are step-by-step instructions on how to conduct an NGT:

First, welcome the participants and explain the structure (do not use the word "rules"), noting that there will be periods of silent work, time in which lists of ideas will be pulled together across the whole group, and time for discussion. It is best not to be heavy handed, but be firm in stressing adherence to structure.

Second, briefly describe the area of concern and then begin a *silent brainstorming* activity. Be specific in your discussion and instructions. For example,

> Today we are going to examine the effects of instituting a teacher merit pay system in this school district. Whenever a major change like this is made, it will have positive and negative effects on teachers, students, the school system, administrators, preservice and inservice training, and society. Your charge is to identify, in your own words, four or more positive effects and then four or more negative effects of this change. Take out a sheet of paper; as you come up with ideas, write the essence of them in a short, single sentence or phrases of under 15 words. This is an activity in which there is no discussion. Please begin.

Allot about 10 to 15 minutes for the silent brainstorming activity.

Next, form the group into a semicircle or circle and explain that you will be going around the group, one person at a time (*round-robin*), asking for their ideas, starting with the positives. State that the purpose is to compile a list of all ideas generated by the group, not to discuss them. Write the main sense of each idea, as closely as possible in the participant's own words, on poster paper or a blackboard, and number each entry. Ask how many individuals had that idea or one that was similar. Instruct them to cross out those items on their individual lists. Record the straw vote beside each item posted on the board.

Next, proceed with the round-robin, building the list of ideas and straw votes until there are no more ideas put forward and participants are passing their turns. (Note: Groups will try to enter into discussion throughout this activity; discourage it by saying, "We'll come back to this idea later" or "There will be ample time for comment and exchange in the discussion phase of the meeting.") This part of the NGT generally requires 20 to 30 minutes.

During the round-robin, note any unclear statements. Ask participants to clarify them with the following type of instruction:

> Prior to our voting on these statements, some clarification is necessary. I may ask you to clarify a point. Provide that clarification in a very short sentence or phrase. Please, at this point, do not attempt to go into a lengthy discussion of your reasoning or advocacy for the point.

After clarification (a relatively short activity), each person votes on the posted items, either by rank-ordering them, selecting three top choices, or allocating a set number of points among them (this is similar to the budget-allocation method described in Chapter 6). Provide a short break at this time to tally the results and determine the highest priorities. Reconvene the group and convey the results to them. Open the floor to a discussion of the ideas and priorities.

From this point on, the NGT becomes less nominal and takes on the characteristics of a small-group process with interaction. After the discussion, another vote may or may not be taken. The presence of a second facilitator is desirable to take notes and observe the discussion. Conclude the meeting with well-deserved thanks and announce that a summary of the meeting will be sent shortly to participants.

FOLLOW-UP

As soon as possible after the session, have the NAC review and summarize the results and collate them with other data from the NA. Send brief summaries, with thanks, to the participants. If there is concern about having results from only one group, replicate the process several times, and communicate a summary across groups.

Here is an example of an NGT:

> A statewide professional society of evaluators used a biennial retreat of its governing board to examine organizational needs for the succeeding 2-year period. An NGT was employed in which board members brainstormed problems or issues confronting the organization. The list was clarified and reconfigured into clusters, such as membership outreach, growth, meetings, and so on, with items

shown for each cluster. The clusters were posted on walls, and board members were allotted a small number of votes (three to five) per cluster to be distributed according to their discretion. Colored marking pens were used to record votes and make apparent any interesting patterns of voting.

Although the process worked well, the governing board—all professionals familiar with NA methodology and evaluation—complained that they did not have the chance to expand on their ideas in the brainstorming session. This occurred despite the fact that the rules were explained prior to the activity. The leader was required to again explain the structure of the meeting and its rules. Once that was done, the group proceeded to generate and prioritize a large list of concerns.

The Focus Group Interview

The focus group interview (FGI) is a structured process for interviewing a small group of individuals, usually between 8 and 12. The purpose is to obtain in-depth views regarding the topic of concern. Obtaining consensus is not the goal; rather, it is to elicit how the participants feel about the topic and to identify the range of perspectives regarding it. This technique provides an opportunity for the kind of probing and follow-up that is common in individual interviews, but, in the focus group, participants can hear the views of others as well. Interaction is generally two-way, between the leader and individuals, but the group members may also interact with each other. Most FGIs require 2 hours on an evening or weekend, and respondents are often remunerated for their time to ensure participation (for a good source on FGI, see Krueger, 1988a).

The FGI had its origin in market research, which explores the values that a given public holds regarding certain products. (Perhaps the ill-fated Edsel would never have been produced if the company had held focus groups!) FGI is now used widely in education and social science research as well as in business to investigate attitudes and opinions about many kinds of topics. FGIs are also conducted to advise public prosecutors and defense attorneys on jury selection.

The general steps in FGI are the same as for other group processes: planning, conducting, and follow-up. The following are some specifics for FGI.

PLANNING

Purposes for using the FGI in NA might be to understand (a) potential needs or concerns of a group in a specified area, (b) the reasons the problem or need exists, (c) how a group might respond to a particular solution strategy, (d) what their general thoughts about an issue are, (e) attitudes toward an institution or program, and (f) the manner in which they refer to the topic.

Sampling criteria for the FGI are somewhat special, generally consisting of (but not always limited to) individuals who are relatively homogeneous regarding some trait or set of traits relevant to the focus of the interview. For example, an NA examining problems or needs of middle-class families with teenagers might choose parents of teenage children who are in traditional families in a middle-class environment (as determined by income) and who are aged 40 to 50 years. If the views of other groups of parents are desired, multiple FGIs might be conducted with homogeneous groups representing other subsections of the population.

The makeup of the sample is dependent on the purpose and topic under consideration. Such samples are generally not determined randomly. Some organizations mail surveys to potential interviewees and follow up with a phone call to see if the individual fits the criteria. Several screening questions are asked, and those individuals who fit are invited to the FGI. Another way to obtain a sample is to contact community organizations for help in identifying participants.

The homogeneity criterion is not always followed. A large West Coast university contracted with a research firm to hold a series of focus groups in a multicity region. The purpose was to determine community perceptions about the university, people's knowledge about its standing in the national research community, and their opinions about the functions it should serve. Participants were chosen randomly from households in different cities in the region and invited by phone. Whichever adult answered the phone call was invited to attend a focus group. There were no criteria of gender, age, income, or educational level.

Leadership of the FGI is highly important. A focus group session is much less structured and more fluid than the NGT, yet it does have certain guiding principles. The leader must be nonjudgmental, create a supportive group atmosphere, be able to keep the interview process going, be a good listener, and be alert to sense when a group is deviating from the prescribed question route in meaningful and non-meaningful directions. The leader must also remember the general questioning route without resorting to notes (although some organizations require a specific set of questions to which the leader may refer). The leader must also summarize as the group progresses and recognize when the group is moving toward closure and the end of its energy.

A skilled leader is able to sense the feelings behind statements and to become aware of terms used by the group that carry emotional connotations or that have more meaning for them than other terms used by specialists in the field. This information can be incorporated into community surveys to make them more relevant to respondents.

Trained FGI leaders are like communication detectives, following the threads that wind in and out of the discussion to detect themes and categories of ideas of which the participants may not themselves be consciously aware. For example, a market researcher who ran FGIs for an auto manufacturer became aware that there were two general categories of car buyers: those who considered a car as merely transportation, and those who considered it an extension of their own homes (and egos). The types of cars and features that each group valued were very different. Focus groups on educational, social, or economic issues will also reveal themes of importance to the NA, which will be detected by the leader who listens carefully and observes both verbal and nonverbal cues.

Although FGI leaders are generally researchers or consultants with special training, Krueger (1988b) found it possible to train community members to lead FGIs. The latter had difficulty, however, with the analysis of group perspectives. Many marketing firms have staff who specialize in the use of this technique.

But specialists are not immune to bias. One of us had an unhappy experience with a man who had been trained by a founder of the technique and who had conducted FGIs for years for large corporations. Our NA project in a school district retained him to lead a focus group of eight high school students. The videotaped playback showed strong negative feelings on the part of the students toward their schools, teachers, cafeteria food, and the curriculum. A debriefing with the students a week after the FGI revealed that they actually had many positive feelings about the schools, but that they thought the leader wanted to hear only the negatives. It then transpired that the leader had hated his own high school experiences (on the opposite coast), had strong feelings that students were in general exploited, and used his own attitudes to influence the course of the session.

This incident occurred over a decade ago. In our more recent experiences with FGIs led by trained researchers, the sponsoring organization has provided a list of suggested questions to the leader, who then makes certain that the group understands that all spectrums of opinion are important, not just negative ones.

The planning phase also includes preparing questions to guide the FGI, arranging for an appropriate setting, and selecting a coleader. The NAC generates a short list of five to eight questions to be used in the session, starting at a general level and moving gradually to more specific aspects of the topic being probed. To develop them, the NAC carefully defines the focus and boundaries of the topic and discusses a potential list of concerns to be explored. These are then put into a logical sequence for the FGI.

As an illustration, in a study of the needs and problems of international graduate students matriculating at a large midwestern university (Yoon, Altschuld, & Hughes, 1995), questions started with what had facilitated or helped students with their studies and what had hindered them. Then, as the interview session flowed, the questioning began to focus on defined areas of difficulty, such as housing, personal relationships, and academics.

FGI questions should be open-ended: What did you think of _____? Why do you feel that way? Describe your experience with that problem. It is best to avoid questions requiring a yes-or-no answer, such as "Did you have experience with that situation?"

Planning also includes close attention to the physical setting. The physical atmosphere of the FGI room should be pleasant and in line with the status and expectations of the interviewees. If possible, provide a rectangular conference table with comfortable, cushioned chairs for adults and somewhat less formal arrangements for teenagers or younger individuals. Provisions should be made for taping or videotaping the interview for later analysis. The obtrusiveness of recording rapidly diminishes as interviewees become engaged with the questions. As we mentioned in Chapter 6, however, the postsession transcription and analysis of tape recordings is time consuming and is even more demanding in a group situation. If the NA has a budget that allows for a consultant group to conduct the FGI and make transcriptions, recording is feasible. If not, having a coleader to record the comments works quite well. The coleader will need coaching on what to record, however.

Some private firms specializing in applications of FGIs have rooms equipped with one-way mirrors and speakers so that a trained observer may watch and listen to the process. Videotaping also takes place behind the mirror. When individuals are first invited, and again at the beginning of the session, the leader must tell participants about the presence of the one-way mirror and the videotaping and promise that individuals' remarks will be held confidential. Only a summary of the proceedings will be given to the sponsor.

Confidentiality and trust are highly important considerations. If the needs assessor or NAC wishes to observe the groups, participants should be so informed. In one recent case, a research firm conducted several focus groups for a large school district and interviewed teachers, students, parents, community leaders, and school staff. The groups of 8 to 12 were observed through a one-way mirror, and the sessions were videotaped—both procedures are standard, and the groups were told about them. Unfortunately, the groups were not told that some of the observers were administrators, only that they were research colleagues.

Some of the teachers complained to the district and their professional association, charging violation of privacy and unethical practices. In subsequent sessions, administrators met first with the focus groups in the same room to answer any questions (Parrish, 1994).

If the sessions are not taped for later reviewing, and because leading a focus group is physically and mentally demanding, we recommend appointing a coleader who will take notes on key and emergent themes and trends. This procedure reduces the strain on the leader and provides another point of view or perspective on the process and the outcomes achieved.

CONDUCTING THE INTERVIEW

Here are step-by-step instructions for leading an FGI.

Begin by thanking the group for their participation and ask them to fill out a name card with their first name in large printed letters to be placed on the table in front of them. Have them briefly introduce themselves to the group. This warm-up gets participants on a familiar basis and sets the tone for actively speaking during the next 2 hours.

State the general purpose of the session: "We have asked you to come here so that we can get your views and ideas regarding the topic we will be discussing today." Establish ground rules: Everyone will be asked to talk during the group discussion; each person's opinions count and each person's opinions may be different from those of others in the group; participants should not interrupt each other; it is permissible to develop ideas and thoughts based on what others in the group may have suggested.

Then move into the *predisposition* phase. In predisposition, the interview proceeds into the area of concern. Guide participants into the questioning by beginning with a general question such as, "Compared to when you were a teenager, what are the problems and concerns confronting teenagers in today's world?" Give the interviewees a few moments to jot down their ideas.

Once ideas are generated, begin the interview by cycling through the group, participant by participant, to elicit perceived problems and concerns. After they are presented, summarize them, making sure that there is agreement with the general structure of the summary. In the summary, note where ideas are similar or different.

At this point, proceed to the specific predetermined questions that compose the rest of the FGI. An example of a question about education might be, "Some of your ideas focus on academic problems. Could you tell me what causes these problems?" In the counseling area, a question might be, "A number of concerns reflect emotional problems; could you describe how teenagers deal with them?"

In conducting the interview, be alert to serendipities that arise during the session. Unusual comments may be made or some participants may build on the comments of others in an unanticipated way. Exercise judgment regarding such occurrences and be willing to probe or move flexibly into unplanned aspects of the topic.

When the questioning is finished, summarize the interview and ask participants to complete a short survey as a check on the screening and demographic characteristics. Then thank them for their involvement.

FOLLOW-UP

The follow-up phase is more technical than for other small-group processes. Analysis is in two phases. As soon as possible, the leader and coleader should debrief and review notes regarding the outcomes of the interview, focusing on the discussion of the initial interview questions, the themes that arose, unanticipated areas that were mentioned, and how the information might be used for the NA.

Within the next day or two (immediacy is important), the leader and recorder should individually review their notes and the recordings before formally analyzing the data. Then, comparisons are made between the two independent analyses (a form of independent replication), differences reconciled, and outcomes determined for the final written report that is submitted to the NAC. It is unwise to attempt widespread generalizations of findings, especially if only one FGI has been conducted. If repeating the process with two or more comparable groups leads to similar findings, then greater faith can be placed in their generalizability.

Last, summaries of findings are distributed to key stakeholders, administrators, and the concerned community at large. Where appropriate, local media coverage should be sought.

EXAMPLES OF FGI USE

Yoon and her colleagues (1995) conducted FGIs at a large midwestern university to determine the perceived needs of international Asian graduate students. Such students represent one of the fastest growing minorities in U.S. universities.

Three groups from a cross-section of Asian countries were interviewed. Students were contacted through the Office of International Students and Scholars. Two groups were evenly balanced between males and females; the third consisted of females only. The leader of the three groups was a woman from Asia who had attended several American universities. Because she recently received a doctorate from the university, it was expected that she would be respected by the participants. The choice of a group leader was especially important in this context as NA planners felt that the students would be more willing to voice their concerns to an individual who had gone through cultural experiences similar to their own and who also was from Asia. This fact was perhaps of even greater importance for the all-female group.

Some findings among the three groups were in the areas of language difficulties (not an unexpected result), lack of cultural sensitivity on the part of U.S. students, unfair dealings by landlords, and rudeness on the part of some staff at the university. The all-female group raised additional concerns about both in-group and external aspects of sexual harassment. (J. S. Yoon, personal communication, July 9, 1993)

It is doubtful that such issues would have arisen in the female-only group if the leader had been either male or outside of the cultural perspective.

Another aspect of the FGI is that it often elicits information and perceptions not easily gained from other data collection techniques. It is unlikely that the data about the sexual harassment issue and its associated dimensions reported by Yoon could have been as readily collected through a survey, observations, or other techniques as the data were in the supportive atmosphere of the FGI.

Gamon et al. (1992) used FGIs in a workshop at an annual conference of the American Evaluation Association (AEA). A general questioning route was followed and pairs of experienced AEA members served as coleaders (one served as a recorder who summarized themes at the end of the interview). One group of participants was composed of students and individuals new to AEA who were attending the conference for the first time. They were interviewed with regard to perspectives, expectations, and needs they had relative to the field of evaluation, the organization, and its conference. This demonstration of the FGI was an excellent way to learn about the technique and provided a forum for newcomers to discuss their needs, concerns, and perceptions.

Krueger (1988b), Sadowske (1988), Casey (1988), and Nefstead (1988) reported on varied uses of the FGI technique: for the Extension Service, strategic planning, and community planning, and for understanding the views and perceptions of rural students entering a large university. Examples in their presentations included how community leaders were trained to conduct focus groups and how to set up the FGI room for students entering a university. In the latter instance, an environment that was somewhat less formal than a round table with cushioned chairs was suggested as being more comfortable for the students.

Other references to FGIs in the literature attest to their versatility and application to many settings and situations. The structure of the

FGI can be varied and can be adapted to NA efforts with children, professionals in highly diverse fields, and the general community.

Combining Group Techniques

"We're Listening to You!" was the theme for a meeting of residents of a large upscale mobile home park that combined features of a community forum, NGT, and FGI. The meeting was sponsored by the park's chapter of Mobile Home Owners of America (MHOA), an association that promotes legislation and services for mobile home owners. The outgoing board decided to do a needs assessment as the basis for membership outreach and program planning for the coming year.

The purpose of the meeting was to involve both members and non-members in giving their opinions about MHOA benefits and suggestions for future programs and projects so that the new officers could be more responsive to their interests.

A 2-hour evening meeting was planned and a general invitation issued to all residents through the park's newsletter. Prior to the session, the president appointed a committee of people willing to assist with the NGT under the leadership of the program chair, who was familiar with the techniques. She trained six group leaders, and the committee prepared a detailed agenda.

The meeting was held in the park clubhouse; six tables were arranged at one side with easels and the facilitator's table at the other. As the 50 participants arrived, they drew numbers for their table to avoid cliques. Each table had one of the trained leaders, and each group chose its own recorder.

Two topics were discussed. Three groups had Topic A: What kinds of programs or topics at MHOA meetings would interest you the most? The other three had Topic B: What do you think MHOA does or has done for mobile home owners? What do you think it should be doing?

For the first 20 minutes, the groups silently jotted down their ideas on the topic, generating as many ideas as possible. Then the recorders entered them on large sheets of paper. As time permitted, the leaders conducted a kind of FGI to probe for more details of how the group felt about the topic.

In the second hour, the participants met in one large group, putting their contributions on the wall. After discussion (clarification and some advocacy), the whole group voted on the ideas that they liked best from each list, using the rule of three.

Before the end of the meeting, the president noted some complaints and suggestions that merited immediate action and appointed committees to do specific follow-up. Two days later, the president and program chair met to organize and review the results and to plan further action. The program areas of most concern to the group included legislation, joint meetings with other comparable parks, knowledge of government agencies, MHOA services, reliable sources for repair and upkeep of homes, and extension services for gardens.

One of the interesting outcomes of the session was that the board found that all but one of the benefits of MHOA desired by the residents were already being offered. As a result, the chapter focused on developing better communication channels with all residents. The programs chosen for the following year and other actions were directly responsive to the priority concerns of the participants in the group session.

Issues in Using Group Processes and Some Tips for Maximizing Success

Many factors can affect the ability of a group to achieve its goals and to furnish useful information for the NA. Problems can occur during the planning stage or during the meeting itself. Scholtes (1990) identifies 10 problems that are common to groups: floundering, overbearing participants, dominating participants, reluctant participants, unquestioned acceptance of opinions as facts, rush to accomplishment, attributing motives to people when we disagree with them or don't understand them, discounting the values of others, digressions, and feuding members. The following is a summary of suggestions for maximizing the success of group processes in NA, both in planning and in implementation.

ADEQUATE PLANNING

Successful groups depend on detailed and careful planning. Experts in the field stress three things:

- Have a goal.
- Be sure the participants understand the goal.
- Have a plan for reaching the goal.

Purposes, agendas, structure, time allocations, and leader and participant selection are critical features of group processes that lead to success. The most productive groups are carefully selected and guided, yet not straitjacketed in their thinking. Of special importance is the definition of purposes for conducting the meeting, making certain that those purposes are clear and clearly communicated to group participants, the provision of a structure with adequate time allocations for achieving purposes, and participant selection in line with intended outcomes.

Here are some tips to facilitate planning:

- Have the meeting purposes and plans reviewed by individuals familiar with the concerns to be addressed and by people representative of those who will be involved.
- Develop forms or handouts that will show participants the generic structure of desired written products.
- Conduct a short tryout of the group process to spot potential problems as well as ways to avoid them and ways to improve the sessions.
- Because groups tend to stray from intended tasks and formats or to move toward solution strategies prior to fully understanding needs, provide written forms that keep the group on task.

For example, if the purpose is to generate and prioritize needs, then develop a page of three types of statements—those that specify discrepancies (needs), those that describe solutions rather than needs, and those that focus on vague concerns rather than needs. Review them with the group and periodically ask participants to review their work to see if it is consistent with the examples given. This creates a norm and allows the group to achieve closure and success as it completes assignments.

SELECTION OF THE GROUP LEADER

The best leader is thoroughly knowledgeable about the purposes of the meeting, the structure designed to attain them, and group processes. The NAC needs to examine carefully its purposes and requirements for the NA before selecting a leader for any group process. The NAC should ask about the leader's prior experience in facilitating groups and the particular technique to be used. An effective small-group facilitator is not necessarily adept at leading large, open forums, and vice versa. Should the leader be someone in the sponsoring organization or external to it? To avoid bias, it is often advisable to retain someone outside the sponsoring organization or agency as the leader.

The potential leader should also ask questions about the nature of the assignment. For example, How will information collected from the group process be used? Is the decision-making group willing to fully examine and consider problems and issues raised by the group process? How will participants be selected? Will subordinate and superordinates be included in the group process? What constituencies (ethnic, socioeconomic, gender) will be represented? Could the representation of some constituencies suppress the willingness of another to speak out and describe its views? Is there an openness and a flexibility on the part of the NAC to restructure and modify the process if necessary?

By means of these questions, the potential leader has an opportunity to learn about the nature of the desired group process and to assess the motivation behind it. Some situations may be inflexible or so highly charged politically that the group process becomes an opportunity to vent frustration or to sidetrack attention from a needs issue rather than to study and understand it. A group leader in these circumstances may be a sacrificial lamb who serves to defuse pressure. Negotiations between the NAC and the potential group leader are important in determining whether the candidate is offered the leadership or accepts it and important to the ultimate success of the group process. (Information from such a negotiation led one of the authors to reject a group process contract.)

Scheidel and Crowell (1979) point out that every leader must *earn* the role, that the leader must reconcile the group goal and individual member goals, that each task of leadership is different, and that even good leadership cannot make every group successful.

SELECTION OF PARTICIPANTS

The selection of participants is always dependent on the purpose of the meeting, the information wanted, and the ability of participants to provide it. It is useful to consider such questions as: Have they thought about the issue? Are they knowledgeable enough to have opinions and comments about it? Are they willing to express their views? One example cited earlier illustrates the importance of sampling. In the all-female FGI interview conducted by Yoon et al. (1995), a different pattern of results was observed when compared with the two mixed-gender groups. Female participants undoubtedly felt freer to offer their feelings and concerns when males were not present and when the facilitator was perceived as able to relate to their experiences and perceptions.

Our advice is to structure the group process, the selection of leadership, and the sampling of participants so that the best understanding of the area of concern will arise. This requires sensitivity to site-specific and other context variables and underscores the importance of planning and negotiation.

Moore (1987) suggests several principles to maximize the work of groups. Among them are these: "Groups are more likely to be satisfied with their work if they have a sense of ownership of that work," "Satisfaction with group participation is enhanced if the group has a sense of closure," and "No technique or process is any better than the people who participate" (pp. 138, 139).

WORKING WITH DIFFERENT PERSONALITY TYPES

Anyone who has led a group is familiar with how different types of individuals participate. Some are reluctant to speak up due to being uncomfortable in groups, feeling that their comments are not valuable, not wanting to offend others with an opposing point of view, or being reticent to contribute when others in the group are more assertive and quicker to respond. Others plunge in with a desire to show what they know or perceive, to win points with or please the leader, or to take charge of the group. Still others require so long to respond and come to the point that the total group begins to experience a sense of ennui.

Wickens (1980) categorized individuals at meetings into types such as those who attempt to dominate, criticize, are reluctant to participate, leave early, leave and then return, come late, carry on a conversation with another, and have a disagreement with another. For each category, he suggested how the facilitator might work to achieve an effective group process. If criticisms are occurring at an incorrect time, the facilitator might say: "Wait a minute; we're going to advocate for or against the items later on. You will have a chance to say what you want then. Right now we're trying to get out as many ideas as possible. We'll evaluate them later" (Wickens, 1980, p. 18).

Or if a person is trying to dominate, the facilitator might use such statements as these: "Could you give us that as briefly as possible?" or "Could you hold that for a moment? I'll get back to you" (Wickens, 1980, p. 18).

Other good sources are Krueger (1988a), on the conduct of FGIs, and Harrison (1987), who describes features for successfully conducting group processes. Scheidel and Crowell (1979) deal with all aspects of group processes in depth.

PREMATURE CLOSURE OF DISCUSSION

In almost all of our work in NA, we have found a strong disposition of groups to focus rapidly on solution strategies when only a vague understanding of the problem (need) was at hand. As individuals and as groups, we seem to find it easier to consider solutions and ways of improving rather than carefully defining and causally analyzing a need. The latter processes appear to slow us down and to be nonproductive. Yet without them, we are in danger of producing superficial solutions to complex problems. To avoid this difficulty, the leader should explain expectations at the start of the meeting, reiterating them and progressing toward their achievement throughout the meeting.

A written agenda with time allotments and other written forms help the group understand the task and keep focused on it. The leader must continually monitor the group process to determine if a premature shift toward solution strategies is occurring. If so, the leader can suggest that the group review its ideas to see whether they are solutions rather than problems and associated causes. Also, the use of examples can keep the group focused on intended outcomes. Prior planning is important for avoiding premature closure of any type. We recommend the use of the Pokey Elevators example (see Chapter 2) at the start of the session to alert the group to this problem.

DEALING WITH HIDDEN
AGENDAS, GRIEVANCES, AND BIAS

A pernicious and particularly troublesome aspect of groups is the emergence of hidden agendas (vested interests), grievances, and preconceptions and biases as the meeting progresses. One way to ameliorate this difficulty is to establish ground rules for the role of participants in the process. Such features as not criticizing, everyone's having an opportunity to speak, not interrupting, and related procedures can go a long way toward creating a climate of openness and respect in the meeting.

Another way to deal with this difficulty is to provide a framework that allows participants to think in alternative and perhaps less fettered ways. Scenarios of the near future can be employed to help the group break out of traditional structures and patterns. The group could explore current demographic patterns based on census data, as an illustration, or trends projected into the future. Case studies could be generated with associated questions requiring a group to delve into many facets of a problem rather than to adhere to a singular perspective.

SUMMARY

When used properly, group processes can be a key element in an NA. We recommend them, especially those incorporated into a comprehensive set of procedures for the identification, prioritization, and causal analysis of needs. They enable the needs assessor and the NAC to get close to involved constituencies and to obtain a sense of their vital concerns stated in their own words and terms. Perhaps most important, they reflect a willingness and openness on the part of needs assessors to explore the feelings, perceptions, and views of those affected by the assessment and ultimate resolution of needs.

We have discussed general guidelines for any group process, described the role of group processes for the NAC as an ongoing task group, and described three basic types that are frequently used in NA: the community forum, the nominal group technique, and the focus group interview. They all require careful planning and implementation in accord with recognized guidelines.

⊗

EIGHT

Specialized Survey and Group Techniques for Data Gathering and Analysis

In addition to surveys and the more common interactive group processes described in Chapters 6 and 7, needs assessors may choose among some specialized techniques suitable for gathering information on various dimensions of need. This chapter presents five such methods: DACUM, the mailed Delphi survey, the group or modified Delphi technique, electronic groups, and concept mapping. The last two rely on the rapid processing capability of computers; although they have not yet been used extensively in NA, they are gaining acceptance as needs assessors see their potential.

Table 8.1 compares the five techniques with respect to these features: structure of the process, purpose in NA, approximate size of the group, sampling considerations, outcomes likely to be achieved, and some advantages and disadvantages.

All but the mailed Delphi survey use more or less interactive group processes. As with all successful group processes, their usefulness in NA depends on adequate leadership, careful planning, active involvement of participants, accurate records of outcomes, and appropriate follow-up. We recommend that the needs assessor review Chapter 7 for the basic principles of effective group processes in addition to

TABLE 8.1 Key Features of Specialized Survey and Electronic Processes

Feature	DACUM	Mailed Delphi Survey	Group/Modified Delphi Technique	Electronic Groups	Concept Maps
General structure	Small-group discussion focused on job tasks	Up to four iterative survey mailings to the same respondents	Iterative feature of Delphi survey applied to group situations	Small- to medium-size group technique relying on computers	Large to moderate group relying on computer analysis of group data
Purpose in NA	Identifying key tasks or "what should be's" for a job	Generating, prioritizing, and obtaining consensus regarding need areas	Similar to the mailed Delphi survey	Generating and prioritizing needs and concerns	Developing a concept map of group perspectives
Approximate size of group	8 to 10	Generally under 50, but more have been used	Generally medium- to small-size groups, 30 or fewer	20 or fewer	50 or fewer
Sampling considerations	Expert job incumbents (a few supervisors could be included)	Most often, individuals with specialized knowledge of area of concern	Similar to the mailed Delphi survey	Heterogeneous, with the ability to mix super- and subordinates in most situations	Heterogeneous

(Continued)

TABLE 8.1 (Continued)

Feature	DACUM	Mailed Delphi Survey	Group/Modified Delphi Technique	Electronic Groups	Concept Maps
Outcomes	Key tasks placed in sequenced order for each job duty	List of ideas/concerns generated by respondents, consensus on scaled items	Similar to the mailed Delphi survey	List of prioritized ideas and group views	Concept maps of idea clusters with strength of cluster and relative degree of independence indicated
Pluses	Expert group rapidly produces job tasks, easily understood outcome chart	Anonymity of respondents, consideration of needs areas over time, reasons for disagreeing with the consensus	Accomplishes Delphi iterations in a short time, no or limited sample loss, face-to-face discussion after final survey results	Many ideas produced, priorities established, group discussion of priorities, dominance removed, anonymity of responses	Produces visual maps of clusters of related concepts that facilitate discussion, limited dominance by one person, all inputs and analyses are supplied by the group
Minuses	Task analysis is not as detailed as other procedures, may not work as well for some jobs, specially trained leader is desirable	Long time required for the procedure, loss of respondents during iterations, subtle pressure to conform with group ratings	Anonymity of respondents cannot be maintained, requires detailed and tightly organized group procedure	Specialized room and software required, ideas are produced on the spot rather than over time, respondents' attention may wander	Specialized equipment and software required, ideas are produced on the spot rather than over time

becoming familiar with those aspects that are peculiar to each technique described in the following sections.

DACUM

DACUM stands for *Developing a Curriculum.* The goal of DACUM is to identify the key tasks necessary for defining or carrying out a job (Norton, in press). In the context of NA, DACUM helps determine the target state or desired condition. The procedure originated in Canada in the 1970s as a way for community colleges, 2-year postsecondary institutions, and postsecondary vocational schools to generate or improve their curricula. Since then, it has enjoyed wide acceptance in the United States for developing training programs in vocational education and in business and industry.

DACUM is a form of task analysis accomplished through a small group that uses group decision-making techniques and focus group interview (FGI) processes (see Chapter 7). In NA, it is particularly appropriate for setting up training programs for new or changing occupations (Level 2, service providers), but it can also be applied at Level 1—for example, to determine the skills that students entering a vocational education program should eventually have.

DACUM assumes that successful job holders are the individuals most knowledgeable about tasks critical to that job. Therefore, the working group assembled for the purpose (about 8 to 10 people) includes successful workers and some supervisors. Participants are selected also for their willingness to take an active part in the group activity and freely express their opinions. The group process lasts for 1 or 2 days, depending on the complexity of the job under consideration.

The DACUM leader should have a thorough understanding of the process but preferably have limited knowledge about or experience with the specific job under consideration. Training for the leader is recommended to reduce and, if possible, eliminate leader bias affecting DACUM outcomes.[1] Some desirable leadership qualities include good listening skills, an ability to draw out each person's ideas over an extended period of time, sensing the pace of the group (allowing more time when needed or pressing ahead as dictated by the situation), and ensuring that the group completes DACUM tasks.

THE DACUM PROCESS

The process consists of the following steps; a brief overview is followed by detailed sections.

1.0 Plan for the meetings.

1.1 Select and invite the DACUM panel.

1.2 Consider logistics: select site, make room arrangements, set up schedules, provide for food, and so on.

2.0 Convene the panel for the DACUM process.

2.1 Introduce purpose, expected outcomes, and ground rules.

2.2 Explain the concept of *bands* for the DACUM chart.

2.3 Delineate task statements for each band.

2.4 Review the completed task statements.

2.5 Place tasks in order for each band.

2.6 Review and reexamine the final structure of the DACUM chart.

3.0 Have DACUM chart verified externally.

Step 1.0—Planning

Criteria for panel selection were given earlier. It should not be difficult to recruit members for the panel. Because DACUM is a task analysis procedure frequently used by business and industry to review current training programs or to develop new ones, corporations often participate by donating the time of their workers. Expert workers may consider it prestigious to be involved and may welcome the opportunity to really talk about their job in detail.

Step 2.0—Convening the Panel

2.1 Introduction to the DACUM Process. This first substep is particularly important for successful implementation. The leader gives a brief overview of the focus of the group deliberations, explains that the product will be a chart showing sequences of tasks or events required for the job or need area to be analyzed, and explains the ground rules governing the meeting. As with other types of discussion, all ideas are important, everyone will be called on to speak over the 2 days, and individuals should not be interrupted when they are speaking. The leader moderates the discussion, keeps the group focused on its assignment, elicits the ideas of reluctant group members, and does not allow any individuals to dominate the meeting.

2.2 Identify Key Areas of Competence. This is where the group begins the substantive work of DACUM. In a round-robin process, group members describe and discuss key areas of competence required for the job under consideration. These become the organizing elements for *horizontal bands* on the DACUM chart. Each band is an analysis of the main tasks necessary to accomplish a duty or to achieve a competence (this will be explained in more detail in the discussion that follows). The areas of competence are posted on the wall or blackboard; then the group delineates specific tasks for each horizontal row.

2.3 Delineate Task Statements for Each Band. Instructions to the group might be patterned on the following:

> What would you need to teach a new recruit to accomplish this main task? Assume that you are writing *short*, action-oriented statements (i.e., using action-oriented verbs such as "calculate," "estimate," "adjust," and so forth). Explain what the person must be able to do. Further assume that each statement starts with the phrase, "the beginner must know or be able to . . ."

One observation of DACUM processes is that groups tend to wander across bands rather than staying focused in one until it is completed. This can dissipate energy and leads to frustration with getting DACUM work accomplished. The leader must monitor the process and, if straying is beyond tolerable limits, refocus the group on one band at a time. If an idea comes up that fits a different band, note it and indicate that it will be stored for incorporation into the appropriate band at a later time.

2.4 Review the Bands. Once the bands and task statements within them are completed, the group reviews them for clarity and appropriate fit with the general area of competence.

2.5 Order the Task Statements Within Bands. In regard to this step, DACUM recognizes that there could be multiple orders or sequences for organizing curricula, instruction, and instructional materials. There is no single right way to do it. Accordingly, the purpose of this sequencing step is to provide a general indication of a possible sequence rather than a mandatory or definitive order.

2.6 Final Review. Now the group takes time for a final review and for making minor adjustments to the chart.

Step 3.0—External Verification

In this last step, the completed chart is externally verified by another DACUM panel or by external experts.

AN EXAMPLE OF DACUM

The outcome of the DACUM process is a single chart. Figure 8.1 shows three bands taken from different areas of a DACUM chart developed for case management for adolescents and young adults with chronic disease (Brink et al., 1989). In this figure, areas of competence are referred to as duties.

The original chart has 10 bands, some with as many as 11 entries. The bands not shown here are for such tasks as the following: provide an individualized health care team, provide disease management education and promote reasonable self-care, ensure appropriateness of medical equipment, address economic and social needs, foster community awareness, and maintain professional competency and awareness.

ADVANTAGES AND DISADVANTAGES OF DACUM

At first glance, DACUM may appear too costly in terms of the high investment of time and staff for an outcome that is simply a chart of general competencies and their associated tasks. Moreover, DACUM usually requires the hiring of a leader specially trained to conduct the process. On the other hand, it results in an easily understood, visual description of "what should be" for a job and is produced relatively quickly compared with other in-depth task analysis procedures (e.g., traditional task analyses or time-motion studies). Because the chart represents the work of one group, the results should be verified (Step 3.0) either by convening another panel or by having the chart reviewed by an outside group familiar with the job. As we mentioned, a DACUM chart is appropriate not only for developing a curriculum but for specifying the target state for either a Level 1 or a Level 2 NA.

Duties	Tasks							
A Establish and Maintain Contact	A-1 Identify target population	A-2 Teach patients about the benefits of health supervision	A-3 Teach patient/ family how to use the team	A-4 Help patient/ family deal with financial barriers	A-5 Establish follow-up methods	A-6 Address barriers to establishing/ maintaining contact		
D Improve Patient's Health Status	D-1 Evaluate and improve metabolic control	D-2 Encourage optimal emotional growth	D-3 Assess physical growth and develop-ment	D-4 Promote physical fitness	D-5 Promote healthy dietary practices	D-6 Evaluate for disease-related complications	D-7 Treat chronic disease complications	D-8 Address risk factors of tobacco, alcohol, drug abuse, and sexual activity
J Keep Office/ Clinic Records	J-1 Obtain graphs and plot blood pressure, height and weight	J-2 Set up and maintain flow sheets	J-3 Set up and maintain up-to-date problems list	J-4 Maintain medical, educational, and psycho-social status	J-5 Collate records from team and consultants	J-6 Ensure adequacy of records for providing rapid review of patient history and status		

Figure 8.1. Example of Three Bars of a DACUM Chart: Case Management for the Adolescent or Young Adult With Chronic Disease

SOURCE: Brink et al., *Competency Profile of Case Management for the Adolescent/Young Adult With Chronic Disease.* Columbus: Center on Education and Training for Employment, The Ohio State University. Copyright © 1989. Used with permission.

DACUM manuals provide excellent guidelines for the develop-ment of specific statements for manipulative, procedural, analytical, interpretative, problem solving, organizing, and managerial tasks. One caveat is in order, however. DACUM identifies general areas of competence and approximately 10 to 15 tasks for each area. It does not specify the details of tasks and their sequences that may be essential for certain types of jobs (e.g., diesel mechanics, surgery, or dentistry). Other procedures (e.g., time-motion studies, observations by skilled observers) may be more appropriate in those instances.

The Mailed Delphi Survey

In Greek mythology, the oracle at Delphi was blessed with the power to see the future. The Delphi technique, as its name implies, was originally developed to predict the future. In NA and other social science applications, the Delphi technique is a set of procedures characterized by the iterative use of a survey over time with the same panel of respondents. During the iterative process, the needs assessor ascertains the degree to which individual respondents agree or disagree with the results from the entire panel, item-by-item, as well as their reasons for disagreement. Respondents consider, review, and rate ideas over an extended time period. Thus, the Delphi technique is used not only to determine consensus but also to enhance consensus building.

THE PROCESS

Like other techniques, the Delphi has three general steps: planning, carrying out the survey, and follow-up. We present a brief outline as an overview and then follow with details for each major step.

1.0 Plan the Delphi.
1.1 Determine the purpose for which information is required.
1.2 Identify a panel of respondents that could produce that information.
1.3 Contact the panel members and solicit their participation.
2.0 Carry out the survey.
2.1 Develop initial open-ended questions for the first survey (Q1).
2.2 Send Q1 to panelists and collect completed forms.
2.3 Analyze the results of Q1 and structure a scaled survey (Q2) from emergent ideas based on Q1 responses.
2.4 Send Q2 to respondents and collect completed Q2s.
2.5 Analyze Q2 and then send the results (Q3) to respondents showing three types of information for each item: the group median, a group measure of spread (Q), and the individual responses to each item. Respondents rerate each item. If their rating is not in agreement with that of the total panel (i.e., in the range of the median plus or minus one Q), they are asked to supply reasons for their disagreement.
2.6 Analyze Q3 and consider the option of repeating (iterating) the process by means of Q4.
3.0 Summarize and report the findings of the Delphi process.

Step 1.0—Planning

Planning for the Delphi is particularly important because of the complexity of the process and the time necessary to complete it. *Iteration*—repeatedly reviewing and rating items—is a feature unique to the Delphi. Although iteration is important and valued, this feature makes it somewhat complex to design and to conduct, and it introduces problems in implementation not encountered in other NA procedures.

1.1 Determine the Purpose. The NAC must carefully look at the goals of the NA and the information desired and then ask, Is the use of the Delphi technique warranted in this situation and is it the best way to obtain this information? Answers are often "yes," when the needs assessment requires the input of experts who are geographically dispersed. For example, in a study for the National Safety Council, Race and Planek (1992) employed the technique to determine recreational boating safety needs for the 1990s. Similarly, Thomas and Altschuld (1988) used it with a national sample to determine the immediate and future training needs of the welding industry. The answer would also be "yes" if the NAC felt that concerns or issues should be revisited more than once by the panel.

1.2 Identify the Panel. The panel normally consists of individuals with specialized knowledge about the topic. The size is usually kept to 50 or fewer, although larger panels have been used. Panel members are identified by the NAC or through contacts with professional organizations or other groups that would know of appropriate specialists.

1.3 Contact and Solicit Participation of Panel Members. This step is crucial to the ultimate success of the Delphi. It is necessary that the same respondents participate in up to four surveys over an extended period of time. Respondent cooperation is absolutely essential for obtaining complete and interpretable data. Once the panel is identified and initially contacted, the needs assessor must make a special effort to obtain their commitment. For their study, Thomas and Altschuld (1988) used two methods of communication: a mailing about the nature of the NA activity and the Delphi survey followed by phone calls to respondents to ensure their involvement.

Step 2.0—Carry Out the Survey

2.1 Develop Q1. The development of the first set of questions (Q1) is not as simple as it may first appear. Q1 has to generate intensive thought and interest on the part of respondents. It needs to contain a brief introduction explaining the nature of the study and one or two open-ended questions with ample space for response. The questions must capture the imagination of respondents and put them in the frame of mind of producing meaningful but not constrained ideas. In a training environment, for example, one could ask respondents to identify and describe current problems confronting training using concrete examples. Then the same question could be asked for problems expected to occur in the next 3 or 5 years.

Figure 8.2 illustrates the format for this type of question. In an educational setting, the questions could focus on forces working to improve education and those working against the field in either current or future times, with the number of years ahead specified. By requesting specific descriptions, the needs assessor encourages the respondents to think as concretely as possible.

2.2 Mail Q1 to Respondents and Collect the Returns. The work done earlier in identifying and contacting the sample begins to pay dividends in this step, and the advantages of using a relatively small sample become clear. A difficulty in mailed survey techniques is poor response rate. In the Delphi technique, that difficulty is magnified fourfold because a maximum of four surveys may be sent to the same panelists. The needs assessor should code response forms to keep track of returns by respondents, even though individual Delphi responses remain confidential and results are reported anonymously.

If some individuals do not respond to the first survey, fewer to the second, and so on, then the quality of the information subsequently produced becomes suspect. With a small sample carefully and personally contacted before implementing the Delphi survey, and with the relative ease of again contacting that small sample if return rates are poor, these difficulties are attenuated.

2.3 Analyze the Data From Q1. This step is accomplished by the needs assessor or by a work group comprised of individuals with specialized knowledge of the field that would be helpful for interpretation. After removing respondent identification, the needs assessor organizes the results into sets by question and gives the sets to members of the work group. They independently review the data, clustering similar thoughts and ideas together, naming clusters, providing key word identifiers or short phrases per cluster, and writing a brief sentence describing the essential nature of each cluster.

Members of the work group discuss their efforts, including differences resulting from their individual analyses. The needs assessor uses the independent work and the outcomes of the discussion as input for the development of Q2—a mailed survey consisting of scaled items that represent the main ideas, themes, and issues generated from the responses to Q1. A variety of scaling approaches could be used such as Likert scales, rank ordering, or the rule of three (selection of the top third or top three items).

2.4 Mail Q2 to the Panel With Appropriate Instructions for Its Completion. In this step, the needs assessor must again be concerned with sample loss and whether results are representative of the views of the entire original panel. Therefore, as completed Q2 surveys are received, the needs assessor monitors who has responded and ensures that surveys are appropriately labeled or identified. Non- or late respondents are rapidly contacted to maintain a high response rate.

2.5 Analyze Data and Create Q3. Q3 will contain Q2 items with the same scaling procedure, with the addition of the survey group's response to each item (generally described in terms of the median value and Q, which is half of the distance between the third and first quartiles). Each individual's response is indicated in relationship to that of the group.

Panelists examine the results and the degree to which their own responses are similar to or different from those of the group. They rerate the items and provide reasons for any ratings that are out of the acceptable range (median plus or minus Q) of Q2 responses. In this manner, the Delphi technique, which is free of the kind of pressure found in interactive face-to-face groups, creates its own pressure for agreeing with the group. The analyst also collects reasons for disagreement when a respondent simply cannot agree with the consensus.

2.6 Examine the Results of Q3. In this step, the needs assessor examines the results to determine if Q4 is necessary. If there is a high level of agreement on Q3, there may be little benefit in developing and sending Q4.

A. Immediate Education and Training Needs

What problems do welding engineers and welding personnel currently experience on the job that need to be addressed (within the next 6 months) through specialized instruction? An *immediate need* is defined as a discrepancy between the current skills of welding personnel and the skills that are necessary for them to do a competent job.

Immediate Problems on the Job	Examples
1.	Examples
2.	Examples
3.	Examples

B. Education and Training Needs in 3 Years

What potential problems or new processes will welding engineers and welding personnel likely encounter on the job that they do *not* currently experience but will need to be addressed through specialized instruction? In this case, a need is a discrepancy between the current skills of welding personnel and those that will be necessary for them to do a competent job in 3 years.

Problems/Processes in 3 Years	Examples
1.	Examples
2.	Examples
3.	Examples

Figure 8.2. Delphi Q1 Questions
SOURCE: Adapted from the work of Thomas and Altschuld (1988).

Step 3.0—Prepare Two Summaries of the Findings

The first summary is a brief one with appropriate thanks for distribution to the respondents. The second is a longer one for the NAC.

SOME EXAMPLES
OF THE MAILED DELPHI SURVEY

Thomas and Altschuld (1988) studied the current and future training needs of the welding industry. Due to cost and time considerations, only Q1 and Q2 were developed and sent to a nationwide panel of 96 respondents from the industry. Seventy-two individuals agreed to participate, five declined due to proprietary considerations, and 19 did not respond. The panel generated more than 400 statements of current and future training needs with descriptions of the problems associated with the need.

Work groups of welding engineers were organized to analyze the data for the preparation of Q2, which was sent to 72 respondents with 64 responding. Q2 required that respondents rate items to two separate surveys—the first, for current needs (30 items) and the second, for future needs (41 items). For each survey, they selected the seven most important items and placed them in rank order. The results from both surveys were presented to an agency advisory board in terms of frequency of item selection and the strength of rankings (see Table 8.2).

Race and Planek (1992) reported the results of a nationwide Delphi study of boating safety needs. They used an analysis technique developed during the course of another Delphi study conducted by Zoski and Jurs (1990). The latter authors suggested that a modified form of a scree test could be adapted for use with Delphi-type data. Figure 8.3 shows the test.

The ordinate represents the percentage of individuals selecting a particular item, and the abscissa depicts the items (numbers) in order of the one selected most frequently to that selected least frequently. Zoski and Jurs point out that the scree test results in a curve with a change in slope such that the key items or needs of high priority will more closely parallel the ordinate and fall to the left of the change in curve slope. The lesser priority items will lie along the curve that more closely parallels the abscissa. A sharp break point differentiating priority from nonpriority items will almost always be visually apparent. Altschuld and Thomas (1991), Zoski and Jurs (1991), and Race and Planek (1992) provide further discussion of this procedure regarding the presentation of data and implications for the selection of the Delphi panel.

In another application of Delphi, Rojewski and Meers (1991) identified research needs facing vocational special needs education in the

TABLE 8.2 Delphi Data Presentation Using Ranks, Points, Number Selecting a Rank, Total Points, Rank Order of Total Points, and Number Selecting an Item in the Top Seven From a Larger List

Original Item Number[a]	Frequency of Occurrence Ranks: 1 2 3 4 5 6 7 Points: 7 6 5 4 3 2 1	Total Points	Rank Order of Total Points	Number Selecting in Top Seven[b]
16. _____	6[c] 6 3 2 2 2 2	113	1	23
21. _____	4 6 2 1 4 4 2	100	2.5	23
15. _____	2 7 4 3 3 0 3	100	2.5	22
6. _____	4 3 4 4 2 3 3	97	4	23

SOURCE: Altschuld and Thomas (1991). Used by permission of Sage Publications.
a. The item numbers, content, and data are from a survey completed by Thomas and Altschuld in 1988. Due to the proprietary nature of the data, specific item content was excluded from the table.
b. Number selecting could easily be converted to percentage of endorsement for scree test purposes.
c. Each number in the display represents the number of respondents selecting a particular ranking for an item.

% Endorsing

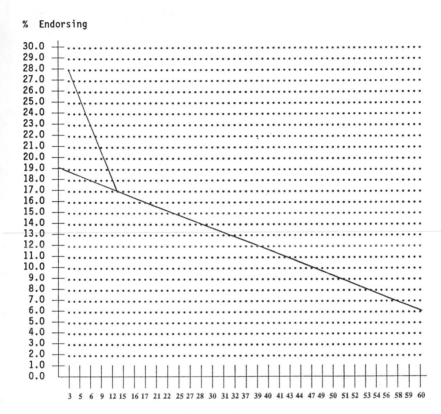

Delphi Item Numbers

Figure 8.3. Example of a Modified Scree Test

SOURCE: Adapted from Zoski and Jurs (1990). Used by permission of Sage Publications.

future (the next 10 years). A small sample (n = 21) of special needs resource personnel was selected, with 18 completing three rounds of a Delphi survey. Q1 yielded 91 unduplicated statements distributed among nine major areas: program evaluation, professional training and development, curriculum and programming, delivery systems, policy issues and related research, collaboration and articulation, instruction or instructional strategies, student-related research, and assessment and related issues. Q2 and Q3 consisted of scaled surveys using a five-point Likert-type scale and procedures similar to those previously described. The authors determined consensus for specific items with the highest being in regard to two critical issues—transition and "at-risk" students. On the basis of their study, Rojewski and Meers suggested a provisional research agenda for their field.

The Group or Modified Delphi Process

The iterative feature of the Delphi survey lends itself to a variety of adaptations with people meeting in a group. For example, with groups that meet regularly (e.g., university classes, professional groups with monthly meetings), it would be relatively easy to conduct a Delphi survey over a 3- to 4-week or 3- to 4-month period without the complications of a mailed survey. Responses could be kept anonymous, and sample loss over time (a weakness of mailed surveys) would be minimal. Of course, even with instructions to the contrary, it might be difficult to prevent informal discussions among individuals outside of the classroom or group setting.

Another adaptation could be carried out at national or regional conferences with a relatively small panel and with a limited expenditure of funds. After determining that the desired panelists will be attending the conference, the needs assessor could complete the Q1 phase of the Delphi technique by mail prior to the conference. Q2 can then be generated. In a pre- or postconference meeting lasting approximately 3 to 4 hours, panelists would reply to Q2. This is followed by about a 20-minute break with instructions not to discuss the survey. Results would be quickly tabulated and Q3 produced. Panelists would then finish Q3, supplying comments for items with which they disagree. A final tally would be made in which priority items were identified and used, in conjunction with the comments of those who disagreed, as the basis for a group discussion. The modified Delphi might also be adapted using electronic meeting software, which is discussed later in this chapter.

AN EXAMPLE OF THE MODIFIED DELPHI

An interesting version of the modified Delphi for educational purposes was developed by Gordon and Pratt (1971). They selected 30 participants representing five constituencies (e.g., teachers, administrators, parents). Members of each constituency wrote their comments on color-coded cards throughout the process so that ideas could easily be associated with a particular constituency. First, an initial list of items (goal statements) was reviewed by participants with the option of suggesting additions to the list on the color-coded cards. The list of additions was posted and then voted on (by secret ballot) by all 30 participants. Additions that received an a priori specified minimum number of votes were appended to the initial list.

In this version, the process continued along the lines of the general steps for the mailed Delphi procedure. However, all comments made about items were recorded on color-coded comment cards and made available to the group. In the next to last step of the process, participants provided comments for both disagreement and agreement with the group in regard to high-priority items. In the final step, the highest priority items were posted along with the color-coded reasons for agreement or disagreement. Each participant was given 1,000 points to distribute as desired among the top vote-getting items. One participant was randomly chosen to present his or her assignment of points as a way of engaging the entire group in an open discussion.

The group or modified Delphi process requires that many details for implementing the meeting, such as rapidly scoring and processing results, scoring rules, and planned breaks, are attended to well in advance of the meeting. Despite our perception that the modified Delphi is less frequently used than the mailed Delphi survey, it does provide a fruitful alternative for using iterative methodology.

As with any group process, it is desirable that the leader have skills in facilitating group discussion as well as particular knowledge about the technique being used.

Electronic Groups

The use of interactive electronic techniques to conduct meetings is widely accepted. Teleconferences employ direct linkages to enable presenters and participants at different sites to interact. As an illustration, the Pennsylvania Department of Education (personal communication, May 25, 1994) held an activity in which panelists had their presentations televised to seven locations in the state. Teachers were invited to attend at the location nearest their home or school. After the presentations, teachers raised questions by means of direct connections to the studio, e-mail (electronic mail), and telephone. Panelists responded through the televised presentation format. The use of e-mail networks for collecting comments and thoughts about issues from selected audiences has also become a routine mechanism for obtaining data.

An NA can also employ electronic technology, but instead of being at different sites, the participants would be in one room and use computers to transmit their comments. Emergent technology facilitates full-scale group interaction by (a) taking advantage of the storage, processing, and speed of transmission capabilities of computers; (b) the maintenance of respondent anonymity; and (c) the potential for rapid feedback. Anonymity is a key feature of the electronic group process, especially in reducing the effects of an individual or a group of individuals dominating the meeting. A needs assessor who wishes to get information or opinions on needs from key informants who are widely dispersed geographically could use e-mail to accomplish the task, but to ensure anonymity, a coding system would have to be set up so that only the needs assessor would see the responses from individual participants.

Networked systems of computer stations for use in meetings have also been designed to reduce the time spent in the group process and to increase the payoff. If we assume (in line with the Pareto principle) that about 20% of the participants do about 80% of the talking in group meetings, the unbalanced participation could effectively foreclose or shut out (could that be "shout down"?) a wealth of ideas and comments that might come from the rest of the group. Furthermore, if 20 people are involved in a 2-hour group meeting, each person has only a maximum of 6 minutes for speaking in the most equitable situation.

A networked system with the appropriate software allows participants to provide comments and ideas anonymously, review the anonymous comments or random samples of comments of others, and rate each item of the total set produced by the group, using rank order, choosing the top three, or using any other rating method desired. Another advantage is that, whereas a networked system requires a leader or facilitator, it does not rely so heavily on the leader's skill in keeping track of ideas and having to summarize them periodically, with perhaps limited recall.

Kirkpatrick (1992) noted that by 1992, IBM had 50 rooms nationwide equipped to accommodate electronic group meetings using its TeamFocus software package. For a rental fee, they are available to other groups wanting to take advantage of the system. Such rooms could be linked together with a large-screen monitor to provide for a simulation of face-to-face involvement of a larger number of people.

The needs assessor gives the same careful attention to detail and goes through the same general steps in planning and implementing electronic groups as for the community group forum, nominal group process, and focus group interview (see Chapter 7). Because each group of participants is in one location, only the methodology for generating NA ideas differs due to the electronic technology. After the ideas are generated and ranked, it would be desirable for a skilled moderator to lead an open discussion without the mediation of the technology.

If for some reason it is not feasible to bring participants together in one place for a phase of the NA, it is possible to use two-way inter-active video, with participants coming to designated locations near them. For a small number of participants (perhaps a group of key informants to verify some aspect of the NA), an audio conference over telephone lines is relatively inexpensive and easy to set up.

Kirkpatrick (1992) described the uses of networked meetings in business and industry settings for improving client satisfaction with services (reflective of Level 1 client needs), for designing new products and processes to meet needs (Levels 2 and 3), and for developing strategic plans (to determine organizational needs, Level 3).

Concept Mapping

Another use of electronic technology is the concept mapping approach developed by Trochim (1989a).[2] It is particularly applicable to an NA that is part of strategic planning, when the group wants to develop a conceptual framework for the needs and display it pictorially. Concept mapping involves both a group process and a computer analysis. Although it is possible to do the analysis as a separate step apart from a meeting environment, the procedure works well when incorporated into a day-long group process in a room containing a computer loaded with the analysis program.

The room should be set up with tables for the group members to work at, with paper, pencil, and a pair of scissors for each participant; a chalkboard or large flip chart in front of the group; a computer loaded with the requisite software and with a printer; an overhead projector and screen; and a palette that connects the computer with the overhead projector. It would be helpful for the needs assessor to have an assistant who is a fast typist and who can help with other organizational tasks.

In concept mapping, a group of 50 or fewer participants engages in brainstorming regarding a problem, issue, or set of concerns. Each individual generates a few brief statements about an issue, which are written on the board or flip chart. They are briefly edited by the group and combined where advisable. There should be no more than 100 statements, as the analysis program cannot process more.

The group takes a break of about 20 minutes, during which the statements are numbered and typed into the computer, and the set is duplicated for each person. When participants return, they are each given a page of numbered statements with instructions to review the list individually and to cluster the statements as they seem to fit together best. Using scissors, each participant cuts apart the statements and places them into cluster piles. After clustering, each person assigns to each statement an importance rating from 1 (highest) to 5 (lowest). The clustered and rated statements are then turned in for concept mapping analysis, and the group breaks for lunch. The computer analysis is done during this time.

If the analyst is skilled with the software and fast in data entry, the analysis should take about 1 hour. To speed up data entry, two people work on the analysis: one to read aloud the clustered data and ratings, and the other to enter the data into the computer.

The analysis procedure uses multidimensional scaling and clustering algorithms to produce map representations in two-dimensional space of the location of statements, the relative strength of their ratings (shown as a third dimension), clusters of statements, and clusters and their relative strength. Figure 8.4 is an example of a concept map developed as part of a strategic planning project of a local planned parenthood organization (Trochim, 1989b). It depicts clusters, their relationship in map space, and the strength of the ratings of each cluster.

In this example, the clusters became logically grouped into broad areas of education, services, finances, environment, and broader issues. The number of layers in each cluster (the depth dimension) indicates the average rating of importance given to the items in the cluster by the participants. Thus, financial planning rated in the 5.4 to 5.8 range, whereas advocacy and community outreach rated from 4.2 to 4.4 in importance.

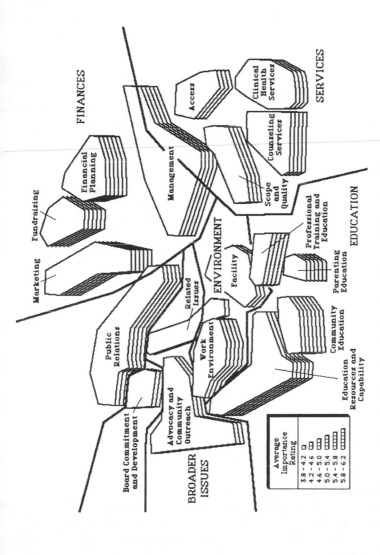

Figure 8.4. Concept Map of a Planning Project for a Planned Parenthood Organization

SOURCE: Reprinted from *Evaluation and Program Planning, 12,* pp. 87-110, by W. M. K. Trochim, "Concept mapping: Soft science or hard art?" Copyright © 1989, with permission from Elsevier Science Ltd., The Boulevard, Langford Lane, Kidlington OX5 1GB, UK.

The visual mapping feature is valuable for NA in understanding the nature of a group's perceptions. The clusters, the number of statements comprising a cluster, and the relative importance of clusters help the group to examine points of commonality and difference. In addition, the distance between clusters—that is, the distance that they are apart or close together—indicates the extent to which the clusters are independent of each other (greater distance means greater independence). Location on the map (north, south, etc.) has no meaning.

With the cluster map projected in front of them, the group explores the clusters and perceptions of their meaning. First, they name or attach a descriptive label to each cluster by examining the statements that comprise the cluster. Then, they inspect clusters with relatively large numbers of statements to see if there are noteworthy subsets within it. They can also discuss the relative independence or dependence of clusters.

In a countywide concept mapping project on needs and concerns of the elderly (Trochim, 1989a), the interpretation led to some interesting insights that had important implications for addressing needs. As the clusters on the map moved in a counterclockwise direction, the issues progressed from needs of the well elderly, to those with varying levels of disability, to those who are severely ill. The group recognized that the issues and concerns are different for each stage. The group also felt that most of the work in advocacy for the elderly is actually done by the well elderly. The map provided a foundation for addressing major concerns at the different stages and for emphasizing the more active involvement of the well elderly in advocating for the full range of concerns.

SUMMARY

The array of resources available to the needs assessor and the NAC has been enhanced by the emergence of techniques such as DACUM, the mailed Delphi survey, and the modified or group Delphi. The use of electronic techniques for groups focusing on NA will accelerate as costs decrease, as technology becomes more readily available and accessible, and as needs assessors become more familiar with them. We see all of the techniques as providing avenues for improving data gathering and analysis in NA, and we encourage needs assessors to consider their value in regard to the information demands of local situations.

Notes

1. The Center on Education and Training for Employment of The Ohio State University offers specialized training for leading DACUM groups. For information on workshops, write: Center on Education and Training for Employment, The Ohio State University, 1900 Kenny Road, Columbus, OH 43210.

2. A computer program is essential for concept maps. Trochim (1989a) describes the software system (CONCEPT) that he has developed for the task and is available from him on request. He also describes general purpose software that can be adapted for concept maps. For information, write: William M. K. Trochim, Concept Systems, P.O. Box 4721, Ithaca, NY 14852, 607-272-1206.

⊗

NINE

Future-Oriented
Needs Assessment Procedures

All NAs contain elements of the future. We conduct NAs to identify and understand problems or deficiencies (discrepancies between what is and what should be) and to make the best use of resources to resolve high-priority needs. In other words, NAs serve as a guide for planning future actions. Although all NAs focus on the future to some degree, some focus more on immediate or current problems, whereas others look specifically 5 or 10 years ahead. Future-oriented NAs require that we adopt a perspective and a set of methods specially suited to questions of the future. Some of the methods described in previous chapters (the Delphi technique and the modified Delphi) are appropriate for future-oriented NAs. Others such as the nominal group technique, surveys and interviews, and focus group interviews can also be used with an orientation for the future.

Obviously, it is not possible to predict the future with complete accuracy, although some types of forecasts in the past have been remarkably prescient, particularly in regard to broad trends. But futures methods have a value beyond accurate prediction. They energize a group to break out of preconceived ideas, to use imagination and creativity in visioning changes, and to recognize and grapple with the complexities of social, educational, and economic problems.

Another reason for considering possible future needs is that there is a danger in focusing exclusively on the present. Programs and interventions intended to address present needs often overlook the fact that other, even more critical needs may be emerging. Considering the rapid pace of change, it is short-sighted to identify needs and plan only for the immediate situation. The mind-set encouraged by futures thinking helps the needs assessor, NAC, and stakeholders to go beyond the obvious and to anticipate potential shifts in priorities.

The procedures that we discuss in this chapter are strategic planning, scenario development, cross-impact analysis, future wheels, and trend analysis. They can be used independently or in combination. For example, information from cross-impact analysis can give input for future wheels, and both can be used as the basis for scenarios. Each of the following sections gives an overview of a process and an example of its use.

Strategic Planning

Organizations employ strategic planning to cope with the dynamics of rapidly changing environments. In contrast to traditional long-range planning, strategic planning is flexible rather than rigidly adhering to a goal or set of goals. It assumes that organizations must monitor and continually adapt to external forces affecting them. At the same time, the organization must be cognizant of its internal processes and willing to analyze and change them in an open and cooperative manner. Figure 9.1 gives an overview of the strategic planning process, adapted from the work of Nutt and Backoff (1992). In the figure, the concept of need is shown by comparing a current situation (the "what is" condition) to a future one (the "what should be" condition). Identifying and attending to need is a basic feature of strategic planning.

The future situation in strategic planning is determined by carefully scanning and examining features of the internal and external environments of the organization. Thus, the perception and understanding of need is tempered by viewing it through the screen of internal processes, with their associated strengths and weaknesses, and by the external screen of environmental opportunities, threats, or constraints. Strategic planning necessitates that an organization engage in an

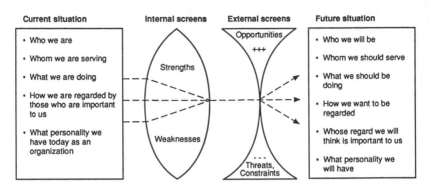

Figure 9.1. Overview of the Strategic Planning Process
SOURCE: Adapted from Nutt and Backoff (1992). Used with permission of Jossey-Bass.

in-depth review of itself and of the individuals and groups with which it interacts. Based on the recognition that change is a constant, ever-present circumstance of life, strategic planning is viewed as an on-going, continuous activity rather than a one-time occurrence.

A strategic planning process might begin with a brief mapping exercise as suggested by Lauffer (1982). Writing from a human services perspective, Lauffer stresses that organizations often have not laid out maps of their interactions with others (individuals, agencies, institutions) or their interagency linkages. Figure 9.2 is an example of an organizational map depicted by Lauffer.

The organization is identified in the center (a short, written statement of the organization's mission attached to the map would be desirable), with consumers or clients, competitors and collaborators, funders or providers of resources, and auspices providers (governing boards, legal or legislative mandates) constituting the four sides. Each cell contains the name of one of the groups with which the organization interacts—for example, the names of suppliers. A linkage is established between the organization and each of the entities in the cells. Linkages are shown in two dimensions—the strength of their *importance* (I) to the organization, and the degree to which they are *amenable* (A) to influence. Lauffer uses a five-point bipolar scale: +2, +1, 0, −1, and −2. An example of a linkage to a supplier in one cell might be I+2 and A−1. That is, this supplier is rated as of the highest importance but as somewhat difficult to influence.

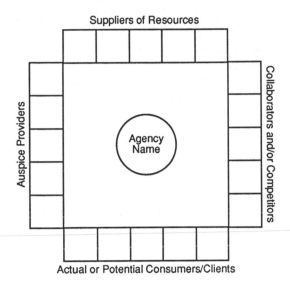

Figure 9.2. Organizational Environment Map
SOURCE: Adapted from Lauffer (1982). Used by permission of Sage Publications.

Planners also identify linkages that do not currently exist but that should exist, along with their importance and amenability ratings. Constructing the map is a relatively short exercise that is helpful in initiating further aspects of strategic planning. Small groups of individuals from the organization might independently develop maps and later compare them as a way of initiating the strategic planning process. The strategic planning process includes the following steps:

1. Obtaining commitment for the effort and deciding on how it will be managed
2. Scanning the internal environment
3. Scanning the external environment
4. Developing a set of strategic issues
5. Prioritizing the strategic issues
6. Developing action plans for high-priority areas
7. Implementing and evaluating the plans
8. Continuing the strategic planning process

Step 1, obtaining commitment, is critical to the success of the process because a concerted effort on the part of the organization and the commitment of every level of staff are required. Moreover, the process requires the allocation of sizable amounts of human and monetary resources and generally will take place over an extended period of time. Strategic planning may uncover problems from the top to the bottom of the organization. It may force change with the potential for restructuring the organization and disrupting (but ultimately improving) the lives of individuals and groups.

In our experience, strategic planning works best when there is a strong personal investment from leadership and staff and when the leaders are active, fully participating (but not controlling) members of working committees. A sense that everyone is involved and has a stake in the outcomes is important. Ownership of results usually enhances the implementation of action plans. For this reason, strategic planning is generally managed by key members of the staff, often with the assistance of consultants. This pattern would be particularly true in small to medium-sized organizations with constrained fiscal resources.

Steps 2 and 3, internal and external scanning, can be carried out simultaneously by separate and independent committees studying the internal and external environments. The internal committee systematically examines activities conducted by the organization in regard to inputs, processes, outcomes, strengths, and weaknesses. The external committee focuses on what may be a more difficult task—examination of the external environment of the organization, which is characterized by a complex set of variables.

For example, Jonsen (1986) indicates that universities and colleges need to monitor these six important and somewhat related components of the environment:

Demographic: Changes in population, such as declines in births, increases in the number of nonnative speakers of English, the aging of certain segments of the population, and so forth

Economic: Trends in economic conditions such as federal, state, and local levels of revenues, changing industrial patterns, changes in tax policies, and the ratio of U.S. imports to exports

Legal-political: Dimensions might include the effects of minority populations on local, regional, and national policies, political issues regarding employment practices, and legislative mandates

Organizational-competitive: The relationship of the organization to its collaborators and its competitors in both the private and public sectors, especially in terms of what the competitors are doing

Sociocultural: Changing cultural patterns, such as dual income families, growth in the number of women who participate in the labor force, the rising need for child care, and trends in work and lifestyles such as more work at home and networking via computers

Technological: The use of computers for instruction, automated teller machines for banking, telecommunications via satellites, electronic mail systems, new automotive systems, and the like

Given time and resource limitations, our recommendation for the external scan is to set priorities on the kinds of information to collect—that is, decide what kinds are most feasible and most pertinent to the specific situation. Much of this information is available from census reports, state and regional studies, local planning groups, and other published documents. Organizations such as the United Way, large corporations, and federal and state governments often conduct future-oriented research and may be willing to share their findings. Librarians are valuable resource persons for locating information related to the external scan.

The collected information is then collated, categorized, and summarized so that the strategic planning process is facilitated. Whereas in the internal scan the focus is on strengths and weaknesses of the organization itself, the external case deals with opportunities afforded to the organization in relation to its environment with its threats and constraints.

In Step 4, developing strategic issues, the results of the internal and external scans are synthesized into strategic issues, problems, or conditions to which the organization or group should react or take action if it is to have future success. In general, the number of strategic issues should be limited to 10 or fewer and placed in priority order (Step 5). The group members can set priorities by individually ranking the issues and collating the ranks, or by voting for the three most important and three least important issues. Setting priorities focuses the organization on the most critical issues to which it must attend for survival.

In Step 6, high-priority issues are examined in terms of concrete activities to be undertaken by the organization. Note: Because of the screening process, the organization may have shifted to completely different needs from those originally perceived, or it may see different dimensions of original needs. In Step 7, actions are implemented, monitored, and evaluated.

Step 8 continues the strategic planning process, emphasizing its cyclical nature. Although the level and intensity of the process may be lessened after the first round of strategic planning, the process should have become integrated into the organizational thinking structure.

EXAMPLES OF STRATEGIC PLANNING

Kluger, Mace, and Lyon (1990) describe a strategic planning process implemented by a large human services agency. Their process included the use of focus groups, nominal groups, surveys, voting procedures, and internal and external scans. The external scan began with a review of 85 trends in society that had relevance for their agency. These were then organized into a smaller set of five with highest importance for the future of the agency. The authors emphasize that results of strategic planning should be reported to all participants, not solely to the decision makers.

Clagett (1989) found three basic approaches to accomplishing environmental scanning in postsecondary institutions: establishing a scanning committee, sponsoring or hosting a scanning conference, or assigning the task to an institutional research and planning office. Clagett gives examples of colleges and community colleges that have used each of the approaches.

A national center for science teaching and learning at a large university embarked on a modified strategic planning process. Because its staff was relatively small and consisted of knowledgeable and experienced science educators and other educational professionals, an internal strategic planning committee decided to use the available expertise as the major source of input for the scans. Staff first completed a survey designed to collect information about the current status of projects in the center. Next, they completed a second open-ended survey that asked for their views regarding internal strengths and weaknesses, external opportunities and threats, and strategic issues they felt were imperative for the center.

Data were analyzed and themes were developed that became input for a day-long retreat—a culminating event held away from the work site to reduce the press of daily concerns affecting strategic deliberations. The retreat focused on how the center should approach the future. Outcomes of the retreat were the following: a very frank, in-depth (cathartic) discussion of the center's future; clarification and reaffirmation of the center's primary research mission; and recognition that the center had too many projects and that some of its activities had drifted away from the central mission of the organization. Thus, strategic planning had therapeutic value for the center as well as directly affecting its future direction.

Scenarios

If a group has engaged in strategic planning, it is moderately easy to extend the information gained from that effort to the generation of future-oriented scenarios. In essence, scenarios are pictures or snapshots of what some specific future event or system will look like. In NA, if we have a vision of the desired target state and compare it to the present situation, we have a need or a discrepancy to be considered as a candidate for resolution.

A scenario is a hypothetical word picture of what a situation may look like in the future. It is generally holistic rather than being too detailed. There are eight major steps in developing a scenario, which become increasingly open to creative thinking as the group moves through the stages.

1. Define the general area of interest or system for the scenario in operational terms.
2. Establish a concrete time frame for the scenario.
3. Identify the external constraints that will affect the area or system of interest.
4. Describe the factors within the system that are likely to increase or decrease its chances of achieving desired goals and objectives.
5. Specify the likelihood of the occurrence of the facilitators of success and the barriers to success in terms of probability.
6. Create one or more scenarios based on different assumptions arising from Steps 3 to 5.
7. Subject the scenario(s) to testing and review by others.
8. Use the scenario for defining policy and future directions for action.

Step 1 focuses the scenario development effort; that is, it provides boundaries. Examples might be to (a) examine societal and technological trends affecting the delivery of vocational education; (b) describe the effects of technological change on instruction and teachers; (c) depict the effects of changing supplies of fossil fuels in developed countries; or (d) project population growth in relation to supply, demand, and use of resources.

Step 2, establishing a time frame, is another way of putting limits on the scenario. It is not easy for us to think in terms of long-term futures, particularly in our educational and social institutions with their constant press for immediate action and with their limited resources for NA, research, and development. In our experience, the optimum time frame for scenarios is for 5- or 10-year periods into the future.

In Step 3, identifying external constraints, we look to the external scan of potential factors, forces, and trends affecting the area of concern, as in strategic planning. We can use combinations of existing forecasts, trend analyses, surveys of experts in the field, the Delphi technique, futures-oriented conferences, comprehensive literature reviews of future-related references, future wheels, or cross-impact analyses. Obviously, this information will have to be distilled into a smaller set of what appear to be the major external events and constraints affecting the area. Regarding trend analysis, the needs assessor might ask whether the trends currently observed will continue into the specified future time frame of our scenario, or whether they will change dramatically—positively or negatively.

Step 4 requires examination of the current status of the situation. Questions to ask include: What processes are in place? To what extent are we accomplishing current goals? What are facilitators of and barriers to success? The answers result in information similar to that collected for an internal scan. In Step 5, the probability of occurrence and the relative importance of the barriers and facilitators described in Step 4 are estimated.

In Step 6, the needs assessor reviews and examines the outputs of the prior steps pursuant to the generation of written scenarios. We recommend that multiple scenarios be generated from the data. One might consider "best case," "worst case," "most likely case," and perhaps even "highly speculative case" scenarios based on the data collected and on assumptions regarding the stability of the identified trends and emergent possibilities for the future. The assumptions underlying each scenario should be explicitly described and included with each scenario.

In Step 7, the scenarios are subjected to outside analysis. Criteria in the form of questions might be used: To what extent does the scenario fit the data? Are the assumptions realistic and valid? How well will the trends hold up during the time period of the scenario? Reviewers' comments are included with the scenarios when they are presented to decision-making groups for use in establishing policies and future directions (Step 8).

AN EXAMPLE OF A SCENARIO

In the late 1970s and the early 1980s, Ruff, Shylo, and Russell (1981) embarked, with federal funding, on an ambitious scenario project. Their purpose was to develop future pictures of the effect of social, demographic, and other related trends on the field of vocational education.

They first studied the futures research literature and identified two basic types of futures forecasting: *exploratory,* in which one defines trends and then extrapolates them into the future, and *normative,* in which a preferred picture of the future is developed and then compared to current status, to then determine ways of attaining the future situation. Methods for exploratory forecasting included trend extrapolation, cross-impact methods, scenarios, and mathematical simulations. For normative forecasting, the methods were relevance trees (essentially traditional program planning methods) and morphological methods. They also cited the Delphi technique as another futures procedure.

The initial year of their project was devoted to identifying trends and issues likely to affect vocational education in the next decade. They used the results from a Delphi survey and the services of a consultant group that had expertise in trend analysis to analyze the future context in terms of demographic, labor force, economic, and education trends, as well as societal expectations. Besides the trends, the consultants highlighted the following areas for policy consideration: high technology, loss of traditional students, rise in importance of new groups, the educationally disadvantaged, student achievement, cultural differences, financial problems, strong future competitors, and curriculum developments.

The final activity of the first year of the project was an alternative futures conference, including an activity in which small groups of participants engaged in discourse based on the data collected about optimistic, pessimistic, and realistic futures for vocational education. The conferees also reviewed and expanded the list of policy issues that had previously been suggested.

As often occurs in futures efforts, the project produced a substantial database that required extensive time and thought to assimilate and collate. Therefore, much of the second year's work dealt with the synthesis of data and the generation of coherent scenarios of vocational education's future. The data were reviewed, a cross-impact analysis was conducted (see a subsequent section of this chapter for an explanation of this technique), and "a *standard 1990 world* scenario and two *alternative 1990 world* scenarios" were created (Ruff et al., 1981, p. 23). The cross-impact analysis helped in determining how key future trends might affect each other.

Figure 9.3 contains a short description used by Ruff et al. (1981) to guide respondents when they were completing the cross-impact analysis. The description is itself an abbreviated form of a scenario of current trends that were affecting vocational education at the time.

Figure 9.4 presents excerpts from the first alternative scenario, and Figure 9.5 contains excerpts from the second one. These different pictures of the future were based on differing assumptions generated from the information in the database. Those assumptions were succinctly delineated at the beginning of each scenario, thus allowing users to make their own judgments about their validity. The scenarios were generally short (several pages in length), in keeping with the guideline that a scenario is holistic rather than detailed in nature. Although they were produced in 1981, the 1990s view of vocational education that was synthesized proved to be remarkably accurate and had a great deal of value for the field.

Full-blown scenario development demands extensive research and often uses a number of varied techniques in data collection. A scenario project requires gathering large amounts of data and sufficient time to perform the complex syntheses. The usefulness of the scenarios depends on many factors, such as the quality of the futures research

The world of vocational education in the 1980s will not be drastically different from that of the 1970s. However, there are some significant changes that are
expected to occur. Due to the drop in the birth rate in the 1960s and 70s, there
will be fewer numbers of young persons and enrollment in secondary vocational education will decline by approximately 13%. Another effect of the changing demographics will be the rising proportion of young people who come from
economically disadvantaged or limited English speaking backgrounds. These
young people will need and demand preparation and jobs in order that they
may join the economic mainstream of American society. The impact of the
women's liberation movement, which changed the face of the labor force as the
1970s progressed, will cause many adult women to be seeking vocational education during the 1980s. Other adults and older persons who are making career
changes will also require additional vocational training.

But factors besides population shifts will cause vocational eduation to become a different entity than it was 10 years ago. Education in general will receive proportionately less of the Gross National Product. Although the actual
number of dollars allocated by the federal and state governments to vocational
education may not decline, inflation and increasing expenditures for energy and
defense will effectively reduce the vocational education budget. However, the
proportion of federal to state and local dollars for vocational education will remain approximately 1 to 10. Education will become a declining industry.

Figure 9.3. Part of a Short Description Used to Guide Respondents for the
Cross-Impact Analysis for the Future of Vocational Education
SOURCE: R. Ruff, B. Shylo, and J. F. Russell, *Vocational Education: A Look Into the Future*, Columbus:
Center on Education and Training for Employment (formerly NCRVE), The Ohio State University.
Copyright © 1981. Used with permission.

that has been conducted and the unique skills, emerging understandings, the vision, and even the artistry of the developer. Given
these circumstances, scenarios of the type shown in the foregoing
examples are most often found in policy-setting contexts where needs
are examined across entire institutions or fields.

In more localized situations, the resources (time, costs, personnel
skill, and experience) for scenario development are generally not as
available, nor would it be reasonable to commit large amounts of local
resources to the endeavor. In many fields, however, it is possible to
locate examples of futures forecasting that can be used to facilitate
local groups in examining and considering futures in their thinking

Elimination of Sex Bias

Vocational educators had made progress in eliminating sex bias and stereo-typing from vocational programs. With the shift to on-site training, a new emphasis was created to assist private sector personnel to maintain the progress achieved in fair hiring practices. The overall effort was supported by increased pressure on employers to respond to equal opportunity and affirmative action legislation and societal attitudes.

Initially, young, nontraditional students encountered difficulty in coping with the stresses of entering training programs for jobs typically held by the opposite sex. However, more displaced homemakers were attracted to nontraditional occupations and as support services were provided to nontraditional students at the work site, enrollments in short-term training programs reflected a more equal distribution of males and females.

Preparation for Employment With
a Specific Focus on Unemployed Youth

The movement toward more on-site training was expected to increase job placement rates. Debate during the 1980s centered on whether the neglect of basic skill development was an appropriate "trade-off" for higher placement rates and lower youth umemployment. The targeted jobs' tax credit programs of the 1980s successfully stimulated private sector employers to provide on-the-job training and cooperative education programs. On-site training tended to enhance work habits and attitude formation, which resulted in higher placement rates and provided a more responsive environment for dropout-prone youth. Detractors, however, claimed that the long-range effects were less positive because of a decreased emphasis on basic skills. They cited examples where academically disadvantaged youth could not meet the minimal skill requirements of industry for entry into training programs. They expressed concern with the lack of socialization skills and academic education that students received, and they questioned whether enough training sites could be found to meet career objectives for all students.

Figure 9.4. Excerpts From the First Alternative Scenario for the Future of Vocational Education

SOURCE: R. Ruff, B. Shylo, and J. F. Russell, *Vocational Education: A Look Into the Future*, Columbus: Center on Education and Training for Employment (formerly NCRVE), The Ohio State University. Copyright © 1981. Used with permission.

about needs and programs. From this point of view, the scenario furnishes an opportunity for groups to capitalize and build on their creative energy in thinking about NA.

**The Elimination of Sex Bias and
Stereotyping Within Programming and Services**

The shifting of federal funds toward providing adult and short-term training programs had little direct effect on the elimination of sex bias and stereotyping within programming and services. In spite of affirmative action and equal employment laws, the attitude of some industrial personnel bordered on resentment toward upwardly aspiring women, especially during the economic and employment downturns experienced throughout the decade. Business and industry leaders were faced with the prospect of having to recruit women into their workforce, and to provide supportive services such as child care facilities, while contending with the changing attitudes toward the role of women in the workforce.

The biggest gains for women were in new occupations that had not been sex stereotyped and in industries or regions where labor shortages existed. While short-term training programs afforded women the opportunity to be trained quickly to enter the labor force, such a movement was not a major contribution to the reduction of sex stereotyping and bias.

**Preparation for Employment With
a Specific Focus on Unemployed Youth**

Accountability demands suggested that training institutions could no longer afford to train students, only to "drop" them into a job market where they might not find employment. Successful training enterprises sought arrangements with business to train youth for specific job opportunites, involved counselors in assessing the needs of youth and in developing training plans, and intensified their placement efforts. Unfortunately, the emphasis on adult and short-term programs had an adverse effect on preparing youth for employment. Short-term training programs tended to ignore the basic educational skill development that youth desperately needed. In many instances, it became apparent that basic skill training was required before the short-term training could begin. There was a trend to direct short-term training programs toward adult subpopulations, such as retired workers and displaced homemakers.

Figure 9.5. Excerpts From the Second Alternative Scenario for the Future of Vocational Education

SOURCE: R. Ruff, B. Shylo, and J. F. Russell, *Vocational Education: A Look Into the Future,* Columbus: Center on Education and Training for Employment (formerly NCRVE), The Ohio State University. Copyright © 1981. Used with permission.

Workforce 2000 (Johnston, 1987) is a case in point. The study describes probable changes in the American labor force in the 21st century that have important implications for employers and educators, especially vocational educators and those who focus on ESL (English as a Second Language) programs. The study could be rapidly summarized, like a scenario, for use with local groups.

Cross-Impact Analysis

Common difficulties in scenario development and strategic planning relate to understanding the vast amount of data that are collected and the effects of trends and factors on each other. Several mechanisms are used to deal with this problem. *Computer simulations* help the needs assessor get a sense of how factors interact. The forecaster can vary the assumptions and levels of quantitative variables to see the effects on other variables. One drawback is that simulations are based on mathematical models and statistical methods, such as regression analysis and linear programming. Needs assessors who may have limited familiarity with such methods should seek expert help.

A second method is to use *spreadsheets,* which allow one to manipulate variables such as levels of inputs, changes in interest rates, changes in inflation and growth rates, and the like. Spreadsheets can provide important information for understanding the changing dimensions of a need. But they too have limitations in that they are mostly focused on financial variables. Like computer simulations, they rely on quantitative variables, and it is difficult to take into account political, organizational, or other qualitative factors.

A third possibility is to use *cross-impact analysis.* The advantages are that it (a) allows the needs assessor to incorporate trends or variables of all types (not just quantitative ones) in the analysis; (b) relies on few, if any, assumptions; (c) is relatively easy to understand; and (d) is readily amenable for use in decision making.

Cross-impact analyses can be conducted in at least three ways. The first type uses the first five steps of scenario development. The needs assessors carefully identify key trends or factors possibly influencing the future. The trends should be limited to under 20 (and preferably under 10), and they should represent what are perceived to be critical factors affecting the future.

The trends are assembled into a matrix with each trend representing a row and a column as shown in Figure 9.6. The matrix is distributed to a panel usually composed of experts in the field. They are instructed

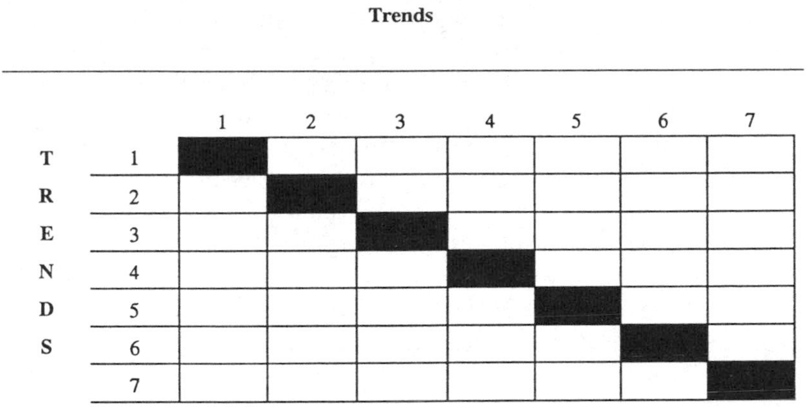

Trends

		1	2	3	4	5	6	7
T	1	■						
R	2		■					
E	3			■				
N	4				■			
D	5					■		
S	6						■	
	7							■

Figure 9.6. General Structure of a Cross-Impact Analysis Matrix

to compare each column entry with each row entry and to rate whether the column factor or trend will have a positive, negative, or neutral effect on the row factor or trend. As with any paired comparison method, the number of comparisons to be made is generally kept small to reduce fatigue and errors. The 7 × 7 matrix of Figure 9.6, for example, requires 42 paired comparisons. A slight increase in size, to a 10 × 10 matrix, requires 90 comparisons, and a 20 × 20 matrix calls for 380, hence the emphasis on limiting the number of factors.

Some cross-impact analyses use a bipolar scale similar to one used by Lauffer (1982) for an organizational map (see the earlier section on strategic planning). The values are as follows:

+2—the probability that one factor or trend is strongly enhanced by the other

+1—the trend is moderately enhanced

0—no effect is likely

−1—the trend is moderately diminished by the other factor

−2—the trend is strongly diminished

To analyze the data, the needs assessor records the scale values assigned by the panel members and the frequencies associated with each value. The assessor then looks for events that seem to be affecting others strongly (positively or negatively) and those that are affecting large numbers of other events.

There are alternatives to using scales containing values or points along a continuum. In one, respondents indicate the *percentage change* that one event may have on another. In another, the analyst assigns a *probability* to an event (row entry) and respondents indicate what that probability would be (increased, decreased, or remaining the same) given that the second event (column entry) exists. Respondents supply the new probability. Analysis consists of calculating the mean of the probabilities assigned by panelists and their spread. Events that have a great likelihood of affecting the original probability are singled out.

A second cross-impact analysis strategy uses a single event as the main column entry with subentries for the column representing years into the future. Each row has an event that could be influenced, over time, by the major column entry. Respondents indicate the effect (percentage increase or decrease) of the column entry on the row event for each year.

A third adaptation of cross-impact analysis, described by Beasley and Johnson (1984), uses computer-based techniques developed by Lipinski and Tydeman (as cited in Beasley & Johnson, 1984) rather than expert comparisons. A model consisting of important variables within a system is developed, and key variables are mathematically compared in terms of their effects on each other. This approach requires these three steps: identify significant variables, specify ranges of value for them, and make decisions about which variables affect others.

In every case, cross-impact analysis directs our attention to the ways in which prime events or factors in the future might have an effect on other events. If one critical factor keeps emerging, it can be used as the central feature for future wheel development.

Future Wheels

The future wheel is intended to guide thinking about a key future event or situation and its potential for affecting other events or situations that may occur in the future. Constructing a future wheel encourages creative, imaginative thought, as the procedure is not constricted by the rigor necessary for some other types of futures methodologies. A group of 8 to 12 individuals participate, using a brainstorming technique that results in a pictorial representation—the hub of a wheel, with spokes radiating from it. If more people participate—for example, 20 or more—they are divided into smaller groups to work independently either on the same future wheel or on other wheels that are of importance to the area of the NA.

The method has some of the characteristics of cross-impact analysis but is a shorter activity that can be implemented rapidly in one group session. As with other futures-oriented techniques, it is dependent on prior work carried out by the needs assessors, the NAC, or both. Key potential future events or trends are identified from the literature, from futures studies, or from cross-impact analyses. The NAC then selects one or more of these events for use in the future wheels activity.

The brainstorming session begins with a 5- to 10-minute warm-up exercise. The group might solve picture or word puzzles, such as are found in newspapers, or consider a question such as, What has happened in your lifetime that you would never have predicted or even dreamed about when you were a teenager? After the warm-up, the facilitator explains the purpose of the future wheels activity. Each event that the NAC has selected is placed on a blackboard, on butcher paper affixed to the wall, or on a flip chart, with the event enclosed in a small circle prominently located in the middle of the space.

The group examines the central event and proposes other events that it could, in turn, affect. These events are also put in circles that radiate from the hub or from other circles to show relationships. All suggestions are welcome; they are not judged but rather are considered as input to the process.

The choice of the central event is critical, as it should not only be relevant to issues that are important to the organization but it should also capture the imagination of the group. One such event or situation might be the aging of the American population. The group is challenged to think of health-related factors in relation to the rising proportion of older people in the country. The panel members consider aging as it affects health, health care delivery, use of resources, demands on the health care system, the training of health care providers, legislation, different health needs of older men and women, and the social fabric of the society. Using the central event and the questions just raised, each member individually jots down related ideas: consequences of the event, the likelihood of the consequences occurring, effects of consequences, and an explanation of their views. Murphy (1982) has developed a short form for this purpose.

Perhaps 10 to 20 minutes are allotted for this part of the future wheels process. Then, using a round-robin procedure, group members read aloud their suggestions, which the group leader enters on the board or chart. Once the list is completed—that is, when the group members have no new ideas to offer—these suggestions can be clustered in an a priori fashion in categories by questions asked or they can be listed and clustered a posteriori by the group. In either case, clusters are identified and labeled. The procedure is repeated for subthemes within clusters.

The group then constructs the future wheel. Labeled clusters are depicted as circles radiating from the center event, with their subthemes entered as small circles emanating from the clusters until the outer level of the large circle is reached. The final future wheel serves as a heuristic device for thinking about the future, discussing its implications, and comparing it to present circumstances. This present-future comparison is obviously valuable for an NA.

AN EXAMPLE OF A FUTURE WHEEL

Figure 9.7 illustrates a future wheel. The subject is the effects of the aging of the population from an educational perspective (Phi Delta Kappa, 1984, p. 11). The insert in the upper left of the figure shows the entire wheel. The portion in black is depicted in the larger figure.

This particular futures exercise turned out to have some predictive value, as noted in the items in the outer set of circles. For example, in 1984, the future wheel suggested that there could be a return to family doctors. As this is written (1994), that trend is showing up—family practice is currently one of the fastest growing health specialties, and the importance of the family doctor has been stressed in the national debate regarding health care. The lower left side of the wheel also depicts major changes in the nature of work, the work force, and training for employment, which we are now seeing.

Future wheels can be used in health, education, mental health, social service, training and development, and other settings. The technique relies heavily on the judgments and understandings of the particular group members involved, who are often quite knowledge-able and who will have thoughtful insights regarding the future. In

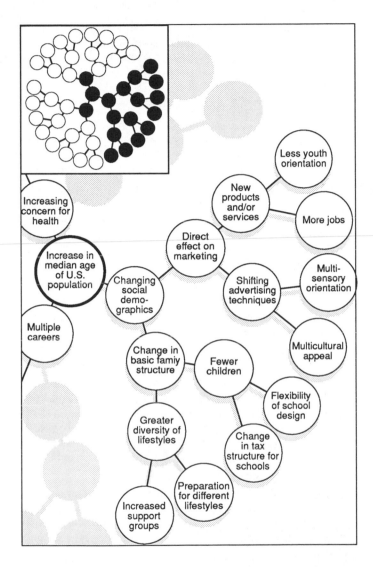

Figure 9.7. Part of a Future Wheel Structure for an Aging Population
SOURCE: Phi Delta Kappa (1984). Used by permission.

contrast with other methods, future wheels consist of ideas generated and organized on the spot, rather than those that are examined over time and with a wealth of data supporting their inclusion in our future thinking. Consequently, they will need to be verified by seeking additional data and information regarding their likelihood of occurrence.

Trend Analysis

Trend analysis (or extrapolation) is a method of determining possible alternative futures by extending a graphed trend of data in several ways, relating each extension to appropriate influential factors. Trend analysis can be applied to strategic planning, scenarios, cross-impact analyses, and future wheels. Identifying and understanding trends is a major ingredient in futures-oriented needs assessment. The data on which to base trend analysis come from such sources as existing records and social indicators (see Chapter 5). This section briefly considers important factors and some cautions.

First, the persons doing trend analysis must have access to historical data that have been regularly collected for an extended period (at least 5 years and preferably more), are appropriate for NA use, and are amenable to the analysis necessary for developing trend lines or functions (time series analysis). Some kinds of historical data meet these criteria to a high degree, but others do not. Even data from the U.S. census present some drawbacks. One problem is underrepresentation of certain segments of the population, such as the homeless and illegal immigrants. In addition, definitions that change or shift with time can cause confusion in interpreting information. Beck (1994) notes that a change in the definition of Native American resulted in a 38% (real or definitional?) growth in the number of individuals in this category from 1980 to 1990.

Information derived from economic and social system databases may also be suspect if there were shifts in how the data were collected (changes in record keeping and the quality of data entry on records, forms, etc.) and how variables were defined (recidivism, mental health and rehabilitation success rates, etc.). Any inconsistency in the criteria for the databases or methods of gathering the data will affect an understanding of the trend.

Interpreting trends is often difficult, depending on both the types of indicators used and the inferences drawn from them. For example, conventional wisdom predicted that the rising federal deficits of the

late 1970s to the 1990s and the export-import imbalance would negatively affect the standard of living and quality of life in the United
States. On the other hand, McKenzie (1994) argues that other indicators suggest that there has not been a decline in living standards. For
example, in the period from 1970 to 1990, life expectancy rose from
about 71 years to over 75 years, the number of Americans finishing high school increased nearly 28%, and the number of recreational boats almost doubled, from 8.8 to 16 million. But interpretation
of trends depends partly on one's perspective. Repeated polls of
middle-class Americans in the 1990s reveal a strong sense of dissatisfaction with their quality of life based on the changing job market and
a concomitant reduced personal standard of living. They would probably quarrel with McKenzie's choice of indicators as well as the
conclusion. To reiterate, the needs assessor must first of all be alert to
issues of choice of indicators, data quality, and interpretation when
doing trend analysis.

A second factor, the relationship of national or regional data to local
concerns, must be considered prior to examining trends and their
relationship to needs. It is unlikely that most local or regional NA
strategies would assess macrotrends (those across states or the country). Such data are often collected and analyzed by agencies such as
the U.S. Bureau of the Census, the Bureau of Labor Statistics, the
National Institutes of Health, and the National Center for Educational
Statistics.

Some organizations conduct specialized national studies on a regular basis. An example in education is the National Assessment of
Educational Progress. Public use data tapes are available for secondary analysis and research.[1] This type of information could be useful
for comparison when analyzing local educational needs, after adjustments for local perspectives and issues. The main question is,
How well do national, state, or regional level data relate to the local
situation?

A third factor relates to having a model of the need area that
specifies important variables, their interrelationships (including
causal ones), and indicators or concrete measures. With a model in
place and once the data have been obtained, observed trends become
part of a comprehensive picture of the need area. In NA, we must go
beyond outcome indicator data provided by the agencies noted. Ideal
data sets would include indicators of various inputs, processes, out-

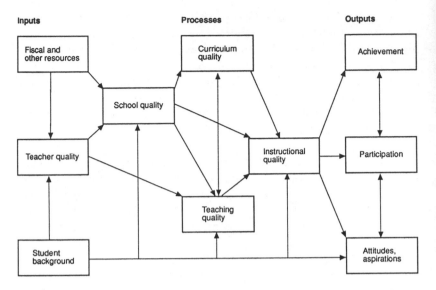

Figure 9.8. Linkages Among the Elements of the Education System

SOURCE: Odden (1990). Copyright © 1990 by the American Educational Research Association. Reprinted by permission of the publisher.

puts, and causal relations organized around a system or model. Seldom do current data collection strategies or sets, even with their wealth of existing data, contain what is required for conducting decision-oriented NA.

Because NA is an important part of the decision-making and program-planning process, we must go beyond the basic specification of discrepancies related to the three levels in a system and their environments. Discrepancies by themselves, without examination of relationships, causal analysis, and the study of the internal and external environments, are inadequate for making decisions.

In education, there is a strong movement to use educational indicators and to link them in such a way that they show the complexity of schooling so that they can be used for policy making. A report by Shavelson, McDonnell, and Oakes for the Rand corporation (as cited in Odden, 1990) proposes a model linking 10 educational indicators and their relationship to inputs, processes, and outputs in an education system (Figure 9.8). The model has been applied to mathematics and science education.

Odden (1990) maintains that we are far from having the strong, data-based type of information system necessary for applying such educational indicators to policy making for schools. Both qualitative and quantitative data regarding system variables would have to be collected and combined into a meaningful, coherent, understandable database—a daunting task.

Therefore, the analysis of future trends in regard to NA has both values and limitations. A major problem is the lack of adequate models to represent meaningfully the dimensions of complex social systems. Even if these dimensions did exist, we probably would not have suitable data for the array of variables that must be taken into account in making decisions. Although it can add an important dimension, the analysis of trends comprises only part of a comprehensive picture of needs.

The fourth factor deals with the determination of trends in the local environment. Mental health agencies, for example, routinely collect and enter into their databases information regarding intake, rates-under-treatment, treatment processes, and results after treatment. The data, however, should be placed in a model or framework that guides the systematic analysis of relationships among variables and will be useful in making decisions regarding programs.

Even so, questions similar to those raised earlier are pertinent to analyzing trends from a local agency database. What kinds of basic data are routinely collected? Are the data sufficient in terms of inputs, processes, and outputs? Is it possible to establish causal linkages and relationships? Have the data always been collected in a systematic fashion? Are variables defined in a consistent manner by different individuals so that they collect essentially the same kinds of data? Have provisions been made for obtaining qualitative data about processes? How much variation is there in such data? How are the entries coded and entered into the database? How are qualitative and quantitative data analyzed, collated, and interpreted?

Although data from local, regional, and national sources can be valuable for understanding trends and needs, we caution that needs assessors use the information with an awareness of the subtleties of data collection and interpretation.

Finally, the fifth factor relates to the analysis and presentation of trend data. Many options are available. One of the most frequently used is the bar chart, a table in which the variable of time (years) is

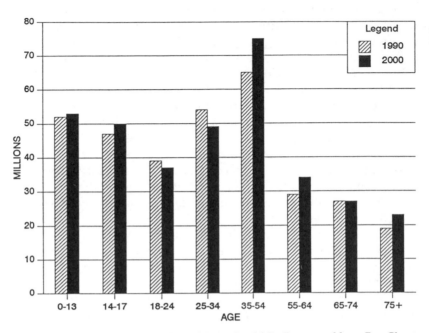

Figure 9.9. Example of How Trend Data Could Be Portrayed by a Bar Chart
SOURCE: Adapted from United Way of America (1989). Reprinted by permission of United Way of America.

represented on the abscissa and the key trend or substantive variable is represented on the ordinate. Figure 9.9 illustrates another use of the bar chart, showing population trends in terms of age (United Way of America, 1989). In this chart, the abscissa represents age spans, the ordinate represents population size, and the height of the bars shows the numbers of people in each age cohort. The bars are in pairs, one reflecting data for 1990, the other extrapolating to the year 2000. Thus, comparisons can be made at a glance regarding which age groups are likely to be larger or smaller at the end of the 10 years.

Another way of presenting the same information is to connect the tops of the bars to create trend lines. Figure 9.10 shows the same data as does Figure 9.9, but with trend lines instead of bars. The lines clearly show that the largest increase in numbers of individuals is likely to be in the age group from 35 to 54 years.

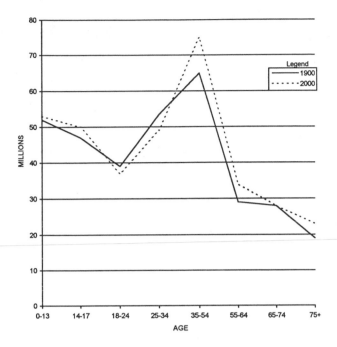

Figure 9.10. Data on Aging Shown as Trend Lines

SOURCE: Adapted from United Way of America (1989). Reprinted by permission of United Way of America.

Assumptions underlying this approach are that (a) there are enough years of data (data points) to define the trend, (b) the trend is readily apparent and understandable by means of straightforward descriptive statistics, and (c) the trend will tend to continue into the near future in the same way it has occurred in the past. More sophisticated versions of analysis calculate the rate of change using a mean value for changes across time, a moving average (successive means across more than a 2-year period), or a slope or regression coefficient determined by linear regression, with time as one of the variables. Other ways of determining a trend rely on procedures such as obtaining the equation of best fit (often accomplished through analysis of variance) or by calculating the degree to which various standard trend functions relate to the observed data (time series analysis—see Monk, 1983).

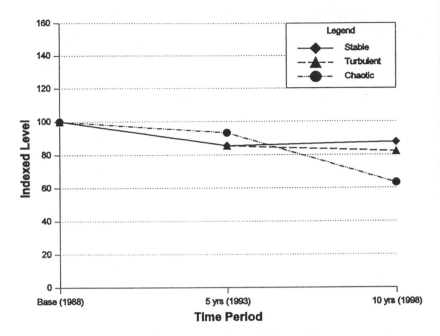

Figure 9.11. Example of Trend Lines Plotted Under Three Assumed Conditions
SOURCE: Adapted from Morrison (1989). Used by permission.

Although all of these procedures for analyzing and visually depicting trends are useful, simple descriptive tables work well enough for the purposes of most needs assessments. Whatever procedure is used, the needs assessor should alert the decision-making group to information pertinent to the quality of the data used for the trend analysis. In addition, any assumptions made in determining the trend should be explicitly provided to the group.

Figure 9.11 shows an analysis in which alternative trend lines were plotted on the basis of three assumed conditions: stable, turbulent, and chaotic (Morrison, 1989; also see Morrison, 1990).

The trends depicted in Figures 9.9, 9.10, and 9.11 were derived from analyses of single variables, rather than sets of variables in which some trends would have effects on others. Using multiple variables is more complex and requires a different type of analysis. For example, if we determine through cross-impact analysis that three or four events will affect another event in both positive and negative ways, we could construct several figures showing the trends for the event of concern as affected by each of the other events. For more advanced analysis, we could apply specialized equations (linear programming or multiple regression techniques) using the three or four events as simultaneous predictors (independent variables) of the other event (the predicted or dependent variable). We could then vary levels of multiple independent variables to ascertain the degree to which the dependent variable is affected by changes in the predictors.

This latter procedure may be particularly useful for a field such as education. In education, we seldom know how changing the input variables will affect desired outcomes or end states. As an illustration, if we decrease the number of students per class and lengthen class periods at the same time, to what extent will the changes affect outcomes in mathematics and science? By using multivariate procedures, we are able to estimate ranges of possible effects that could occur in the future.

SUMMARY

In our examination of hundreds of needs assessments reported in the 1980s and early 1990s, we found that the overwhelming majority focused on the present. Although all NAs using a discrepancy approach consider the future to some extent—in terms of relating a present state to a desirable state that is not now present—they overlook the fact that both parts of the equation are likely to change; existing states alter for better or worse, and the vision of desirable states may change in unexpected ways.

Although we cannot predict the future with certainty, we can predict that change will certainly occur. In this chapter, we have described five methods by which needs assessors and stakeholders can think about the future and about the shape of needs to come. They are strategic planning, futures scenarios, cross-impact analysis, future wheels, and trend analysis. In varying degrees, they call on the imagination and creativity of groups to project themselves beyond the present and thus to open up new possibilities for addressing both present and future needs.

Note

1. Contact Doug Rhodes, National Assessment of Educational Progress, P.O. Box 6710, Princeton, NJ 08541, 800-223-0267. This organization provides census-like data for major learning areas at various educational levels, which are periodically reassessed.

TEN

Causal Analysis

You, the needs assessor, and the NAC have identified a set of needs of varying criticality. Now you ask, How come those needs were not addressed (or problems solved) 10 years ago? Or, How come we did not see the present needs emerging? And if we take the long view into the future, what can we do now to prevent the needs from getting worse?

The tools for addressing these questions reside in the domain of causal analysis (CA). We are well aware that the whole notion of cause and effect in the social sciences has been seriously questioned. In other fields, researchers can establish cause-effect relationships (or at least strong correlations with predictive value) through statistical studies—for example, that smoking is a major causal factor in a certain percentage of cases of lung cancer, or that hydrocarbon emissions from automobiles are a causal factor of airborne particulates that result in smog in the Los Angeles basin. But when it comes to social systems, we are wary about ascribing particular effects to certain causes and vice versa.

Uses of Causal Analysis in Needs Assessment

We are using the term *causal analysis* to refer broadly to techniques that describe or analyze factors or conditions that contribute to the

239

existence or perpetuation of a need or an unresolved problem. In this context, causal analysis does not refer to the rigorous methods of mathematical causal path analysis but, rather, consists of largely qualitative procedures intended to answer such questions as: What factors have operated to perpetuate an unsatisfactory situation? What conditions have prevented the needs from being met? If solutions were tried, why didn't they work? Is the need really a need, or just a symptom of something more basic? Causal analysis is used to uncover factors underlying the symptoms and to bring planners and evaluators closer to the real needs.

From this point of view, an essential component of a complete NA—yet one of the most neglected in practice—is analysis of causes, which usually occurs in Phase 2, the main assessment. Figure 3.1 in Chapter 3 shows the place of causal analysis in the total activity flow. After identifying and prioritizing Level 1 (primary) needs, the needs assessor and NAC perform one or more causal analyses. They examine factors in Levels 1, 2, and 3, as well as factors outside the system that have probably caused the need or contributed to its maintenance. They also examine reasons why previous attempts to meet the needs have failed.

Inferences about causes at any of the three levels are combined with discrepancy data and other information to establish priorities of unmet or inadequately met needs and to anticipate what types of solutions are most likely to meet those needs. One of the criteria used in weighing the merits of alternate solutions is the extent to which one will address one or more of the causes or contributing factors.

Before we describe some causal analysis techniques, let us briefly discuss two other concepts: *systems,* and the *Pareto principle.*

Systems and Causal Analysis

Needs do not exist in a vacuum. They exist in a system context—whether educational, familial, social service, governmental, or business.[1] And a prime truth about systems is that all elements in a system are interrelated. Thus, anything that affects one part of the system has repercussions throughout. In addition, systems interact with other systems in complex ways. The causal analyses that we will present, particularly fault tree analysis, reflect this system concept. Keep this interrelatedness in mind as we discuss the techniques.

Some notion of the complexity of causes and system interactions is conveyed by the following illustration of the problem of discipline in the schools, which

> requires attention to an immediate cause ("angry, apathetic children"), which in turn is apparently influenced by "hopelessly poor" achievement among certain students, which in turn is traced to automatic promotions, themselves one result of a conveyor-belt mentality, which itself may be a defense mechanism in response to schools' inability to deal with problems of teacher education, selection of principals, motivating the unmotivated, achieving educational equality . . . and so forth. And probably each problem-solution has multiple, sometimes unanticipated effects and relationships with other conditions and problems. (Sikorski, Oakley, & Lloyd-Kolkin, 1977, p. 16)

Another example is that well-intentioned school programs intended to decrease dropouts have often had an unintended effect: Many students who stay in school do not master basic skills, which in turn brings a new set of problems, such as angry children and poor discipline.

The Pareto Principle

The three methods that we will describe are based to a certain extent on the Pareto principle: that only a few contributors to the problem are responsible for the bulk of the problem (Juran & Gryna, 1988). The Pareto principle is often invoked in such statements as, "90% of repeated violent crimes are caused by 10% of the population," or "In a group meeting, 20% of the participants will do 80% of the talking." The principle has been well established in such diverse fields as quality control in manufacturing and assembly, administrative and support services, service industries, and analysis of customer needs, about which Juran and Gryna (1988) remark:

> Customers are not equally important. Their importance follows the Pareto principle: a relative few of the customers absorb most of the effect. The planning process requires that these vital few customers be identified so that their needs will become known and met.
>
> Customers' stated needs often differ from the real needs. For example, an internal department asks the finance office for a change in some

cost standard. The real reason may be to avoid criticism for cost overruns.

Customers' perceptions often differ from those of suppliers. For example, a personnel office perceives the need to train the work force in some specialty. However, the line managers do not perceive such training as helping their departments meet departmental goals. (p. 21.9)

"Customers" in this quotation could be any groups at Level 1 or Level 2 in our schema of NA levels. A large part of the work of NA, including causal analysis, aims to disentangle people's perceptions of their needs from the real needs at any of the three levels and to consider the reasons for misperceptions of their own needs. The following example illustrates a common type of misperception of Level 2 needs.

Professional staff in an educational service district office provided a large variety of workshops and seminars to teachers in a multicounty area, offering the latest in teaching technology and applications of learning theory. After a time, the staff noticed an interesting pattern of enrollment: a certain proportion of teachers attended workshops on the same or similar topic over and over but avoided those on new and emerging techniques that had more relevance to their work. Informal questioning of a sample of teachers uncovered several reasons for the avoidance: The teachers had a high comfort level for concepts with which they were familiar, they were afraid of new techniques that might challenge their ability to adapt, they felt overwhelmed by new ideas and techniques that they had little time to absorb and put into practice, they saw no need to add other methods to their repertoire, and, in some cases, they attended the sessions mainly for continuing education credit, not for adding to their own skills or knowledge. These teachers' "real" needs—in relation to their teaching goals and responsibilities—were probably very different from their perceived needs in attending the workshops that they chose.

The foregoing example illustrates why we caution against basing NAs on wish lists alone. The multicomponent NA model described in Chapter 4 (Misanchuk, 1984; Schwier, 1986) was designed in part to deal with such misperceptions and resistance to change in Level 2 (training) needs.

METHODS OF CAUSAL ANALYSIS FOR NA

There are many ways of doing causal analysis. The simplest is for a group to brainstorm possible causes, discuss them, and vote on the most probable. In this chapter, however, we present three methods that are structured to give more precise information for decision making than simple brainstorming. They capitalize on expert information of group members and are nonthreatening because they ascribe causes to processes and components in the system rather than to individuals or to attitudes.

The three methods are *fishboning, cause and consequence analysis,* and *fault tree analysis.* We will give an overview of each method, show the types of information it provides, suggest how the method can be used in different phases of the NA, point out advantages and disadvantages of its use, and provide examples of application.

CA is useful from two perspectives in the NA: looking backward and looking ahead. We can look backward to discover precipitating factors of the need, factors perpetuating the need, previous or present barriers to solutions, previous attempts at solutions that have failed and the reasons why, and even previous solutions that did what they were supposed to, yet the need still exists. Two methods are applicable: fishboning and fault tree analysis.

We can also use causal analysis to look forward: in Phase 1, when designing the management plan for the NA, and in Phase 3, when considering criteria for solutions. This predictive function will be discussed under cause and consequence analysis and fault tree analysis.

Fishboning

Fishboning is an easy and effective technique for identifying causes of existing needs. Ishikawa (1983)[2] describes it as a way to examine the failure of manufacturing systems to produce goods at the level of quality desired. Ishikawa devised a fishbone diagram for analyzing the causes of poor quality products. In accordance with the Pareto principle, the fishbone can be very useful with a relatively small number of causes.

PROCEDURE

Here is the procedure for fishboning. Figure 10.1 shows the basic fishbone diagram, with the head of a fish at the right side of the page and the spine and ribs extending to the left. The need or problem is written on the head. Because Ishikawa was working in quality control in manufacturing, the labels that he placed on the ribs above and below the spine were "materials," "methods," "machines," and "workers." These four categories represent potential sources of manufacturing failures leading to product defects. Although other ribs could be included in the fishbone diagram, generally their number is kept under 10 and is often limited to 4 or 5.

This technique is used in informal groups of usually 10 or 12 individuals who are familiar with the need area. More than one group may be used, either at different times or concurrently in different rooms or sections of a large room, with a facilitator for each group. Materials needed are a large diagram of the fish skeleton drawn on stiff paper and displayed on a wall or easel where everyone can easily see it, colored felt pens for the facilitator, and pads of paper and pencils for the group members. The fishbone displays the general need, and four or five ribs selected by the needs assessor or the NAC are drawn and labeled before the session. (An alternate method is for the ribs to be drawn in before the meeting, but not labeled until later; see description that follows.)

The facilitator briefly describes the reason for the session and the nature of the specific need to be addressed. Each person then individually writes down as many causes of the problem or need as are possible from her or his perspective. (This could be the time when the facilitator writes in the labels for the four ribs. It is better if the group members do not think about the labels of the ribs as they generate lists of causes.)

After about 10 minutes or when individuals are no longer writing, the facilitator asks each person in turn to name one cause and indicate where it should be placed on the diagram. Causes can be shown radiating from lines (twigs) extending from the four ribs of the skeleton or from other twigs. All causes are considered equally plausible at this stage, and each person's ideas are placed on the diagram

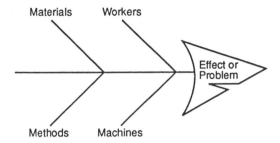

Figure 10.1. General Fishbone Structure

SOURCE: Adapted from *Guide to Quality Control* by Kaoru Ishikawa. Copyright © 1982 by Asian Productivity Organization. Reprinted by permission of the Asian Productivity Organization. Distributed in North America, the United Kingdom, and Western Europe by Quality Resources. NOTE: The head represents a problem (gap or need) and the spines show possible key factors related to causes of the problem.

without commentary or discussion. The process is continued until no more ideas are offered.

The group then reviews the diagram to decide whether it needs restructuring. The facilitator writes in the changes until there is consensus that the relationships of the causes to the ribs are generally accurate.

Next, the facilitator reads out each cause and asks the group to decide, by a show of hands, whether they believe it to be an important cause of the need. Entries receiving no votes are crossed out. Each member then assigns a number to each remaining item indicating the degree of likelihood that the event or situation is a cause of the need, with 1 being the most likely and 5 being the least. One way of doing this is for the facilitator to read each cause again and call for votes (e.g., How many give it a 1? a 2? etc.). When the votes are tallied for each item, the facilitator uses colored pens to mark the clusters of causes in order of likelihood.

Finally, there is general discussion of the fishbone diagram. If the group members work at the site of the meeting (e.g., teachers in a school or employees of a business), the diagram could be posted on a wall for a few days so that all concerned can think about the findings.

A completed fishbone for a problem that often occurs in large offices—bad-tasting coffee—might look like Figure 10.2 (adapted from Jones & Limes, 1988). Bad-tasting coffee is depicted as being caused by only five main factors (machinery, materials, measurement,

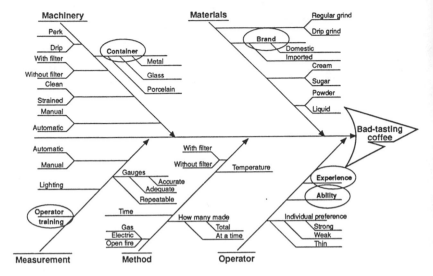

Figure 10.2. Fishbone Diagram for the Problem, "Bad-Tasting Coffee"
SOURCE: Adapted from Jones and Limes (1988).
NOTE: Circled entries are major potential causes highlighted by the group.

method, and operator); the five circled items indicate the group's opinion as to the most important subfactors that contribute to the main causal factors.

USES OF THE DATA

Fishboning is a relatively easy and quick method for looking below the surface of an expressed need for probable causes and contributing factors. As an exploratory method, it could be used in the preassessment phase to help narrow the focus of the assessment. After the fishboning session(s), the NAC can review the causes receiving the highest ranks and decide what kinds of indicators would verify the existence or accuracy of the causes. Then methods of verification could be built into the design of the actual assessment in Phase 2.

Figure 10.3 shows a production example (Ishikawa, 1983) structured around processes, rather than factors or components as in Figures 10.1 and 10.2. In Figure 10.3, key steps in the process are placed in order on the spine, and causes of problems within a process become

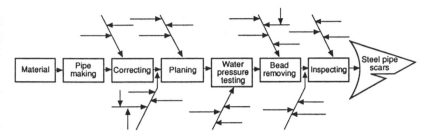

Figure 10.3. Fishbone Diagram for Determining Causes of a Production Defect—"Steel Pipe Scars"

SOURCE: Adapted from *Guide to Quality Control* by Kaoru Ishikawa. Copyright © 1982 by Asian Productivity Organization. Reprinted by permission of the Asian Productivity Organization. Distributed in North America, the United Kingdom, and Western Europe by Quality Resources.

the ribs. An advantage of this type of fishbone diagram, particularly for analysis of a time-phased production problem, is that it provides a complete picture of the production process from start to finish. Even experienced workers are sometimes not knowledgeable regarding all the steps involved in production. The diagram can help them to gain understanding of how their work fits into the total production. A fishbone diagram could be constructed for the process of writing and publishing a book, staging a play, or doing an NA project.

Figure 10.4 depicts the use of fishboning for an hypothetical educational problem. A large college of education has evaluated its graduate program and found that approximately half of its doctoral candidates are not completing their degrees. The costs associated with this problem are extensive in terms of faculty time invested in students and the psychological pressures that students and advisers experience. The college selects the fishboning technique as a way to look into causes of the problem. Several fishboning sessions are conducted with small groups of past and current graduate students and faculty members.

Figure 10.4 shows four main factors causally related to the problem, with five circled subfactors as the key focus for strategies to alleviate the problem. As in other approaches, some causes that are identified (personal or family factors) are not easily amenable to solution by changes in programs or program activities. They are beyond the control of the system. The fishbone diagram, however, offers insights that contribute to understanding the needs, shows potential areas for

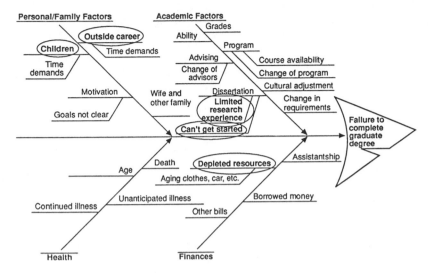

Figure 10.4. Fishbone Diagram for the Problem, "Failure to Complete the Graduate Degree"

NOTE: Circled items are the most likely causes, which were chosen by the group after completing the fishbone process.

efforts to reduce the problem, and forms a basis for counseling with students.

ADVANTAGES AND DISADVANTAGES OF FISHBONING

Advantages. Fishboning is adaptable to analyzing causes of many kinds in a variety of settings, in addition to its successful application in business and industry. Groups find the method enjoyable, they can usually complete the work in a session lasting 1 to 2 hours, and they have a strong sense of involvement in resolving problems and in ownership of results. Facilitators need little training to implement the procedure.

Disadvantages. Although groups can quickly determine potential causes, fishboning does not usually clarify sequences of causes; the causes identified require verification; and the magnitude and probability of a cause contributing to a need are not established. Another disadvantage may be low validity of the inputs. As a check on both validity and reliability, two or more groups familiar with the need area can be formed. Before incorporating the information into the major NA design, the NAC can compare and synthesize the results from several fishbone analyses.

Cause and Consequence Analysis

Problems or needs can sometimes be viewed as causes and sometimes as effects, but neither causes nor effects should be considered in isolation. Cause and consequence analysis (CCA) is a strategy for uncovering both the causes and effects of present needs to determine factors contributing to the present situation, and for potential effects in the future.

CCA is a form of risk assessment (see Chapter 4) and is especially useful after the NAC has identified major needs. It works best with small groups of key informants who have varying perspectives on the system and its needs. An important output from the process is a priority ranking of needs based on severity of causes and potential consequences of not eliminating the causes and meeting the needs.

PROCEDURE

The inputs for CCA are developed by small groups working separately, discussing need areas and entering pertinent data on large charts ruled into five columns, as in Figure 10.5.

In Column 1: List *needs* that were previously identified in the NA.

In Column 2: List all possible *causes* of each concern or need, itemized separately for each need. A given need may have more than one cause.

In Column 3: List *consequences* if the cause is not removed and the need is not met, also itemized separately for each need. There may be more than one consequence for each need.

In Column 4: Enter a rating (low, medium, or high) of the *difficulty of correcting the problem* once it has occurred.

In Column 5: Enter a rating, on a scale of 1 to 5, of the degree of *criticality* of the need if it is not met, with 5 being the most critical.

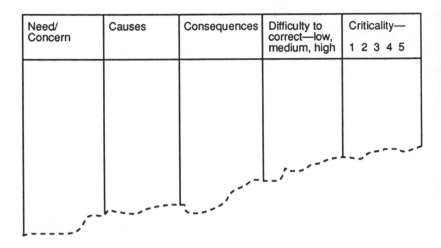

Need/ Concern	Causes	Consequences	Difficulty to correct—low, medium, high	Criticality— 1 2 3 4 5

Figure 10.5. Form for Cause and Consequence Analysis (CCA)

If a large group is convened, the facilitator explains the process to the group as a whole, which then decides what statements of need to enter in Column 1. Then, small groups of five to eight members make entries in Columns 2 through 5, each group working at a table with its own chart on which the needs have been entered in Column 1. The facilitator synthesizes the inputs from all groups on a master sheet displayed on a wall or easel where all can see it; then the entire group makes judgments to be entered in Column 4 (difficulty to correct) and Column 5 (degree of criticality).

To derive consensus on the items in Columns 4 and 5, each participant makes individual judgments using rating sheets with numbers keyed to the needs or concerns on the master chart. The facilitator tallies the votes as they are read off and records the most frequent response as the group judgment. Although any need may have several sets of causes and consequences, only the need itself is judged for difficulty to correct and degree of criticality.

USES OF THE DATA—SETTING PRIORITIES

One of the major uses of CCA is to set priorities of needs in Phase 2 based on both the causal analysis and the severity of consequences if the needs are not met. The first step is to combine the data from

Columns 4 and 5. For short-term planning, the highest priority might be given to those needs that have a high rating on the "criticality" scale and a low or moderately low rating on the "difficulty to correct" scale. Such needs could probably be met more easily than those with high ratings on both scales. The two ratings are then reviewed in light of other data from the NA, such as magnitude of the discrepancies between present and desired states. Information from the CCA is also useful in Phase 3, when setting criteria for solutions and action plans. The highest-priority needs can be further analyzed by having groups generate suggestions for strategies that not only address the causes but also prevent undesirable consequences from occurring.

For longer-range planning, list those needs that are high in criticality and also difficult to correct. By examining reasons for the difficulty, and perhaps applying force field analysis (see Chapter 4) to the problem, planners and managers may discover creative solutions that had not before been evident. As we mentioned previously, the needs assessor and NAC can also identify causal factors within the control of the organization or system and those beyond its control. In the latter category, sometimes information from the CCA and fault tree analysis (see the following section) will suggest where to look for countervailing measures.

ADVANTAGES AND DISADVANTAGES OF CCA

Advantages. Groups enjoy working with CCA. The procedure is not difficult, it encourages lively discussion, and the task of considering possible consequences if the need is not met adds an important dimension that is often overlooked in NA. The results provide concrete material for consideration in setting priorities and moving to solution strategies.

Disadvantages. The major disadvantage of CCA is that groups sometimes get mired in details. Each need may have more than one cause, and a given cause may be related to more than one need. (This shows the concept of interrelatedness in a system. A cause related to more than one need is likely to be of high importance when considering criteria for meeting the need.) Also, in CCAs of educational and social needs, there is the problem of separating out causes rooted in the family and society (about which school systems or social agencies can generally do very little) from more proximal causes that might be amenable to amelioration by the system. Using the term *contributing factors* rather than causes sometimes clarifies the point and prevents the group from getting bogged down in useless discussion.

Fault Tree Analysis

Fault tree analysis (FTA) uses a system-centered approach. It promotes thinking about needs as existing in a network of contributing factors. FTA is the most complex of the three methods described in this chapter, but it is also one of the most fascinating as well as the most powerful for identifying causes. Like CCA, FTA is a form of risk assessment. The ultimate purpose of FTA is failure avoidance and the enhancement of success.

BACKGROUND AND PURPOSE OF FTA

FTA was so named because the product of the analysis is a logic diagram consisting of *failure events* in boxes that are related to each other by logic gates. The diagram looks somewhat like a tree, with a single *undesired event* (UE) at the top and branches with other events descending from it, spreading horizontally wider and wider as the analysis continues to develop several levels below.

FTA was developed originally to trace potential failures in a complex system, such as a manned space vehicle, and to predict the most probable ways that a catastrophic event might occur—for example, loss of the vehicle with all lives. The analysis provides the basis for redesigning or monitoring the system to prevent or significantly reduce the likelihood of the UE occurring. Since the 1960s, FTA has been an important part of systems-safety analysis and design in such fields as aerospace engineering, nuclear reactor studies, industrial accidents, and highway safety. The technique was first adapted to educational and social systems by Witkin and Stephens (1968, 1973). Since 1967, they and others have applied FTA to hundreds of planning, management, and evaluation problems in education, business, government, organizational communication, and other social contexts.

We said earlier that causal analysis may be used either to look backward or to look forward. FTA is highly appropriate for analyzing causes of known needs at Level 1, 2, or 3, looking *backward* to discover reasons for the existence of the needs or why they failed to be addressed earlier, and for analyzing causes of specific failure events that have recently occurred, such as the bankruptcy of a whole county government, the loss of accreditation by a school system or university, or failure of voters to approve school bond levies 5 years in a row.

FTA is also a powerful technique for looking forward, to project causes of possible future needs (see Chapter 9), or to predict possible ways in which a system or program designed to meet a need might fail, in order to redesign or monitor the program and thus enhance the probability of success. FTA is also an excellent technique for managing and evaluating the NA project itself—for anticipating problems that could arise in the course of the NA. The needs assessor can then decide what additional resources or contingency plans to add to increase the likelihood that the NA will meet its goals.

The FTA method of logic diagramming considers multiple causality and relates the contribution of each causal sequence to all others. Each event on the tree is considered a potential failure or a contributor to the UE.

FTA METHODOLOGY—GENERAL PRINCIPLES

FTA is usually performed by an expert in the technique who gathers information from people who know the system or need area to be analyzed. We will refer to these people as the FTA team. They usually include the needs assessor, members of the NAC, and other key informants.

The NAC lays the groundwork for failure analysis by first stipulating the "what should be" dimension of the need. This can take several forms: a mission statement and a set of goals for a projected program, a success map, or criteria for a desired state of affairs. This step, called *success analysis*, will be explained and illustrated in a later section.

After postulating a UE based on the success analysis, the analyst and FTA team construct logic diagrams that relate combinations of possible events in a system, or subsystems within a system, to show how they interact to produce the UE. There are two principal types of analysis—qualitative and quantitative. The qualitative analysis produces the logic diagram, or tree, consisting of clear statements of inputs that are related to each other in a systematic fashion. In other words, any UE may be caused by two or more events, each of which in turn could be caused by two or more other events, and so on for as many levels as the analyst wishes to go. In the quantitative analysis, the FTA team assigns nominal values to each event on the tree and relates all events and logic gates mathematically to derive *strategic paths*—that is, those chains of events that have the highest likelihood of contributing to the occurrence of the UE, in the order of their probability.

QUALITATIVE ANALYSIS—CONSTRUCTION OF THE TREE

Qualitative failure avoidance analysis generally occurs in four stages: performance of a success analysis, selection of one or more UEs, the gathering of concerns focused on the UE, and construction of the fault tree.

Step 1: Perform Success Analysis. Success analysis helps establish the "what should be" dimension of a need. As we saw in Chapters 3 and 4, the NAC assists decision makers in specifying the criteria for a program or project that would meet the needs. The needs assessor, working with the FTA team, constructs a flow chart (that we here designate a *success map*) that shows graphically the goals of the new program or service and the events necessary to achieve those goals. A detailed success map of the projected flow of events depicts relationships of activities, gives a basis for realistic time lines, clarifies ambiguities, illuminates areas of misunderstanding or disagreement among staff, shows where probable overloads on staff or clients might occur, and highlights areas needing more thorough planning or a change in design, backup, or monitoring.

A typical success map of a complex project could depict 20 to 30 or more events in various relationships. The flow chart can be displayed on a wall to monitor the implementation of a program. The same type of success mapping is also very useful for planning the NA itself. (See Figure 10.8 later in this chapter for an example of a rudimentary success map.)

If the need area is not related to a new program or project but to a general concern—for example, unemployment of youth in an inner city or lack of available and affordable child care for working single mothers—a success map may not be appropriate. The FTA team could instead list some major criteria that would indicate success in meeting the need, such as adequate employment or appropriate child care in that geographic area and social context.

Step 2: Select One or More UEs for the FTA. The FTA team can derive major UEs from several sources: a success analysis, a CCA, or other people knowledgeable about the need. If a success map is used, the UE will relate to some failure to achieve the goal of the project or program depicted on the map. If data are derived from a CCA, the group reviews the probable consequences if the needs are not met and chooses one or more needs from events that have high ratings of both criticality and difficulty to correct. In the case of the child care need, where a success map was not appropriate, a UE was selected by a group of mothers and other community people familiar with the problem.

Step 3: Gather Concerns and Supporting Data Regarding the UE. These can be converted to events on the fault tree.

Step 4: Synthesize the Events by Constructing a Fault Tree. This step is explained in the next section.

PRINCIPLES OF FAULT TREE CONSTRUCTION

Event Symbols and Logic Gates

As noted earlier, a fault tree is a logic diagram consisting of statements of actual or potential events interrelated by logic gates and resulting in complex pathways. The analysis begins at the top with the major UE and proceeds downward. Inputs at each level are failure events that contribute to the event immediately above it in a cause-effect relationship. Potential failure events are depicted by boxes of different shapes, mainly rectangles, diamonds, and circles. Our examples will use only rectangles, which represent events that result from a combination of lesser events related through logic gates. (Diamonds represent events that could be developed further, if desired, and circles indicate basic failures that need no further analysis, such as a dead battery.)

Logic gates depict relationships among events. The use of logic gates is one of the features that distinguish FTA from other forms of graphic analysis, such as functional flow charts and decision trees, and from other causal methods, such as fishboning. The two principal types of logic gates are the *OR* gate and the *AND* gate. The OR gate is used when any one of two or more possible inputs to an event could alone produce the output event. The AND gate is used when two or more events must coexist to produce the UE. At least two inputs must be present for both kinds of gates.

The symbols of FTA described here are the basic features needed to construct simple fault trees. Other logic gates are available to depict complex relationships, such as inhibit gates, priority AND gates that specify a sequence of events, matrix gates, and conditional gates. But for nearly all analyses of social systems (rather than of aerospace systems, for example), the rectangle and two kinds of logic gates provide ample information. (For additional information on logic gates, input events, and constructing fault trees, see Witkin & Stephens, 1968, 1973.)

The tree is constructed from the top down, beginning, "The failure of the UE could be caused by . . . " and specifying two or more causes as input events, each of which becomes the top of a branch for further inputs and analysis. The single event above each logic gate is an output event; the two or more events below each gate are input events. The general method and uses of the AND and OR gates are illustrated in the figures that follow.

Figure 10.6 shows two input events related to an output event through an OR gate. It is read: "The undesired event can be caused *either* by event A *or* by event B, or both." Alternately, one can say that either event A or event B alone will produce the UE. For example, if a passing grade in a college course requires both a term paper and a C on the final exam, the FTA would show that failure to receive a passing grade (the UE) can be caused either by failure to submit a term paper *or* by failure to earn a C on the final exam, or both. In other words, the logic of events on the fault tree is the opposite of the logic relationships of events in a success analysis.

Figure 10.7 shows two input events related to an output event through an AND gate, using the same events as in Figure 10.6, but based on a different success analysis. It reads: "The undesired event can be caused *only* if failure events A *and* B *both* occur; that is, failure events A and B must coexist to produce the UE." For example, if a student has two options for earning a passing grade—either by writing a term paper or by receiving a C on the final exam—the FTA would

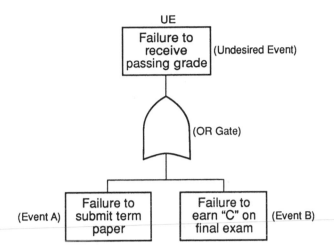

Figure 10.6. Illustration of an OR Gate
NOTE: The undesired event (UE) could be caused by either Event A or Event B if both requirements are mandatory.

read: "Failure to receive a passing grade can occur only if the student fails to submit a term paper *and* fails to earn a C on the final exam."
To summarize:

1. If two or more events are required to achieve success, then the failure of either one of them will cause failure of the objective—shown by an OR gate on the fault tree.
2. If a person can achieve success by choosing one of two or more options, then all of the options would have to fail to cause failure of the objective—shown by an AND gate.

In social and behavioral systems, the AND relationship most commonly occurs when backup systems or alternative paths to success are incorporated in the design (success map) of the system. That is, if a program allows for two or more alternate paths to reach an objective, then failure to reach the objective should occur only if all paths fail. On the other hand, if the program provides no alternatives or backup systems, then the failure of any event in the system would logically lead to the failure of the principal objective. The latter situation is indicated by an OR gate connecting two or more events at each level.

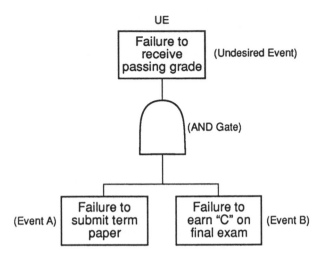

Figure 10.7. Illustration of an AND Gate

NOTE: The undesired event (UE) could occur only if both Event A and Event B occur, if the events are alternative options.

Also, if a fault tree branch contains only OR gates down to the lowest level, then any event on that branch could cause the failure of the UE.

Generating Input Events to the Tree

Fault trees of complex systems often have several hundred events, all related through logic gates. The generation of inputs at each level continues until the causal factors are sufficiently delineated to provide the basis for later recommendations regarding priority of needs.

As noted earlier, events on the tree may be derived from a success map. When planning or mapping for success, one usually thinks from a beginning point to an end point or goal sometime in the future. When analyzing for potential failures, one begins at the end and works backward through the system, either in time or in space.

Another useful method for generating events is systematically to ask questions regarding possible *input, processing,* and *output failures* for each event in turn. That is, failures of a given component or subsystem might be attributable to (a) failures of input from another part of the system or from outside the system, (b) failures of processing within the component or subsystem, or (c) failures of output to another part of the system. Inputs may be internal or external to the system, but the closer the inputs in time or space to the event being analyzed, the more powerful the analysis. If internal failures are due to external events, they will usually appear at the points of interface between the system and its environment. It should be noted that when a fault tree is systematically developed from the top down, a potential failure event may occur in more than one branch of the tree. The occurrence of redundant events in different parts of the tree is important. It indicates that the particular event or potential occurrence can have serious consequences for the success of the program or is a significant contributor to the existence or maintenance of the need.

Illustrations of Success and Failure Analysis

These two cases illustrate the use of both success and failure analysis for two projects designed to meet critical needs. In the first example, even without a full-scale FTA, the fault tree logic showed its predictive value by identifying potentially serious problems that did occur.

A two-county consortium, with the help of a major university, received a grant to provide specialized counseling and vocational services to young adults with learning disabilities. The need for such a program was critical and had been amply demonstrated. The project was funded for less than 2 years, but 6 months elapsed before a director and staff could be hired. At that time, a consultant was retained to work with core staff members responsible for the project to do a predictive analysis based on FTA principles. In a series of meetings over a 3-day period, the consultant helped the staff translate their narrative descriptions of the project into clear success maps that showed the steps necessary to ensure the success of the project.

Although inadequate resources precluded doing a complete FTA, careful examination of the success map revealed several factors that might lead to failure of the project. They included short time lines for completion of design elements and installation of the program, almost no alternatives or backup systems, and the possibility of failures occurring from interaction of the project with outside systems, such as the funding agency and community groups. The staff also divided potential failures into three categories: those events completely under project control, those partially under control, and those completely outside of project control. The consultant worked with the staff to identify steps they might take to redesign components with high likelihood of failure and to figure out ways of minimizing failures that might occur due to factors beyond their control.

Unfortunately, pressures of time and inadequate numbers of staff combined to frustrate much of the redesign effort. At the end of the project, it was found that several major predicted failures, mainly related to factors outside project control, had in fact occurred. By doggedly pursuing the "success" path outlined, and largely ignoring potential failures, the project failed to meet its objectives and further funding was withdrawn.

The following illustrates how a success map and a qualitative FTA furnish the basis for project redesign.

A nationwide moving company decided to develop a wellness program for its employees designed to prevent or reduce back injuries and related problems. The company's objective was that 90% of the employees in each of its regions would enroll in the program and engage regularly in one or more options for physical therapy, and that 70% of those enrolled would report major satisfaction with the program after 1 year. The plan for the program, as well as success and failure analyses, was developed by a panel composed of company administrators, representatives of the employees and their labor organizations, and appropriate health professionals.

Figure 10.8 depicts a rudimentary success map for the program, with two concurrent flows of events. The company must design the wellness program and must also persuade 90% of its employees to enroll. The design included two *mandated* features in the wellness program: a set of diagnostic options and a set of physical therapy options. The program also provided two *alternatives* by which employees may engage in the program: the company would either install facilities on site at its plants or provide funds for employees to join a health club.

The flow of events from left to right indicates that they occurred in that order. Thus, in the bottom flow, the company first developed an

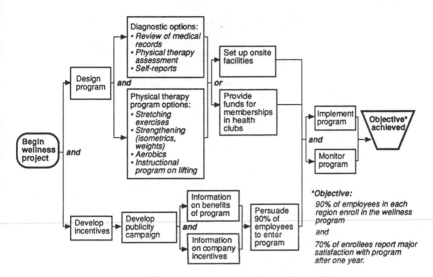

Figure 10.8. Rudimentary Success Map for a Program Designed to Reduce the Back Problems of Employees of a Nationwide Moving Company

incentive plan, then publicized it, and then persuaded employees to enroll. All of the events in both the program design and incentive plans lead into the final phase of implementing and monitoring the program.

In the full plan, there would be many more events in the success map, with indications of time lines, details of design and implementation, identity of those responsible for development or management of the main components, contractual arrangements, and the like.

Figure 10.9 shows an example of a fault tree branch for the program depicted in Figure 10.8, using an OR gate. The UE (failure of the company to achieve the objectives of the wellness program) could be caused by any one or more of three major failures: failure of the program itself, failure of enrollment, or failure of the satisfaction criterion. The logic thus indicates that there are many potential opportunities for failure of the program to reach its objectives.

Figure 10.10 illustrates a different situation, as well as the use of the AND gate. We saw in Figure 10.8 that the program furnished four options for physical therapy. Because the employee could choose any one of them, the wellness goal would fail to be reached *only* if 90% of

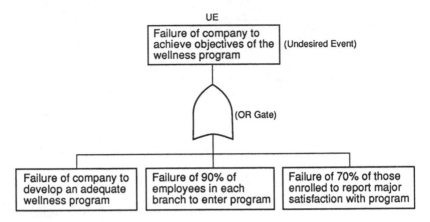

Figure 10.9. Rudimentary Fault Tree Branch Using an OR Gate

NOTE: Derived from events on the success map, Figure 10.8.

the employees failed to choose *any* option. The tree can be read: Failure of an individual to achieve the wellness goal through the physical therapy program would occur only through the *coexistence of all four* specified failures. The existence of the AND gate relationship shows a strong feature of the program.

Now look at the success map (Figure 10.8) in relation to Figure 10.9 and Figure 10.10. The presence of mostly OR gates reflects greater rigidity in the success map and few alternatives available for reaching the goal. Situations that reveal many AND gate relationships are always preferable because they indicate the presence of multiple pathways to a goal. Thus, providing alternatives in the success plan reduces the probability of failure to reach an objective.

Figure 10.11 depicts two branches and four levels of a fault tree of the moving company's new program, based mainly on the success map of Figure 10.8. The OR gate at the top indicates that the program could fail to attain its goal *either* because the program itself fails to reduce back problems *or* because 90% of the employees fail to enroll in the program. Each of those two branches is further developed (analyzed), and each of the events (in rectangles) at the bottom of each branch could have been analyzed further for input causes. During the discussion of potential sources of failure, the FTA team also identified outcome indicators for verifying program success and continuing dimensions of need, in addition to the specification of the two major

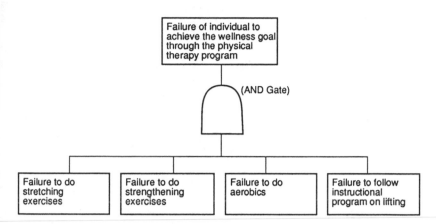

Figure 10.10. Rudimentary Fault Tree Branch Using an AND Gate
NOTE: Derived from events on the success map, Figure 10.8.

objectives. Some indicators were reductions in injuries and days lost due to injuries, lower medical costs and workmen's compensation rates, improved morale, higher motivation (the company cares about its employees), fewer related medical problems, general improvement in wellness, and a greater individual sense of well-being. Any of those indicators could have appeared on the success map as well as on the fault tree.

As noted earlier, most of the events in the fault tree are related through OR gates—that is, the system design offers few alternatives to achieve the goal. A good rule of thumb is: The more AND gates that occur in the tree (because of features in the success map or of inferences that can be drawn from how the program might work), the greater the likelihood of success.

Also note that certain events at the bottom of the tree, but on different branches, are related to each other. At the fourth level on the left branch, the two inputs to the AND gate not only are an integral part of the program design but also contribute an incentive—that is, employees would not have to provide their own funds for the exercise or therapy program. That feature is related to the incentive section on the right-hand branch, although it is not explicitly shown. It may be that employees do not consider the availability of facilities an adequate incentive to join the program. If there is a high likelihood that

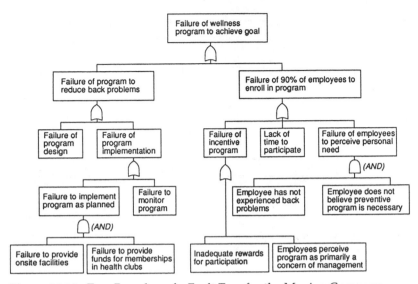

Figure 10.11. Two Branches of a Fault Tree for the Moving Company Wellness Program

NOTE: Events based on the success map, Figure 10.8.

failures related to incentives might occur, the redundancy of input events signals that the program designers should consider adding factors that will enhance the probability of success of the program. Even from a rudimentary analysis, the fault tree shows that motivation and incentives will be important for the successful implementation of the new program, particularly for employees who see no need for a preventive program for themselves.

It might appear from these examples that failure analysis is simply the mirror image of success analysis. This is somewhat true, in that the likelihood of a UE occurring is reduced by changing the events identified in key paths that potentially lead to failure. Thus, when a project is still in the design stage (as in the moving company example), the planner has the opportunity to enhance the potential for program success and increase the probability that the system will meet client needs.

But note also that the failure analysis shown in Figure 10.11 identified factors that did not appear on the success map—for example, the employee has not yet experienced back problems or lacks time to participate. Data from analysis of complex systems reveal that FTA gives perspectives that go beyond the simple inversion of success to failure analysis. In performing a failure analysis, one is not limited to the events portrayed in the success map. In fact, FTA often generates causal events that are not readily apparent from a success analysis. It raises questions about the system, program, project, or area of need that usually fail to arise in success planning alone, or in the stages of NA that precede the causal analysis.

Some basic principles to remember about qualitative FTA:

- A success map is your plan for getting from the beginning of a program or project to the end or objective.
- A fault tree helps predict how you could fail to reach an objective.
- The UE may be based on the failure of the major objective or it may be related to some other factor in the system (perhaps derived from the success analysis). Analyses may be made for more than one UE.
- The more backup systems or alternative paths in the success map, the greater the likelihood of success.
- Failures can occur anywhere within the system, and events outside the system can cause failures within the system.
- Important potential problem areas often occur at the boundaries (interfaces) between subsystems, or between the system/project and an external system. The more that the success of a venture depends on inputs or cooperation from people outside the system, the more likely that critical failures will occur due to lack of attention to the linkages at the interfaces.
- Much useful information can be generated by sorting potential critical failures into three groups: those events completely within the control of the manager/project staff, those partially within control, and those entirely outside such control. In the first two instances, it may be possible to redesign the success plan or to build in a monitor. In the last, it is important to anticipate the conditions under which the external effect might occur and build in monitors or contingency plans.

In the foregoing section on qualitative analysis, we have focused mainly on how FTA can be used to anticipate events in the future or the potential failure of a new system. FTA has also been used extensively to analyze failures that have already occurred, such as the meltdown in the nuclear facility at Three Mile Island. In the context of NA, a qualitative fault tree could be constructed to analyze the contributing factors to a present critical, unmet need, using the same techniques of failure events and logic gates. The information for the tree would come from a group of key informants who could find actual data to validate their perceptions.

For example, a school district might want to know why the voters have failed to approve a bond issue for much-needed repairs and maintenance on school buildings for 4 years in a row. A group of stakeholders that includes school administrators, parents of students, citizens with no children in the schools, and experts on public involvement could give inputs to the FTA. Analysis might reveal strategic paths with a high probability of leading to the failure of the bond issue—and those events would be the ones to focus on before the next election.

QUANTITATIVE ANALYSIS

A full FTA uses quantitative analyses to derive strategic paths in order of criticality—that is, it assigns estimates of various kinds to each event on the tree, computes probabilities for each path or sequence of events, and then traces the sequence of events that have the highest probability of contributing to the UE or to the failure of the objective. In complex hardware systems, values are assigned to each event based on actual data, such as failure rates of components. In social systems, such as education, service agencies, and business, people knowledgeable about the system make expert judgments about each event's contribution to the event above it in the tree. Research has shown that such judgments have high validity.

It is beyond the scope of this book to explain how to derive strategic paths. In brief, individuals on FTA teams assign ratings of importance, frequency of occurrence, and difficulty of rectification of the failure to events on the tree. These estimates are combined mathematically using Boolean formulas, with values attributed to the different types of logic gates, resulting in a probability estimate assigned to each event (Stephens, 1972). The analyst highlights those sequences of events with the highest probabilities to indicate paths of events in the order of their potential contribution to the major UE.[3] The magnitude of the probability estimates is not crucial. When FTA is used to determine causal factors for NA purposes, the rank ordering of strategic paths is sufficient to supply a rational basis for determining priorities of need, regardless of the probability of occurrence of any of the causal sequences.

An important feature of FTA is that any or all events depicted *could* happen, given certain conditions and relationships. In an ideal situation and if the system or program functions perfectly, none of the potential failures will occur. But in the real, imperfect world, perfection rarely occurs. The occurrence of a failure event anywhere in the tree contributes in some way to the potential for occurrence of the top UE. On the other hand, following the Pareto principle, it is common to find that only a few key events or strategic paths contribute to the highest likelihood of the failure of the top UE.

The establishment of priorities of failure event sequences is a function of many factors. Fault trees relate every event in a system to every other event, so that the analysis behaves more like a network than a simple cause-effect sequence. Judgments of frequency and importance are independent of each other. An event of high frequency but low importance will probably contribute little to the occurrence of a major UE, whereas an event of high importance but low frequency can have serious consequences if it does happen.

In well-designed systems of the kind to which FTA was originally applied, such as aerospace systems, the probability of a catastrophic failure is very low—although when one does occur, it has disastrous consequences. In social systems, however, serious failures have a much higher likelihood of occurrence, and even those less serious, if the frequency rate is high, can have undesirable cumulative effects.

USING FTA TO ENHANCE THE LIKELIHOOD OF SUCCESS IN MEETING NEEDS

Even without quantifying the events on a tree in order to derive strategic paths, the needs assessor and FTA team get much important information from a qualitative analysis alone, as noted earlier. In addition, the NAC can inspect the completed fault tree and ask such questions as these:

- Are there any AND gates? If there are few or none, can the success plan be altered to provide backup systems, alternatives, or offsetting strategies?
- Are some events depicted that expert judgment indicates could be very critical in contributing to the overall UE? If so, highlight those. If the

same or similar highlighted events or paths occur in more than one branch of the tree, are they related to each other? Redundant events magnify the criticality of potential failures manyfold.

- Are there any events that might occur because of the effect from external sources, such as regulatory agencies or some environmental hazard? Are offsetting strategies available?
- What about the timing of a potential event? If a student fails a required course in the last quarter of the senior year, the event is much more critical than if it occurred a year earlier. The "difficulty of rectification" factor increases in magnitude.
- Did you choose the right UE?

The following case illustrates the importance of carefully defining the UE to enhance the probability of success of the mission.

A multiyear project designed to improve specific listening skills in elementary school children included an FTA on the UE: "Failure of the students in the experimental group to make significantly greater improvement in [specified] listening skills than the control group." The project met its stated goal but was refused funding for national dissemination because the students did not also demonstrate sig- nificantly improved *reading ability*—a requirement that was impor- tant to the state department of education that monitored the project but not to the federal agency that granted the funds. If the UE had been worded to reflect the concerns of external agencies, the proj- ect might have included some direct instruction in how students could transfer the newly acquired, specialized auditory skills to the visual act of reading. (Nevertheless, because of their quality, the program materials continued to be in demand for many years, far beyond the geographic area of the original project.)

Sometimes, however, the best success and failure analyses in the world cannot rescue a project. Murphy's Law—"anything that can go wrong will"—was operating in the interagency NA described in Chapter 3. Although the project identified priorities of critical needs and made specific recommendations for joint interagency action (the whole project underwent an extensive FTA), the long-term aspects of the collaboration failed due to factors outside of the control of the project or the agencies involved. The school district lost its accredita- tion and fired the superintendent; the two most supportive city council members were recalled; decreased tax revenues for one of the county offices led to the dismissal of a key staff member, an expert on social indicators; and policies for the city and school district that affected the NA were set by the chief of police, who was not officially involved in the NA but turned out to be the unofficial power broker of the city. Even though the project met the major goals of the NA, the findings failed to be used as planned.

The more complex the project, or the more that the NA and its subsequent implementation depend on political or other factors beyond the project's control, the greater the probability of failure. On the whole, however, experience has proved that appropriate causal analyses, when tied to project redesign, close monitoring, or both, do increase the likelihood of success. We emphasize Phase 3 of NA because the most common failure is in the area of use—which should be a major focus of any failure avoidance analysis.

Applications of Causal Analysis

FTA and other kinds of causal analysis provide an important bridge from identification of needs to the development of solutions. Without causal analysis, it is all too easy to settle for solutions or programs that do not really meet the need. True, it is often necessary to take steps to ameliorate a social problem without waiting to address the underlying causes. For example, advocates of stricter regulations on possession of handguns and assault weapons to curb violence assert that we cannot wait until the root causes of violence—poverty, unemployment, the drug culture, breakup of the family—are solved.

Nevertheless, in most NAs, it is important to go beyond symptoms of need to causes or contributing factors, as the following examples show:

A. The need for adequate and affordable child care services and facilities was apparent in a small city with a high proportion of low-income families headed by a single parent or in which both parents worked. Before undertaking an FTA, the NA team set up some criteria for an ideal situation: that there should be options available for parents who worked early morning or evening hours, that child care should be available for school-age children before and after school, and so on. In this case, a success map was not appropriate.

For some time, leaders in the community had been advocating the establishment of a licensed child care center. The FTA, however, showed that the most critical need was for evening and early morning child care, when centers were not normally open. Another strategic path identified barriers that prevented parents from arranging their work schedules to take advantage of child care at times when it was available. The predisposition of child care center advocates to consider only one solution had prevented them from considering other measures that might more readily meet the actual needs.

B. An employment FTA identified factors in the local school system and local industry that could be improved through cooperative action in a three-way partnership—the schools, the city government, and an existing industry-education council. This possibility had previously been unrecognized.

C. A task force of teachers, students, and administrators in a suburban high school was working to refine goals and identify needs, one of which was related to a high incidence of single-period absences from class. The problem had reached alarming proportions. Jumping from the problem to solutions, the task force recommended stronger discipline and various punishments for unexcused class absences. A couple of sessions of causal analysis with the task force, however, showed that the absences were only one symptom of a complex set of student needs and that the proposed "get-tough" policy was unlikely to meet the needs, even if it temporarily reduced the absences. The causal analysis led to consideration of alternatives that were more likely to solve the problem in the long run.

ADVANTAGES AND DISADVANTAGES OF FTA

Advantages. FTA is a powerful technique for analyzing contributing factors to present or future needs as well as anticipating causes that might arise to frustrate the successful attainment of a goal. When linked with success analysis, FTA plays an important role in both failure avoidance and the enhancement of success. Both success maps and fault trees can be displayed to decision-making groups to stimulate their thinking about use of NA data and to inspire creative approaches to meeting critical needs. FTA is also very useful for designing and managing the NA itself (see next section). The technology has a long history of successful application in such diverse fields as education, health and social services, environmental pollution, epidemiologic studies, industrial operations, and government departments.

Disadvantages. Developing the logic diagrams requires more technical skill and time than either fishboning or CCA. Whereas fishboning takes only 1 to 2 hours, and CCA from one half of a day to 1 day, FTA may take several days. In addition, software for deriving strategic path analyses is not in the public domain, although it is available to interested clients.[4]

Use of Causal Analysis in Managing and Evaluating the Needs Assessment

Causal analysis, and particularly FTA, is highly useful for designing and managing the NA itself (in Phase 2) and as a basis for evaluating the effort (in Phase 3). If the scope of the NA is large, we recommend that the needs assessor and NAC produce a fairly detailed success map of the steps required to complete it. The success map should set out a clear and measurable goal (how you will know that the NA is successful), show the sequence of events that must occur to reach the goal, indicate what activities or events must occur in a series and which ones are concurrent or have alternatives, and design backup systems (e.g., phone calls following a mailed survey to raise the response rate).

The success map can be used to monitor the project by displaying time lines on a parallel line above the map, as well as noting special resources needed at appropriate points below the map. Both professional and support staff responsible for implementing a new project enjoy working with the success map and checking off activities as they are completed.

Before the main NA begins (usually at the end of Phase 1), the NAC can review the success map for potential failure events and may construct a few levels of a fault tree. If it is obvious that the tree consists mostly of OR gates, the NAC can inspect the success map to see where backups or alternate routes can be provided and redesign the NA plan to incorporate the changes. If few or no alternatives are possible, we advise that the needs assessor provide careful monitoring of the NA throughout Phases 2 and 3.

In Phase 3, the evaluation report can refer briefly to the designated goal(s) of the NA, the principal events that were intended for success of the project, and the extent to which those events occurred as planned. If parts of the NA were unsuccessful, the needs assessor has information from both the success map and the causal analyses to document the reasons.

Application of Success and Failure Analysis to a Complex Project

A regional laboratory for educational research and development was charged with developing a program to meet a critical need in career education, with funding from the National Institute of Education (NIE). The mission statement was: "To develop a model of employer-based career education (EBCE) that will demonstrate the potential of improving the individual's interaction with the economic sector—for example, selection, entry, advancement, and satisfaction in a career." This was a multiyear, complex project with many components in design and field testing.

Criteria for the program were that the model demonstrate sound educational design, that it achieve stabilization and furnish documentation for replicability, and that it demonstrate *transportability*—the potential for usefulness in other venues.

Constraints on the project were (a) to follow the guidelines of the NIE; (b) to reduce the cost of the program, after pilot-testing, to $2,500 per pupil, or show how it can be done by a specified date; and (c) to operate in cooperation with specified school districts and with the economic sector of the same area during a particular fiscal year.

Decision makers involved were NIE consultants and personnel from the regional research and development laboratory, the state department of education, local school districts that were pilot-testing the program, and the private sector.

The analysis began with construction of a detailed success map of the entire project, showing the many events that had to occur from the project's inception to completion. Entries for the map were derived from inspection of the narrative project application and extensive interviews with the project director and key staff members. From the mission statement and the success map, a fault tree of several hundred events was constructed.

The UE could have been, "Failure to develop and demonstrate a successful EBCE model." Instead, it was felt that even if the model were successful, the ultimate goal was replicability and transportability. Therefore, the major UE chosen was, "Laboratory fails to provide information to educational decision makers regarding future viability of the EBCE model to achieve its mission." The top branches of the tree were "failure of management to receive information regarding viability," "failure of management to document information adequately," or "failure of management to communicate information adequately to decision makers." The three branches represented input, processing, and output failures, respectively. Failures associated with the design or implementation of the model itself occurred in later, lower stages of the fault tree. In other words, management could fail to receive, document, or communicate the adequacy of the EBCE model because of failures in the model itself. If the project had not been charged with demonstrating transportability and convincing other decision makers of the EBCE model excellence, the tree could have been devoted solely to analyzing possible failures of the EBCE model. The fault tree did highlight potential failures from external sources, which the project was able to avoid through some redesign and offsetting strategies.

SUMMARY

Causal analysis can be used either to identify unrecognized needs or to analyze contributing factors to known needs as well as presumed barriers to meeting those needs. This chapter describes three kinds of causal analysis and illustrates their applications: fishboning, cause and consequence analysis (CCA), and fault tree analysis (FTA). The chapter discusses the relationship between success and failure analyses and recommends using a success map combined with FTA as a predictive device when designing and managing the NA itself and to ensure use in Phase 3.

Notes

1. We use the term *system* here in the context of assessing needs for program planning or evaluation—not of diagnosing needs of individuals per se. Newer approaches to assessing needs of individuals and families, however—such as medical, economic, or social—do take the systems approach. The individual or the family is regarded as a complex system that also interacts with other people and the environment in a system relationship.

2. The contact in the United States for Ishikawa's materials is UNIPUB, One Water Street, White Plains, NY 10601.

3. For more information on strategic path analysis and risk assessment, contact Dr. Kent Stephens, President, CEO Sciences, P.O. Box 950, Springville, UT 84663, phone: 801-489-0078, FAX: 801-489-0079. Stephens has developed related methodologies such as Success Enhancement Evaluation (SEE), Success Enhancement Analysis (SEA), and Risk Identification Evaluation and Minimization (RIEM), all applicable to NA.

4. Sage Analytics International is a company that specializes in methods of failure avoidance using FTA (their term is *Sage Analysis*) in NA, focusing on affordability of the technology for both education and the corporate sector. It is particularly interested in NAs of K-12 school systems. The company has proprietary software designed to determine strategic paths but offers training that enables its clients to use the software. For information, contact Dr. Joseph Petterle, President, 2150 River Plain Drive, Suite 105, Sacramento, CA 95833, phone: 800-582-4134, FAX: 916-648-1152.

Postscript

Before you, the needs assessor, close the book, we would like to sit down and have a little chat. We've covered a lot of ground, and now we want to consider what it all adds up to.

As we collaborated on this guide, endeavoring to keep you in mind, we found that our thinking changed over the months of planning and writing. Ideas that seemed clear in the conceptual stage turned out to need a lot of explanation and, often, drastic revisions. Part of this postscript will serve as a reminder of those ideas that we feel are essential for successful NAs.

We have drawn on our years of experience with NA to suggest some guidelines for converting theory to practice. This postscript is not so much a road map as a commentary on hazards and roadside attractions. We cannot anticipate every bump in the road, but we can identify where major detours and hangups en route are likely to occur. We hope that our insights will make the NA trip more fun, more exciting, less stressful, and more enjoyable.

Highlights and Insights

BALANCE: WALKING THE NA TIGHTROPE

We didn't emphasize it much, but you can get overloaded with work in the NA process, and systems can get overloaded with information. Somehow, you must strike a balance between gathering too much information and gathering too little—between supplying mounds of data in a comprehensive NA and providing only the minimum of information necessary for making decisions in a limited area. At times you may have to make practical tradeoffs—using fewer data sources, reducing sample size, and so on, to get the job done. We have had to do it in the past and have sometimes felt uncomfortable. Be stoic, relax—balance and tradeoffs are part of the real world of NA.

A major problem with large-scale NAs in the past has been burnout of all concerned. We have known communities that spent so much time achieving a consensus on goals that there was no energy left for actually assessing the needs related to those goals. More than one city has engaged in a 2- or 3-year comprehensive NA, only to put the report on the shelf without using the results, because everyone was tired of the whole thing.

LEVEL 1 NEEDS ARE IT!

In a review of hundreds of NAs that took place from 1981 to 1993, Witkin (1994) found that nearly 55% were narrowly targeted at training needs of service providers (Level 2) or preferences for solutions or delivery systems (Level 3). Where were the needs of the service recipients or clients for whom organizations and agencies exist? We cannot always assume that focusing on training or delivery systems will fill the needs at Level 1. Sometimes organizations and agencies have a vested interest in preserving and extending existing services when other types of services or programs would be more appropriate if Level 1 needs were reanalyzed.

We encourage you to stop periodically during the NA process, step back from it, and examine whether the needs at Level 1 are still of prime importance.

VALUES, VALUES EVERYWHERE

Kaufman (1992) has repeatedly stressed the importance of aligning NA with societal values and goals. But sometimes an NA brings to light competing or conflicting values, on occasion leading to conflict and confrontation. The "what should be" dimension of the discrepancy definition of needs is often an expression of strongly held values and beliefs from which the exponents do not want to back down.

You will be challenged to create a positive and open atmosphere for discussing values, especially when you use highly interactive group techniques. Consider the use of games, scenarios, and future-oriented methods to free the creative energy in the group, and establish a win-win atmosphere. The hints we have furnished on leadership of groups, listening, and consensus formation should also assist you when considering values.

THE PLANNING GRIDLOCK (INERTIA) AND THE "P" WORD—POLITICS

So you did all the NA work and nothing happened? What could have gone wrong?

At the core of NA is the likelihood of change, and the allocation of resources to one set of needs to the (probable) disadvantage of another. Change requires new foci, thought processes, and ways of interacting with others. There may be an uncomfortable degree of upheaval, with change being perceived as harmful. Resistance to change can lead to inertia regarding participation in the NA and a half-hearted commitment to new priorities and programs. The work on action plans may be tabled or sent to committees that drag on endlessly, until enthusiasm for the effort wanes.

As you try to translate priorities of need into action plans, you may feel yourself drowning in the organizational, community, or governmental cauldron of politics. Two factors operate here. Either there are cries of pain as precious resources are switched from one area of need to another, or someone with political clout insists on pushing through a pet project, regardless of the fact that the NA showed it would be irrelevant in meeting the need. One of us helped a community study its recreational needs. Although the NA showed that the top priority was for a well-equipped playground and baseball diamond for young people, the city council decided to build a community swimming pool, which rated very low on the NA.

Our current national debates over the provision of health care, the funding and nature of public education, and the provision of services to the homeless all bear witness to the relationship between needs and politics at many levels.

There are strategies you can use. If larger, more sweeping changes will encounter resistance, start small. Break a large program into smaller, more easily accepted parts. Success from small changes establishes a positive climate for subsequent larger changes and a willingness to examine needs in the future. But be warned. Installing changes piecemeal may result in the needs being inadequately met, and you may lose momentum for more important initiatives in the future.

Another strategy is to involve a cross-section of concerned stakeholders, key administrators, and decision makers in all phases of the NA process. Involvement should be meaningful and frequent, especially at key points in the life of the NA. Active involvement develops both an understanding of and a sense of ownership in the NA and the decisions regarding priorities. It also is the basis for commitment to and support of programs designed to alleviate needs. Both informal mechanisms (hallway conversations, phone calls, short status memos) and formal ones (scheduled meetings, full status reports) should be used.

Finally, make sure that stakeholders do not feel that there are hidden agendas. In setting up the NA plans, judiciously point out that the study may lead to new priorities, improved programs, or altogether different programs or services than those now in place, with potential reallocation of resources or the search for new ones. Reiterate the point as needed throughout the NA. This broad-based participation should go far to counteract the possibility of decisions being made on the basis of purely political factors. If possible, enlist the cooperation of power brokers who wield influence behind the scenes.

THE LONELY, ISOLATED NA

If you are engaged in a comprehensive NA that takes several months to complete, you may develop tunnel vision. The NA occupies your entire field. It may become separated from other organizational activities and decision making.

We discourage this mind-set. NA is integral to program planning and implementation, as well as program evaluation and accountability. NA clarifies the nature of underlying problems and helps establish criteria for selecting solution strategies. An in-depth NA using the three-phase model creates an imperative for action, galvanizes the energy of the organization, and serves as a catalyst for improvement and organizational renewal. Keep in mind the relation of the NA to the context and the rest of the organization's activities.

MULTIPLE DATA SOURCES—HELP OR HINDRANCE?

Chapter 5 contains an example in which data from one source (records of underutilization of a mental health facility) were not sufficient for understanding the nature of a need.

Only when qualitative observations were added did a clearer picture of the need emerge.

There is some research to support the claim that you should use more than one method for identifying and analyzing needs. But there are problems. Multiple methods add time and costs to the NA, and the results may be contradictory and interpretation difficult. A written survey may reveal priorities of needs quite different from the results of focus group interviews or a Delphi process.

Despite such problems, we do recommend that you use more than one data source or method, particularly for regional or large-scale NAs with adequate funding, and that you balance quantitative methods with qualitative ones. Data from any single method (surveys, interviews, focus groups, or analysis of existing records) are generally insufficient to provide an adequate basis for understanding needs and making decisions on priorities.

With smaller NAs and fewer resources, think of inexpensive ways to collect different types of data. If existing records were the primary source for an NA of library services, the information could be easily supplemented by making some observations on site; interviewing a few longtime as well as new patrons of the library; and interviewing the director and some librarians.

Combining qualitative with quantitative data not only provides what navigators term *triangulation* to focus better on the nature of the needs but also provides a basis for brief anecdotes that you could include in your final report to decision makers, putting a human face on the abstract collection of data, and facilitating better decisions.

RIGID RULES DON'T WORK; A GENERAL NA MODEL DOES

NA is an applied methodology—it is far from an exact science. We have based our three-phase model and recommendations for data-gathering tools on what we have found that works—not in terms of some abstract theory, but because those procedures have consistently demonstrated the most likelihood of furnishing reliable and useful information about needs and their contributing factors.

So, as we said in Chapter 2, *start from where you are* and choose the options that make the most sense in the light of what the organization has already done and what decisions you want to make on the basis of the NA. Keep your eye on the ball. Why are you undertaking the NA? How does it fit in with organizational or agency planning or evaluation? Once you have identified major discrepancies (the needs) and their contributing factors, what then? The three-phase model is a guide, within which you have considerable scope for creative approaches to achieve the ends desired.

Does this mean that anything goes? Not at all. Some methods are better than others, and throughout the book we have pointed out the advantages and disadvantages of each and their applications in context.

What Does the
Future Hold for Needs Assessment?

We are enthusiastic about the future of NA. It represents a rational way of approaching the identification and analysis of complex needs that emerge in rapidly changing societies such as ours. Although we have focused on NA in the United States, reports from Canada, the United Kingdom, and many other countries indicate that the use of NA is on the rise. But what will it look like?

SOCIAL TRANSFORMATION

In the November 1994 issue of *Atlantic Monthly*, Peter F. Drucker surveyed the epoch that began early in this century and described the present age as one of "social transformation," with far-reaching consequences for the future. His thesis is that since World War I, the social structure of the United States has changed radically, but that the character and magnitude of change have gone almost unnoticed. Among the major transformations were the rise and fall of the blue-collar worker, the rise of the knowledge worker, and the emerging knowledge society, which puts a premium on lifelong learning and on psychological and intellectual skills that are not readily transferable from an industrial setting.

The rise of a knowledge society, displacing an industrial society, has profound implications for education, employment of all kinds, human services, and technology, and may lead to new kinds of class conflict. Drucker asserts that no other society in history has faced these challenges, but that equally, there are new opportunities previously unknown.

How does NA fit into this? In at least two ways: First, more than ever, NA should not only seek to identify present needs but also anticipate future needs in the context of social transformation. Even though we do not know the exact shape of the future, there are enough clues in the present to indicate the probable directions of change. And second, as the nature of employment and of job and career opportunities alters, you will probably encounter even more clashes of values over priorities and allocation of resources than before. The NA process, however, with its emphasis on a broad base of stakeholder involvement, can furnish an important milieu for debating values, concerns, and priorities of need.

We have urged you many times to focus first on the assessment of need before jumping to solutions. In the coming decades, that advice will be even more important, as different groups of stakeholders insist on their favorite solutions to complex problems—whether it be voucher systems for public education, "three strikes and you're out" for repeat criminal offenders, or refusing social services to both legal and illegal immigrants.

TECHNOLOGY TO THE FOREFRONT

The computer revolution, changes in potential for data analysis, and the escalation in electronic communication channels and technology hold promise for NA. The new technologies should facilitate the rapid gathering and analysis of information from disparate groups of stakeholders.

On the cutting edge of technology are NA by groups communicating electronically, new strategies for concept mapping, and analysis of Delphi responses. Accessing census and other large databases and using geographical mapping will help you better understand location and pattern of needs. Technology is also making it more feasible to install management information systems in which data can be entered to furnish a basis for ongoing or cyclical NAs, as well as to spot trends and signal important changes in needs or the emergence of new ones. But the systems will not work unless managers give careful thought to the kinds of indicators that are necessary to define both present and future areas of need. Qualitative data will be as important as quantitative for these purposes.

Although technology alone will not ensure valid NAs, we recommend that you watch the developments and adapt the most useful tools to your needs.

HELP! MORE RESEARCH IS NEEDED

There has been very little empirical research on NA. A few recent studies compare different methods of data gathering, of analyzing survey data, and of validating methods of estimating need for services. Many more such comparative studies are needed, as well as syntheses of different research efforts. We also lack research on certain technical questions about designing and analyzing survey questionnaires for NA (rather than for general opinion polling), including whether different scaling options really yield different priorities.

Additional questions of interest are, What are the practical consequences of using different models of NA? What kinds of effects do NAs have on organizations and on target groups? Do organizations use the results of internal NAs differently from those conducted by third-party consultants? Is it possible to find the "real" needs—to validate people's perceptions of their own or others' needs through some objective means? What are the consequences when large-scale programs to alleviate needs are instituted without adequate assessment, especially in regard to analysis of causal factors? The stronger the research base, the more likely that more effective NA practices will arise in the future.

TRAINING IN NA—THE OPPORTUNITY

In a national study of the preparation of professional evaluators, Altschuld, Engle, Cullen, Kim, and Macce (1994) found few evaluation courses devoted solely to preparing students to conduct NAs. Furthermore, there may be only a small number of NA courses taught in fields other than evaluation, such as program planning. We hope that this situation will change. We have had a great deal of satisfaction and success in teaching about NA, with students coming from health and allied health fields, all areas of education, agriculture, social work, public policy and administration, business schools, training and development, and organizational development. Obviously there is an interest that cuts across disciplines, and we hope to see many more training opportunities in the future.

COLLABORATIVE NAs—THE WAVE OF THE FUTURE?

As the scope of problems increases and resources either remain the same or diminish, collaborative and interagency NAs would seem to make good sense. The question is how to weigh the needs of individuals and groups whose problems do not fall into neat compartments that match the boundaries of schools or agencies or municipalities against the natural desire of educators, human service workers, and city councils to protect their turf. Many needs are too complex for single organizations to deal with and require collaborative effort both for assessment and for devising solution strategies.

Will we be able to cede "territorial" claims and some control over our own domains in order to work cooperatively in assessing needs and seeking resolution? The imperative is there. Will we seize the initiative?

A FINAL NOTE

You, as an individual needs assessor, may not be able to answer the questions raised in this postscript. But if our dialogue has stimulated your thinking about these issues, we will have fulfilled one of our main goals. After you have had a chance to work with the concepts and methods in this book, we invite you to continue the dialogue from your own point of view. We welcome your feedback.

References

Alteck, P. L., & Settle, R. B. (1985). *The survey research handbook*. Homewood, IL: Irwin.

Altschuld, J. W., Engle, M., Cullen, C., Kim, L., & Macce, B. R. (1994). The 1994 directory of evaluation training programs. *New Directions in Program Evaluation, 62*, 71-94.

Altschuld, J. W., & Thomas, P. M. (1991). Considerations in the application of a modified scree test for Delphi survey data. *Evaluation Review, 15*(2), 179-188.

Altschuld, J. W., Thomas, P. M., McColskey, W. H., Smith, D. W., Wiesmann, W. W., & Lower, M. A. (1992). Mailed evaluation questionnaire: Replications of a 96 percent return rate procedure. *Evaluation and Program Planning, 15*, 239-246.

Americans With Disabilities Act of 1990, 42 U.S.C.A. § 12101 *et seq.* (West 1993).

Banathy, B. H. (1978). *A guide to interorganizational linkage in education* (ITS Monograph Series, No. 78-1). San Francisco: Far West Laboratory for Educational Research and Development.

Barnes, J. L., & Landy, F. J. (1979). Scaling behavioral anchors. *Applied Psychological Measurement, 3*, 193-200.

Beasley, J. E., & Johnson, R. (1984). Forecasting environmental protection legislation using cross-impact analysis. *Long Range Planning, 17*, 132-138.

Beck, J. (1994, June 28). Diversity can be both boon, bane. *Columbus Dispatch*, p. 28.

Bradburn, N. M., & Sudman, S. (1988). *Polls and surveys: Understanding what they tell us*. San Francisco: Jossey-Bass.

Brink, S., Bubb, J., Drash, A., Gray, D., Golden, M., Orr, D., Owens, R., Rosenbloom, A., Travis, L., Zipf, W., & Lankard, B. (1989). *Competency profile of case management for the adolescent/young adult with chronic disease*. Columbus: Ohio State University, Center on Education and Training for Employment.

Casey, M. A. (1988, October). *Focus group interviews with students: Overview and assessment*. Paper presented at the annual meeting of the American Evaluation Association, New Orleans, LA.

Clagett, C. A. (1989). A practical guide to environmental scanning: Approaches, sources, and selected techniques. *Planning for Higher Education, 17*(2), 19-28.

Davis, L. N., & McCallon, E. (1974). *Planning, conducting, and evaluating workshops.* Austin, TX: Learning Concepts.

Demarest, L., Holey, L., & Leatherman, S. (1984, October). *The use of multiple methods to assess continuing education needs.* Paper presented at the annual meeting of the Evaluation Network, San Francisco.

Drucker, P. F. (1994). The age of social trasformation. *Atlantic Monthly, 274*(5), 53-80.

Eaton, W. W., Holzer, C. E., Von Korff, M., Anthony, J. C., Helzer, J. E., George, L., Burnam, A., Boyd, J. H., Kessler, L. G., & Locke, B. Z. (1984). The design of the epidemiologic catchment area surveys: The control and measurement of error. *Archives of General Psychiatry, 41*, 942-948.

Edwards, J. E., & Thomas, M. D. (1993). The organizational survey process. *American Behavioral Scientist, 36*(4), 419-442.

Epstein, A. (1994, May 19). Liberals divided in their reactions to Breyer's record. *Seattle Times*, p. A3.

Fivars, G. (Ed.). (1980). *The critical incident technique: A bibliography* (2nd ed.). Palo Alto, CA: American Institutes for Research.

Forester, J. (1989). *Planning in the face of power.* Berkeley: University of California Press.

Freeman, V., & Farel, A. (1990). *The incidence and prevalence of conditions in children: A sourcebook of rates and state-specific estimates for DHHS Region IV* (U.S. Department of Mental Health and Human Services, Grant Number MCJ 375031). Chapel Hill: University of North Carolina, Graham Child Development Center.

Gamon, J., Altschuld, J. W., Eastmond, J. N., Kirkhart, K., Morris, M., & Ory, J. (1992, November). *A focus group on using focus groups in the teaching of evaluation.* Workshop presented at the annual meeting of the American Evaluation Association, Seattle, WA.

Garfinkel, H. (1967). *Studies in ethnomethodology.* Englewood Cliffs, NJ: Prentice Hall.

Goldhaber, G. M., & Richetto, G. (1977). *ICA communication audit of Wichita State University.* Wichita, KS: Wichita State University, Communication Audit Liaison Team.

Goldhaber, G. M., & Rogers, D. P. (1979). *Auditing organizational communication systems: The ICA communication audit.* Dubuque, IA: Kendall/Hunt.

Gordon, J. J., & Pratt, L. K. (1971). *Group Delphi goals* [Technique training guide]. Durham, NC: National Laboratory for Higher Education.

Grussing, P. G., Valuck, R. J., & Williams, R. G. (1994). Development and validation of behaviorally anchored rating scales for student evaluation of pharmacy instruction. *American Journal of Pharmaceutical Education, 58*, 25-37.

Hall, O., & Royse, D. (1987). Mental health needs assessment with social indicators: An empirical study. *Administration in Mental Health, 15*(8), 36-46.

Harrison, M. I. (1987). *Diagnosing organizations: Methods, models, and processes.* Newbury Park, CA: Sage.

Henry, G. T. (1990). *Practical sampling.* Newbury Park, CA: Sage.

Herman, J. L., Morris, L. L., & Fitz-Gibbon, C. T. (1987). *Evaluator's handbook.* Newbury Park, CA: Sage.

Hersey, P., & Blanchard, K. H. (1977). *Management of organizational behavior: Utilizing human resources* (3rd ed.). Englewood Cliffs, NJ: Prentice Hall.

Ishikawa, K. (1983). *Guide to quality control.* Tokyo: Asian Productivity Organization.

Jagtiani, A. (1994, August 1). Generation gap widens at OSU with increase of older students. *Ohio State Lantern, 179,* 1-2.

Johnston, W. B. (1987). *Workforce 2000: Work and workers for the 21st century.* Indianapolis, IN: Hudson Institute.

Jones, M., & Limes, K. (1988). *Gone fishing.* Unpublished manuscript, Ohio State University, Educational Services and Research Deptartment, Columbus.

Jonsen, R. W. (1986). The environmental context for postsecondary education. *New Directions for Institutional Research, 52,* 5-19.

Juran, J. M., & Gryna, F. M. (Eds.). (1988). *Juran's quality control handbook* (4th ed.). New York: McGraw-Hill.

Kaufman, R. (1988). *Planning educational systems: A results-based approach.* Lancaster, PA: Technomic.

Kaufman, R. (1992). *Strategic planning plus: An organizational guide.* Newbury Park, CA: Sage.

Kaufman, R., Rojas, A. M., & Mayer, H. (1993). *Needs assessment: A user's guide.* Englewood Cliffs, NJ: Educational Technology.

King, J., Morris, L. L., & Fitz-Gibbon, J. T. (1987). *How to measure program implementation.* Beverly Hills, CA: Sage.

Kirkpatrick, D. (1992, March 23). Here comes the payoff from PCs. *Fortune,* 93-102.

Kluger, M. P., Mace, P., & Lyon, E. (1990, October). *Strategic planning: How to do it.* Presession at the annual meeting of the American Evaluation Association, Washington, DC.

Krueger, R. A. (1988a). *Focus groups: A practical guide for applied research.* Newbury Park, CA: Sage.

Krueger, R. A. (1988b, October). *Focus groups for community needs assessment: Overview and assessment.* Paper presented at the annual meeting of the American Evaluation Association, New Orleans, LA.

Lauffer, A. (1982). *Assessment tools: For practitioners, managers, and trainers.* Beverly Hills, CA: Sage.

Lewin, K. (1947). Frontiers in group dynamics: Concept, method, and reality in social science, social equilibria, and social change. *Human Relations, 1,* 5-41.

Lundy, J. L. (1986). *Lead, follow, or get out of the way.* New York: Berkley.

McCollough, T. (1975). *Project redesign.* Palo Alto, CA: Palo Alto Unified School District.

McKenzie, R. (1994, June 28). Decline in U.S. living standards is politicians' myth. *Columbus Dispatch,* p. 28.

McKillip, J. (1987). *Needs analysis: Tools for the human services and education.* Newbury Park, CA: Sage.

Misanchuk, E. R. (1984). Analysis of multi-component educational and training needs. *Journal of Instructional Development, 7*(1), 28-34.

Monk, J. S. (1983). *Using an intensive time-series design to examine achievement and attitude of eighth- and ninth-grade earth science students grouped by cognitive tendency, sex, and IQ.* Unpublished doctoral dissertation, Ohio State University, Columbus.

Moore, C. M. (1987). *Group techniques for idea building.* Newbury Park, CA: Sage.

Morrison, J. L. (1989). *The alternative futures approach to planning: Implications for institutional research offices.* Chapel Hill: University of North Carolina Press.

Morrison, J. L. (1990). *Using futures research in college and university planning: A handbook for institutional researchers.* Chapel Hill: University of North Carolina.

Murphy, E. (1982). *Teacher's guide to the future*. Washington, DC: Population Reference Bureau.

Nefstead, S. (1988, October). *Focus groups with educational programs: Overview and assessment*. Paper presented at the annual meeting of the American Evaluation Association, New Orleans, LA.

Norton, R. E. (in press). *DACUM handbook*. Columbus: Ohio State University, Center on Education and Training for Employment.

Nutt, P. C., & Backoff, R. W. (1992). *Strategic management of public and third sector organizations: A handbook for leaders*. San Francisco: Jossey-Bass.

Odden, A. (1990). Educational indicators in the United States: The need for analysis. *Educational Researcher, 19*(5), 24-29.

Orlich, D. D. (1978). *Designing sensible surveys*. Pleasantville, NY: Redgrave.

Parrish, W. Y. (1994, March 1). Teachers raise stink over being observed. *Seattle Times*, p. B3.

Patton, M. Q. (1990, May). Workshop presentation at the annual spring workshop. Ohio Program Evaluators' Group, Columbus, OH.

Phi Delta Kappa. (1984). *Handbook for conducting future studies in education*. Bloomington, IN: Author, Commission on Schooling for the 21st Century.

Race, K. E. H., & Planek, T. W. (1992). Modified scree test: Further considerations on its application to Delphi study data. *Evaluation Review, 16*(2), 171-183.

Rojewski, J. W., & Meers, G. D. (1991). Research priorities in vocational special needs education: A Delphi approach. *Journal for Vocational Special Needs Education, 13*(2), 33-38.

Rosenfeld, P., Edwards, J. E., & Thomas, M. D. (Eds.). (1993). Improving organizational surveys: New directions and methods. *American Behavioral Scientist, 36*(4).

Ruff, R., Shylo, B., & Russell, J. F. (1981). *Vocational education: A look into the future*. Columbus: Ohio State University, Center on Education and Training for Employment.

Sadowske, S. (1988, October). *Focus groups for state strategic planning: Overview and assessment*. Paper presented at the annual meeting of the American Evaluation Association, New Orleans, LA.

Scheidel, T. M., & Crowell, L. (1979). *Discussing and deciding: A desk book for group leaders and members*. New York: Macmillan.

Scholtes, P. R. (1990). *The team handbook*. Madison, WI: Joiner Associates.

Schwier, R. A. (1986). Extracting training implications from multi-component needs assessments: Extension of the R-C-D model. *Canadian Journal of Educational Communication, 15*(2), 91-104.

Sikorski, L. A., Oakley, G., & Lloyd-Kolkin, D. (1977). *A report of the research and development exchange: The feasibility of using existing data as feedforward information*. San Francisco: Far West Laboratory for Educational Research and Development.

Smith, N. L. (Ed.). (1982). *Communication strategies in evaluation: New perspectives in evaluation* (Vol. 3). Beverly Hills, CA: Sage.

Sork, T. J. (1982). *Determining priorities*. Vancouver, Canada: University of British Columbia.

Stephens, K. G. (1972). *A fault tree approach to analysis of educational systems as demonstrated in vocational education*. Unpublished doctoral dissertation, University of Washington, Department of Educational Administration, Seattle.

Stephens, M. (1991, January 30). Proficiency test results are grim. *Columbus Dispatch*, pp. 1-2.

Sudman, S., & Bradburn, N. M. (1982). *Asking questions: A practical guide to questionnaire design*. San Francisco: Jossey-Bass.

Taite, G. L. (1990, April). *Identifying the at-risk student: Do legislators know best?* Paper presented at the annual meeting of the American Educational Research Association, Boston. (ERIC Document Reproduction Service No. ED 322 644)

Tang, T. (1993, October 17). School voucher plans offer only trouble, not solutions. *Seattle Times*, p. B6.

Theiss, J., Anderson, J. M., & Gideon, J. L. (1991, October). *Exploring maps as a way to represent needs assessment data*. Paper presented at the annual meeting of the American Evaluation Association, Boston.

Thomas, P. M., & Altschuld, J. W. (1988). *A survey of education and training needs of welding personnel* [Research report for members only]. Columbus, OH: Edison Welding Institute.

Tri-Met Public Affairs. (1994, June). *Tri-Met "wish list" results*. Portland, OR: Author.

Trochim, W. M. K. (1989a). An introduction to concept mapping for planning and evaluation. *Evaluation and Program Planning, 12*, 1-16.

Trochim, W. M. K. (1989b). Concept mapping: Soft science or hard art? *Evaluation and Program Planning, 12*, 87-110.

Tweed, D. L., & Ciarlo, J. A. (1992). Social indicator models for indirectly assessing mental health service needs. *Evaluation and Program Planning, 15*(2), 165-180.

U.S. Department of Commerce. (1990). *Hidden treasures: Census bureau data and where to find it!* (Available from U.S. Bureau of the Census, Customer Service Branch, Washington, DC 20233)

United Way of America. (1989). *What lies ahead: Countdown to the 21st century*. Washington, DC: Author.

Wickens, D. (1980). *Games people oughta play: A group process for needs assessment and decision-making for elementary and secondary schools* [Facilitator's manual]. Hayward, CA: Alameda County Office of Education. (ERIC Document Reproduction Service No. ED 189 089)

Willis, B. (Ed.). (1994). *Distance education: Strategies and tools*. Englewood Cliffs, NJ: Educational Technology.

Witkin, B. R. (Ed.). (1979). *A comprehensive needs assessment module* (Rev. ed.) [Manual]. Hayward, CA: Office of the Alameda County Superintendent of Schools.

Witkin, B. R. (1984). *Assessing needs in educational and social programs: Using information to make decisions, set priorities, and allocate resources*. San Francisco: Jossey-Bass.

Witkin, B. R. (1991). Setting priorities: Needs assessment in a time of change. In R. V. Carlson & G. Awkerman (Eds.), *Educational planning: Concepts, strategies, and practices* (pp. 241-266). White Plains, NY: Longman.

Witkin, B. R. (1994). Needs assessment since 1981: The state of the practice. *Evaluation Practice, 15*(1), 17-27.

Witkin, B. R., & Eastmond, J. N., Jr. (1988). Bringing focus to the needs assessment: The pre-assessment phase. *Educational Planning, 6*(4), 12-23.

Witkin, B. R., & Richardson, J. (1983). *APEX: Needs assessment for secondary schools* [Manual]. Hayward, CA: Office of the Alameda County Superintendent of Schools.

Witkin, B. R., Richardson, J., Sherman, N., & Lehnen, P. (1979). *APEX: Needs assessment for secondary schools* [Student survey]. Hayward, CA: Office of the Alameda County Superintendent of Schools. (APEX consists of survey booklets for students, teachers, and parents, and an administrators' manual)

Witkin, B. R., & Stephens, K. G. (1968). *Fault tree analysis: A research tool for educational planning* (Technical Report No. 1). Hayward, CA: Alameda County PACE Center. (ERIC Document Reproduction Service No. ED 029 379)

Witkin, B. R., & Stephens, K. G. (1973). *Fault tree analysis: A management science technique for educational planning and evaluation.* Hayward, CA: Office of the Alameda County Superintendent of Schools.

Yoon, J. S., Altschuld, J. W., & Hughes, V. (1995, Spring). Needs of Asian foreign students: Focus group interviews. *Phi Beta Delta International Review, 5,* 1-14.

Zoski, K., & Jurs, S. (1990). Priority determination in surveys: An application of the scree test. *Evaluation Review, 14*(2), 214-219.

Zoski, K., & Jurs, S. (1991). Applications for the modified scree test revisited. *Evaluation Review, 15*(2), 189-190.

Recommended Reading

Adams, D. (1991). Planning models and paradigms. In R. V. Carlson & G. Awkerman (Eds.), *Educational planning: Concepts, strategies, and practices* (pp. 5-29). White Plains, NY: Longman.

Altschuld, J. W., & Engle, M. (Eds.). (1994). The preparation of professional evaluators: Issues, perspectives, and current status. *New Directions in Program Evaluation, 62.*

Benveniste, G. (1989). *Mastering the politics of planning.* San Francisco: Jossey-Bass.

Borisoff, D., & Purdy, M. (1991). *Listening in everyday life: A personal and professional approach.* Lanham, MD: University Press of America.

Carlson, R. V., & Awkerman, G. (Eds.). (1991). *Educational planning: Concepts, strategies, and practices.* White Plains, NY: Longman.

Delbecq, A. L., Van de Van, A. H., & Gustafson, D. H. (1976). *Group techniques for program planning: A guide to nominal group and delphi processes.* Glenview, IL: Scott, Foresman.

Doyle, M., & Straus, D. (1993). *How to make meetings work: The new interaction method.* New York: Berkley.

Eastmond, N. (1994). Assessing needs, developing instruction, and evaluating results. In B. Willis (Ed.), *Distance education: Strategies and tools* (pp. 87-107). Englewood Cliffs, NJ: Educational Technology.

Fowler, F. J., & Mangione, T. W. (1990). *Standardized survey interviewing: Minimizing interviewer-related error.* Newbury Park, CA: Sage.

Hagedorn, H. J. (1980, November). A working manual of simple program evaluation techniques for community mental health programs. In A. Fink & J. Kosecoff (Eds.), *How to evaluate educational programs* (No. 39). Washington, DC: Capitol Publications.

Hamilton, D. N. (1991). An alternative to rational planning models. In R. V. Carlson & G. Awkerman (Eds.), *Educational planning: Concepts, strategies, and practices* (pp. 21-47). New York: Longman.

Henerson, M. E., Morris, L. L., & Fitz-Gibbon, C. T. (1987). *How to measure attitudes* (2nd ed.). Newbury Park, CA: Sage.

Hirschhorn, L., & Associates. (1985). *Cutting back: Retrenchment and redevelopment in human and community services.* San Francisco: Jossey-Bass.

Johnson, D. E., Meiller, L. R., Miller, L. C., & Summers, G. F. (1987). *Needs assessment: Theory and methods.* Ames: University of Iowa Press.

Kaufman, R., & Herman, J. (1991). *Strategic planning in education: Rethinking, restructuring, revitalizing.* Lancaster, PA: Technomic.

Lipinski, H., & Tydeman, J. (1979). Cross-impact analysis: Extended KSIM. *Futures, 11,* 151-154.

Miles, M. B., & Huberman, A. M. (1994). *Qualitative data analysis: An expanded sourcebook* (2nd ed.). Thousand Oaks, CA: Sage.

Neuber, K. A. (1985). *Needs assessment: A model for community planning* (Sage Human Services Guide #14). Beverly Hills, CA: Sage.

Paolucci-Whitcomb, P., Bright, W. E., & Carlson, R. V. (1991). Interactive leadership: Processes for improving planning. In R. V. Carlson & G. Awkerman (Eds.), *Educational planning: Concepts, strategies, and practices* (pp. 221-239). New York: Longman.

Patton, M. Q. (1990). *Qualitative evaluation and research methods* (2nd ed.). Newbury Park, CA: Sage.

Schwab, D. P., Heneman, H. G., III, & DeCotiis, T. A. (1975). Behaviorally anchored rating scales: A review of the literature. *Personnel Psychology, 28,* 549-562.

Shavelson, R. J., McDonnell, L. M., & Oakes, J. (Eds.). (1989). *Indicators for monitoring mathematics and science education.* Santa Monica, CA: RAND.

Tesch, R. (1990). *Qualitative research: Analysis types and software tools.* Bristol, PA: Falmer.

Wolfe, P., Wetzel, M., Harris, G., Mazour, T., & Riplinger, J. (1991). *Job task analysis: Guide to good practice.* Englewood Cliffs, NJ: Educational Technology.

Index

293

About the Authors

Belle Ruth Witkin is a visiting scholar in the Department of Speech Communication at the University of Washington. She has been engaged in research, teaching, and consultation on needs assessment, program planning, and evaluation since 1966, when she joined the staff of a regional educational planning agency in Alameda County, California, of which she later became director. She has designed and field-tested several models of needs assessment, directed needs assessments in educational and community settings, and convened the first national conference on needs assessment. She was codeveloper of the first applications of systems safety analysis to planning and evaluation in education and the social sciences. She has been a consultant on needs assessment and evaluation for school districts, universities, corporations, and government agencies, including the U.S. Department of Agriculture and the National Institute of Education. Her book, *Assessing Needs in Educational and Social Programs,* became a major resource in the field. She has also published a book chapter and many articles on needs assessment in professional journals, the latest of which was "Needs Assessment Since 1981: The State of the Practice." She was president of the California Association for Program Evaluation and serves on the editorial review board of *Educational Planning* and *Evaluation Practice.* She received her doctorate in Speech Science from the University of Washington, where she taught communication courses for several years. Her interest in communication, particularly group processes and listening, is reflected in her applications of communication theory to needs assessment.

James W. Altschuld received his doctorate in Educational Research and Evaluation from The Ohio State University (OSU). He has been an evaluator for the Columbus, Ohio, public schools, a supervisor in the Delaware Department of Public Instruction, and a research specialist at the Center for Vocational Education at OSU. Currently, he is Professor in Educational Research and Evaluation, and the evaluation coordinator for the National Center for Science Teaching and Learning, both at OSU. His teaching, research interests, extensive publications, and conference presentations focus on needs assessment, evaluation methodology, and the development of evaluation as a field. Recent published articles and presentations include "The Utilization of Needs Assessment Results," "Needs of Asian Foreign Students: Focus Group Interviews," and "Teaching of Needs Assessment Across the Disciplines." In 1994, he coedited an issue of *New Directions for Program Evaluation* devoted to "The Preparation of Professional Evaluators: Issues, Perspectives, and Programs." He has served as president of the Ohio Program Evaluators' Group and as chair of the Topical Interest Groups, in teaching of evaluation and needs assessment, of the American Evaluation Association. He has received major state and university awards for his teaching and his work in evaluation.